A Drawing A Day

By *Helane*

Written and Illustrated by
Helane Freeman

Edited by Steve Schwab
Cover drawing by Helane Freeman
Cover drawing signed by Charlie Sheen

Helane Designs
Agoura Hills, CA
helanedesigns@gmail.com
helanedesigns.com

Printed in the United States of America

Library of Congress Control Number: 2015903551

ISBN 978-0-9961516-4-1

First Edition
10 9 8 7 6 5 4 3 2 1

The Story

I don't remember the exact moment I fell in love with art, but I do remember the moment it profoundly changed my life. It was September 25, 1978, which happened to be my 14th birthday. I realized that creating art was what I loved to do – and needed to do – and decided then that I was going to be a professional artist. For me, as well as many other artists, it started as a love affair with a sketchbook. I learned to draw by carrying my sketchbook and clear-handled BIC pen everywhere I went, the way some people walk around carrying the latest bestseller. My obsession with drawing and painting paid off six months later, when I got my first job as an illustrator, and I committed myself to turning my passion into a career.

I have happily spent the last 36 years working as an artist, while continuously honing my craft along the way. What I'm sharing with you in this book is my passion: the pure joy of drawing. This is what I do for fun! Now, what to draw?

Many artists who do portraits or likenesses use a projected image, so all they need to do is trace it. Some look down on that, but it's more like a trade secret among professional illustrators, even though it does have a stigma attached to it. To me, there's a certain stiffness in a traced drawing that I don't find pleasing to the eye. I decided to learn how to draw people and nail their likeness just by looking at their picture.

In college, we were encouraged to collect art reference materials, such as images and portraits clipped from catalogs, books and magazines. Now, everything is online, and as fabulous as it is to have any image you can think of appear at the click of a mouse, I'm not sure I would have stumbled upon the things I did if there had been an Internet when I was starting out. What I did have was my older brother's subscription to Mad magazine and our family's TV Guide, giving me a weekly opportunity to cut out photos and illustrations of famous people and anything else I thought was interesting enough to look at and attempt to copy. I kept several pictures tucked securely inside my sketchbook, so I always had something to draw if my environment or imagination didn't inspire me.

I found myself drawing as often as I could. It became an amazing escape for me as I raised my two children. If I was stuck in the dentist's office waiting room for an hour, that gave me an hour to draw. Sitting high up in the stands at a football game? More time to draw. Tutoring? Cheerleading practice? Drawing and drawing. I recently renewed my personal commitment to drawing every day, and I hope you'll be inspired to do the same.

My method of learning turned me into a huge admirer and student of many famous artists. I find inspiration across a wide variety of illustrators and painters; from the greats of the Renaissance to some of today's top illustrators. Among my favorites are Mort Drucker, Richard Amsel, Jack Davis, Bob Peak, Al Hirschfeld, Drew Struzan, Norman Rockwell, Leonardo da Vinci and Leyendecker.

I believe it's very important to practice imitating the drawings of other artists that you admire. By learning how an artist achieves their personal style, I can better understand the way they think. I see how every shape and line reflects their personality, and I become very connected to an artist by doing that. For example, you can see how Mort Drucker draws loop-de-loops in his illustrations to define a half-tone shadow, and discover that Charles Schulz used manic scribbles to represent grass in his Peanuts cartoons.

And sometimes, it's pure admiration; I absolutely love the back rim lighting in a Drew Struzan portrait!

My "A Drawing a Day by Helane" project started innocently enough back in September, 2010. I didn't know about e-mail marketing campaigns, so I sent out an e-mail to about 50-75 friends and family with my five favorite drawings I had done that week. I invited everyone to forward and share my pictures, hoping to reach a wider audience. I didn't realize how popular it would become.

By April, 2011, "A Drawing a Day by Helane" had grown to over 1,000 subscribers! I learned that my work was being forwarded all across the country, and art students in three colleges were taking on my challenge to draw every day. It was an amazing experience, but since I was sending it out through personal e-mail accounts, I kept blowing out e-mail servers. I opened a few more e-mail accounts, and sent a few hundred through each of them, but after a few days, those stopped working as well. I needed a reliable e-mail address so I could spend more time creating art, and less time solving technology problems. I now use e-mail marketing software, so you can visit my website at helanedesigns.com and sign up for my monthly letter and artwork directly from there! Hooray for modern technology!

Do you want to learn how to draw? The only way to do it is to pick up a pen, jump in, and give it a try. Who knows? You may discover a hidden talent you never knew you had! So, here's my challenge to you: Draw something every day. It doesn't matter what it is. A doodle or an abstract shape while you're chatting on the phone is a perfect start. Draw anything that inspires you, but make it a point to draw every day.

This book contains the same BIC ballpoint pen drawings that I sent out each week to the original subscribers of my "A Drawing a Day by Helane" e-mail club. Some of the portraits are of famous people, but others are not. There are drawings that came from my imagination, and drawings I made from photos. You'll see characters I designed from scratch, and others that I copied from other artists that I admire. I also included studies of nature and movement. I hope you find them inspiring and entertaining. Enjoy them all!

-Helane
helanedesigns.com

Check out my YouTube page and watch me draw:
https://www.youtube.com/results?search_
query=helanedesigns

Thank you to my family and friends
for your loving support!

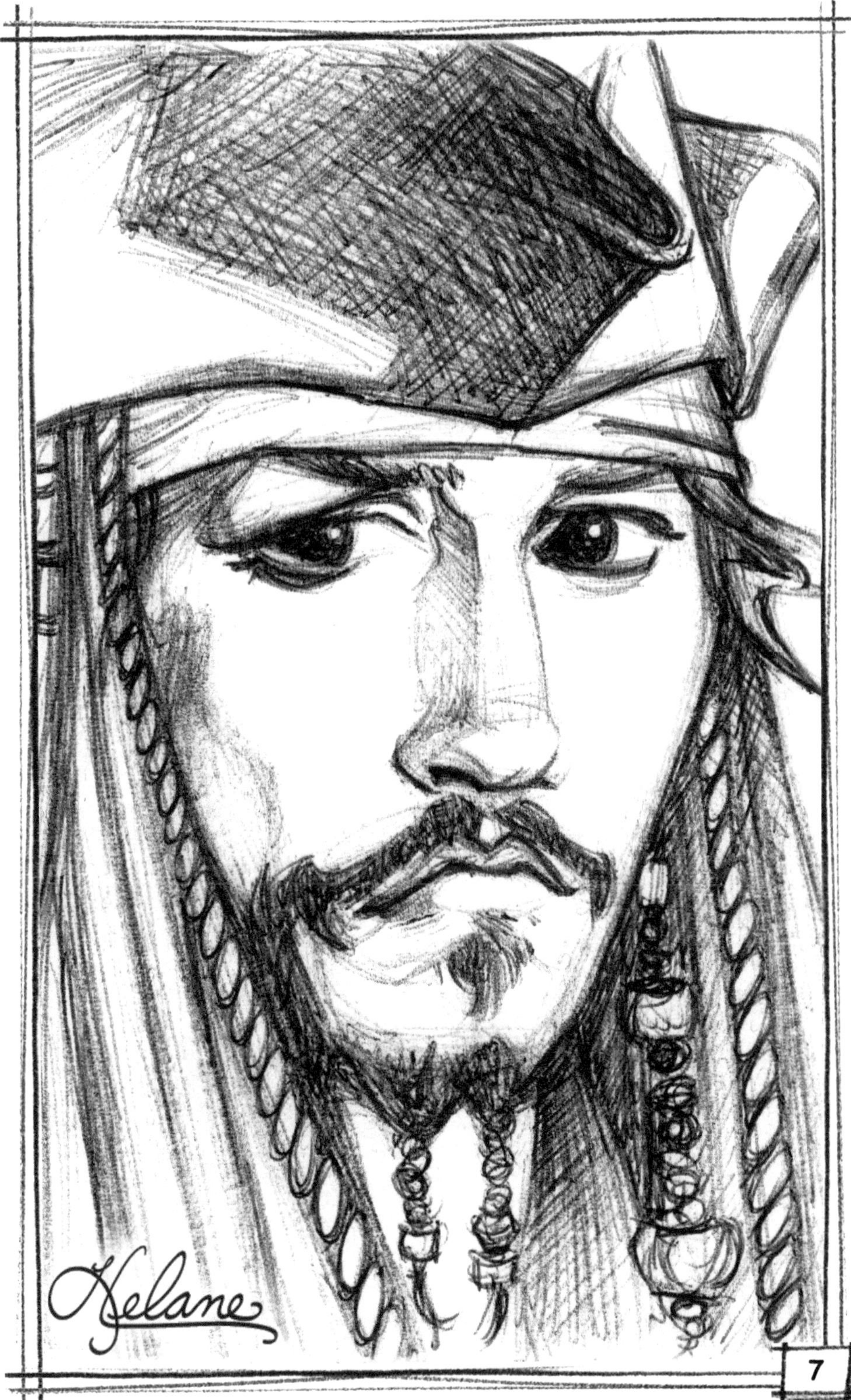
Kelane

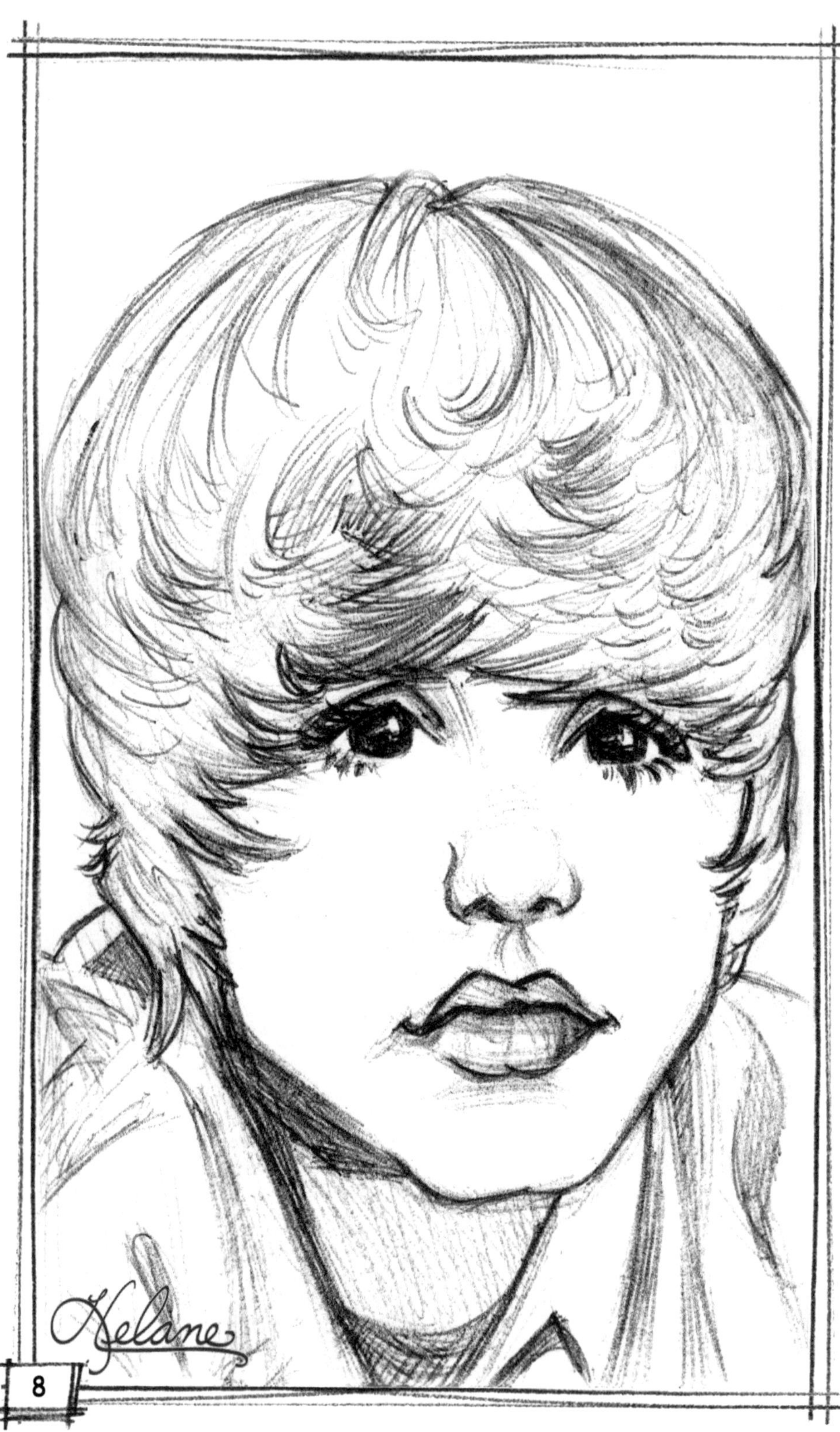
Helane

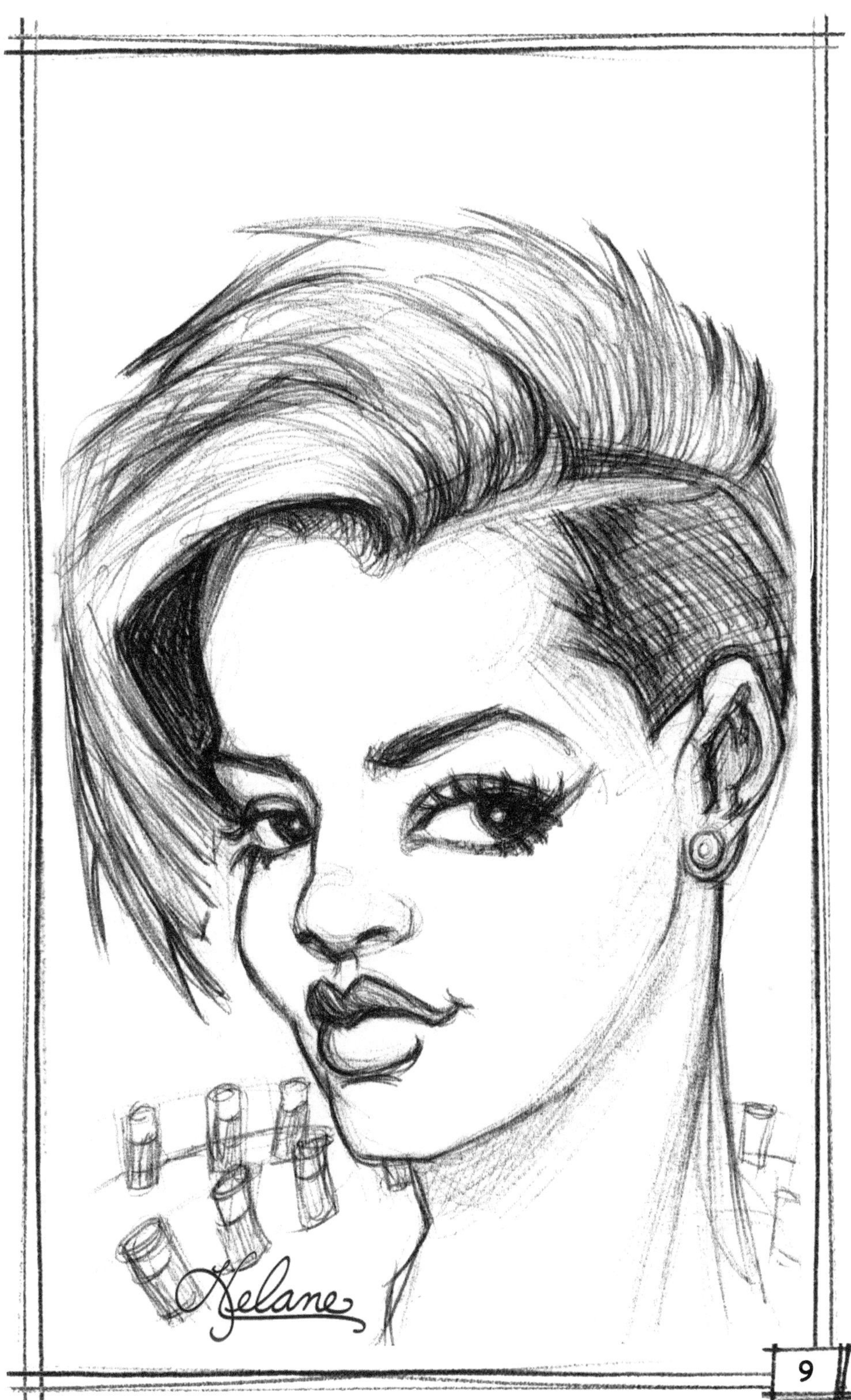

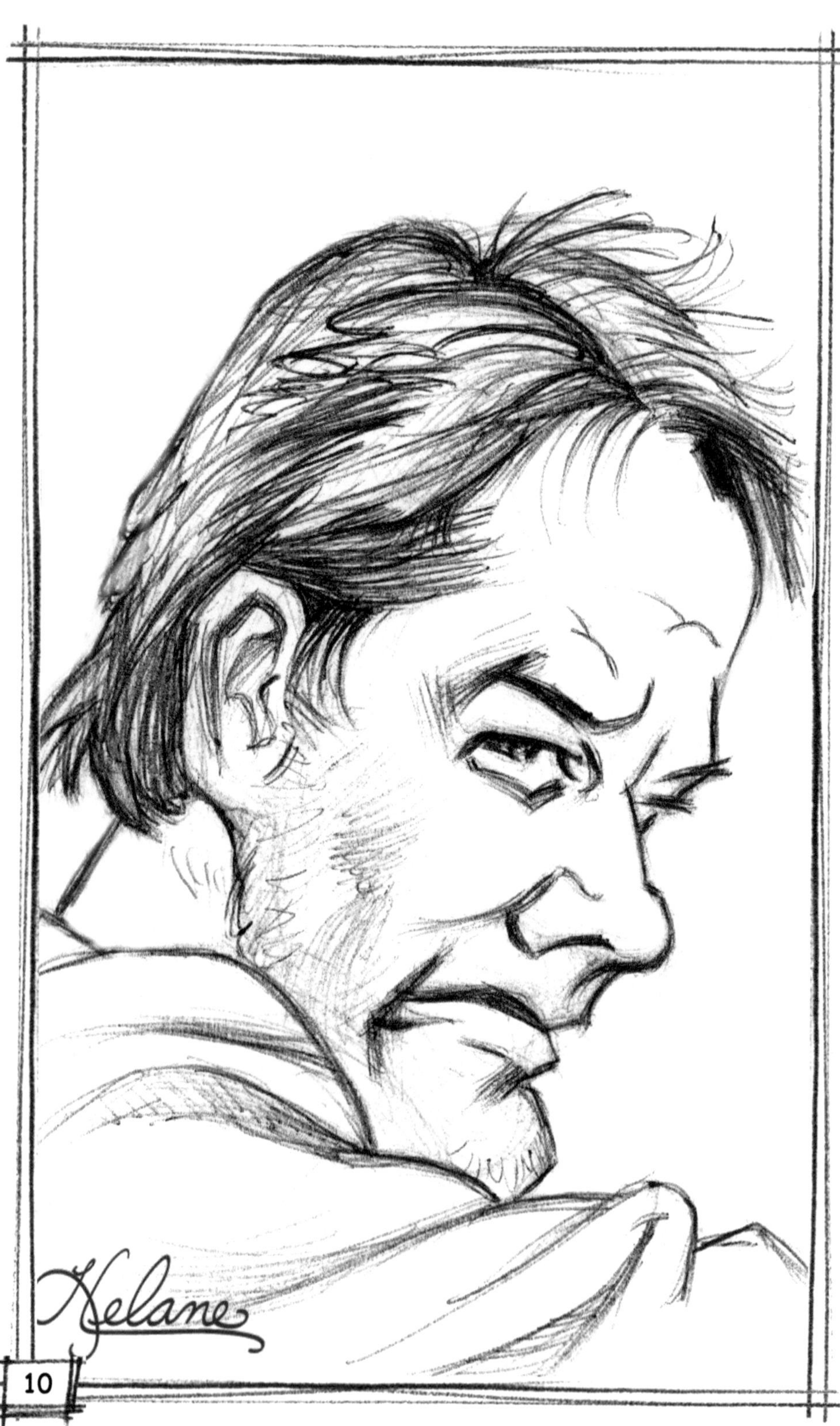

Kelane

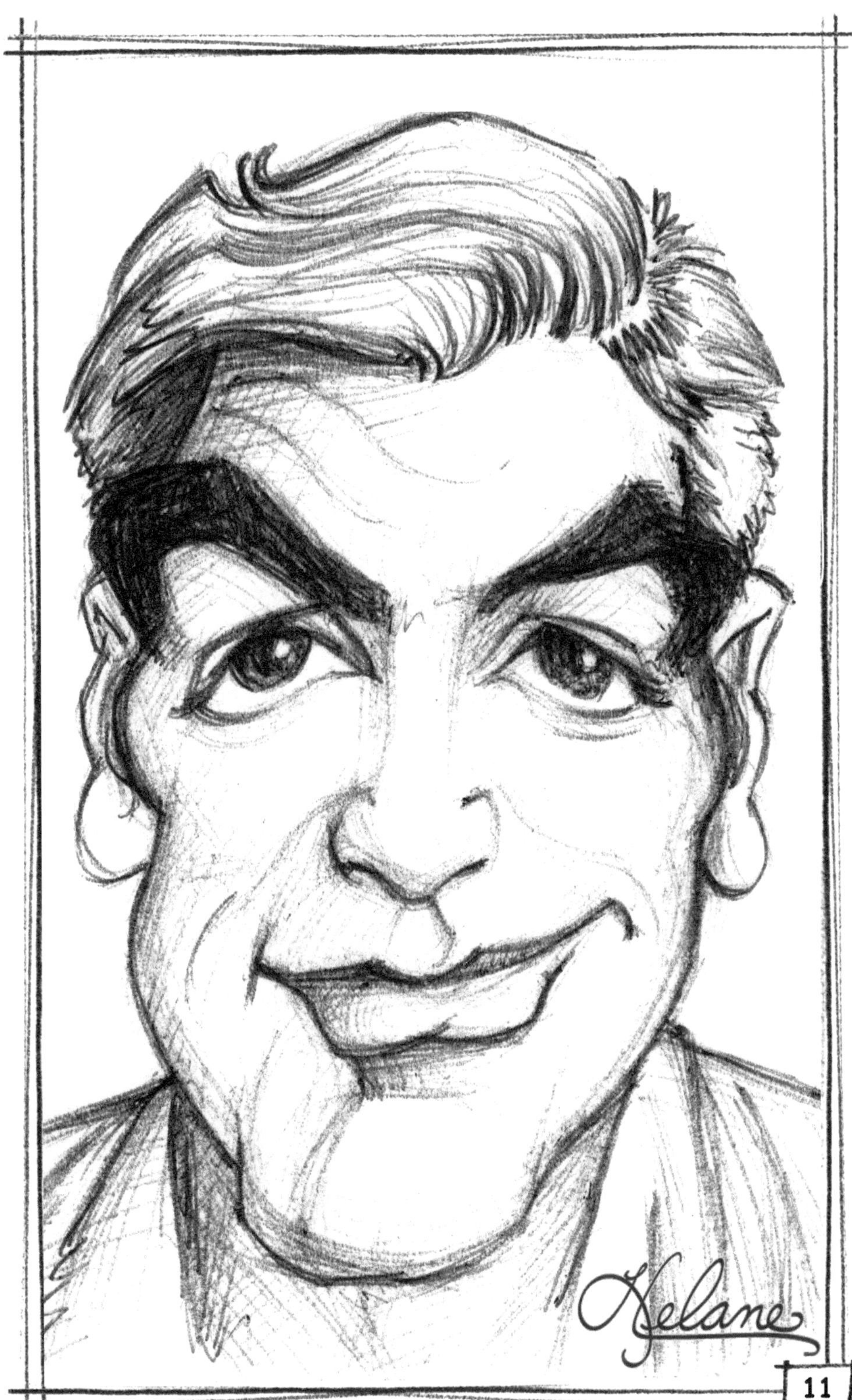

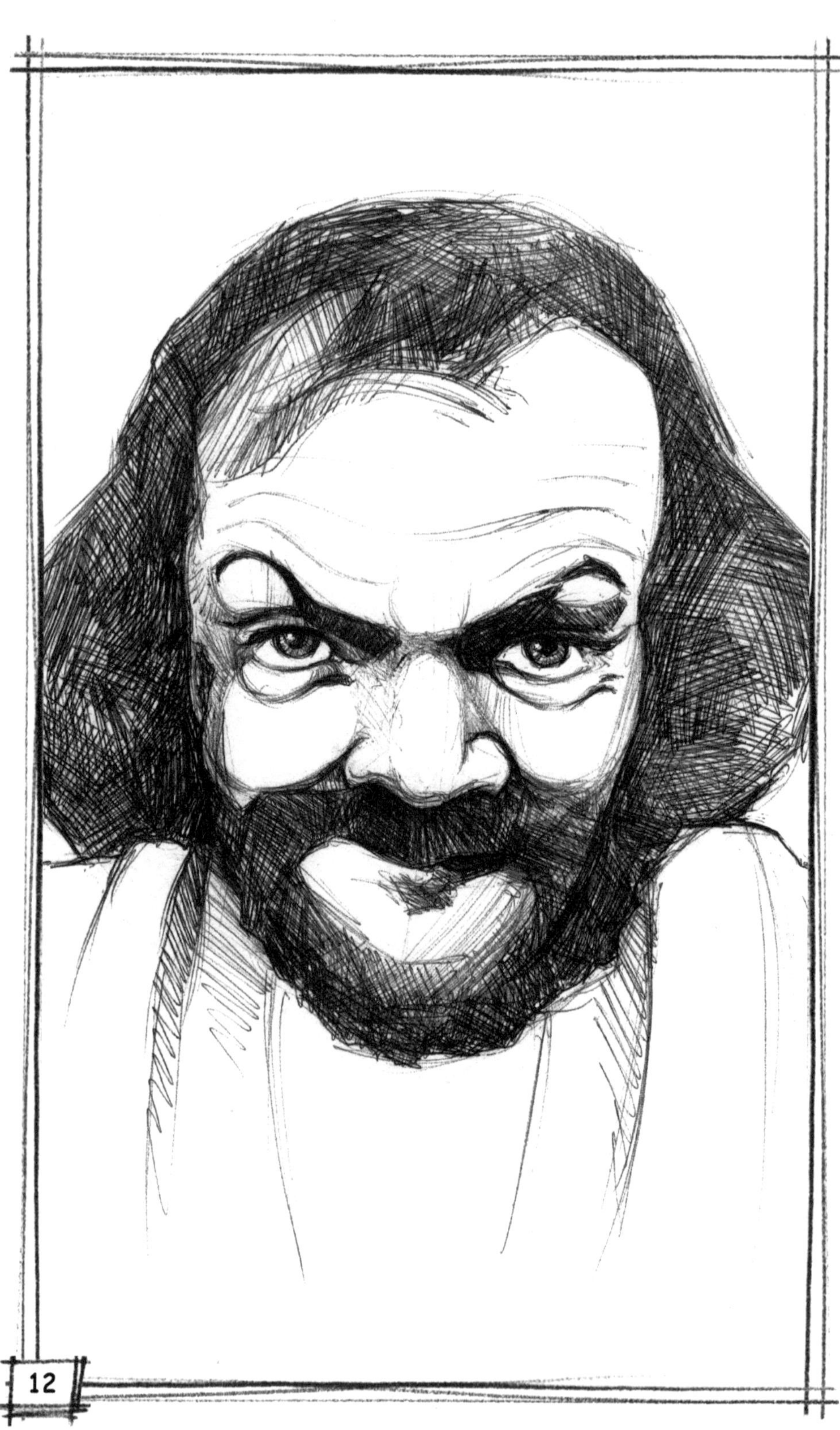

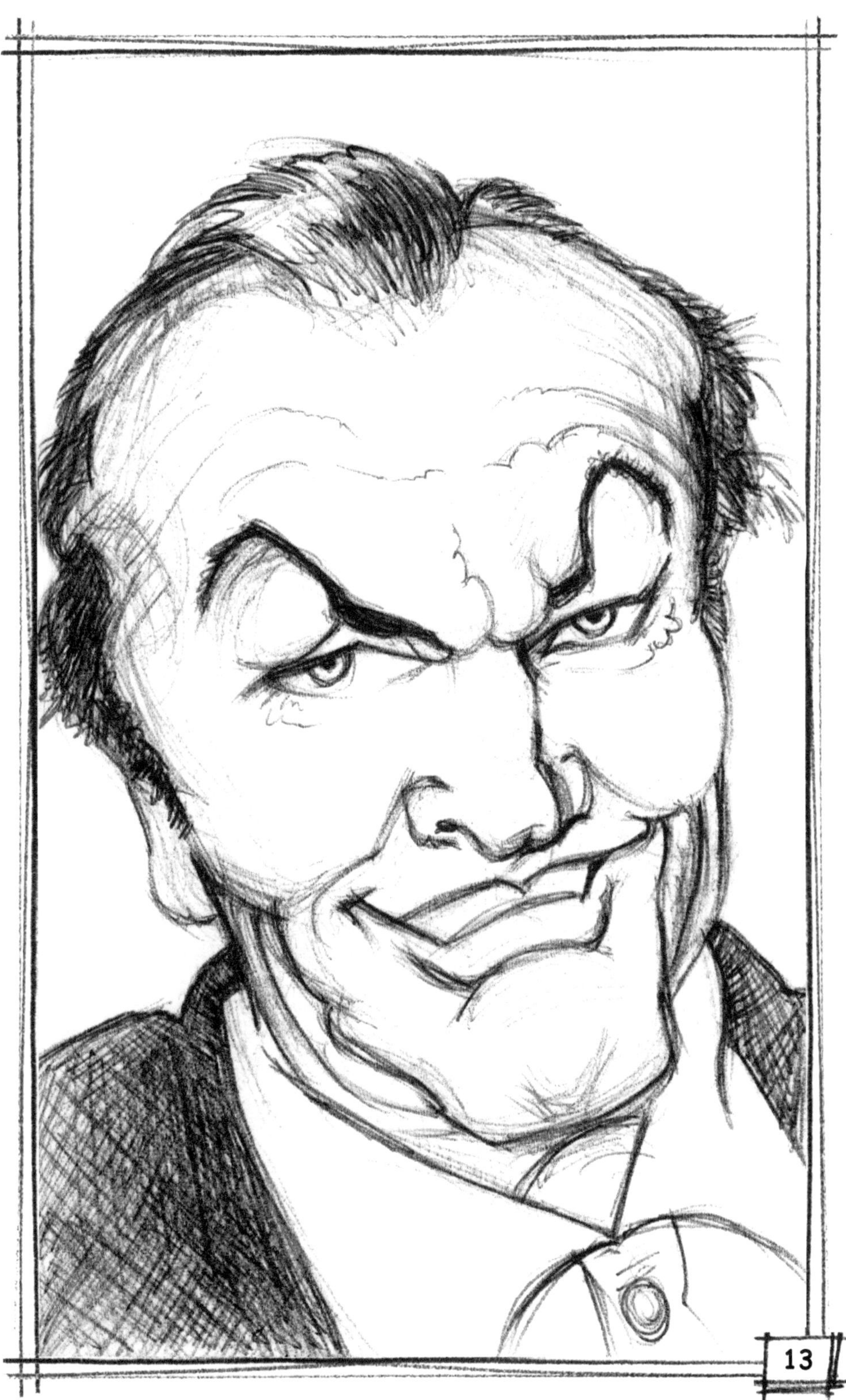

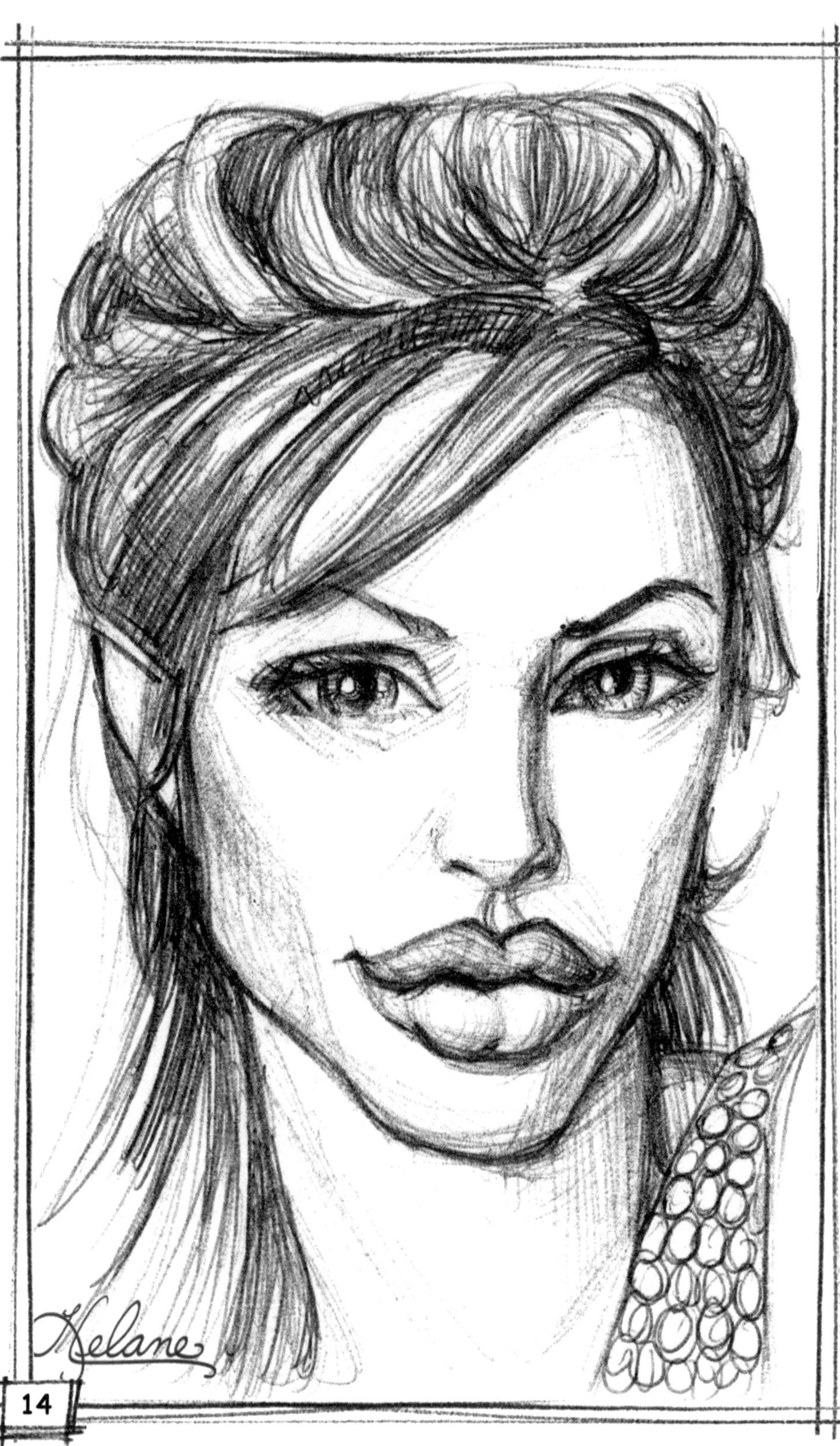

Kelane

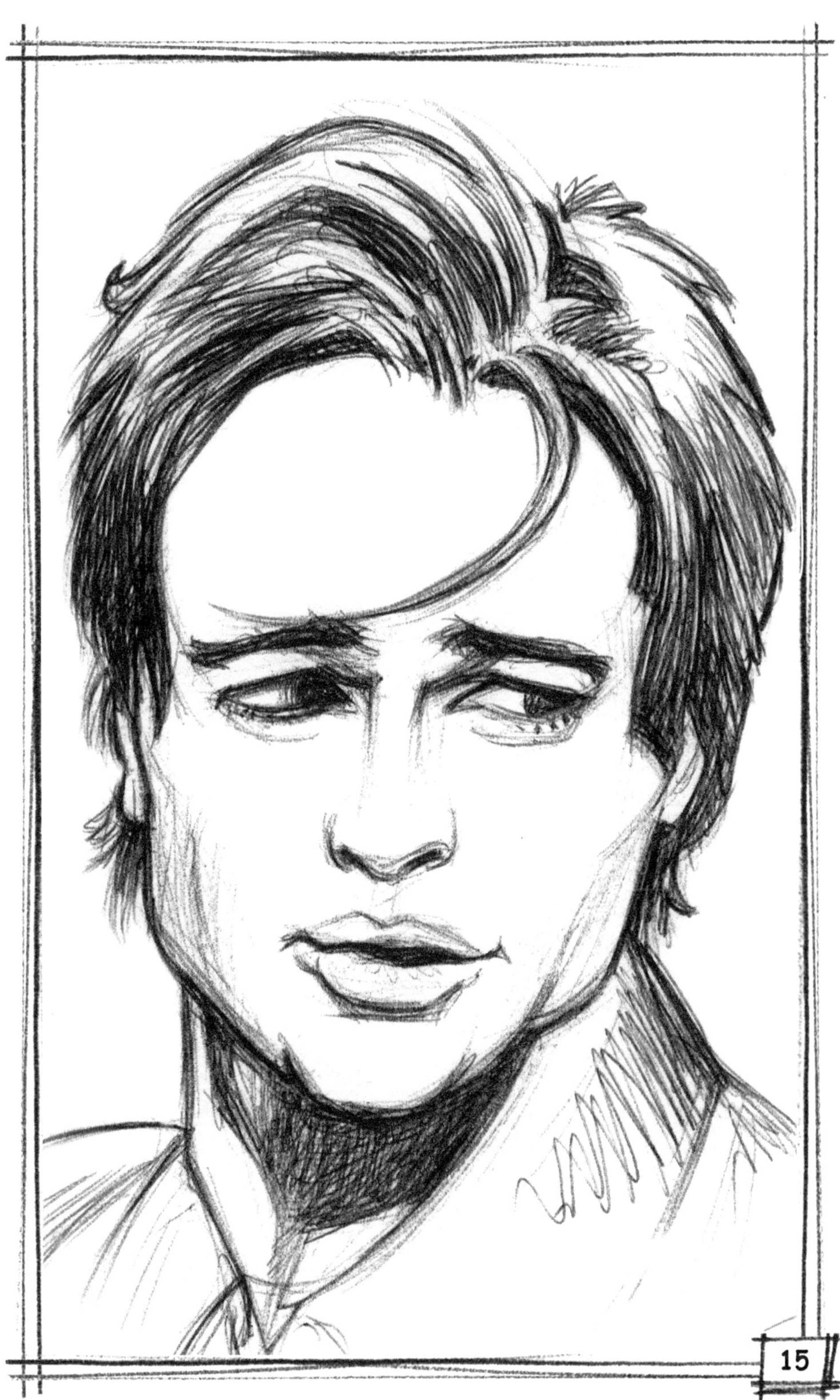

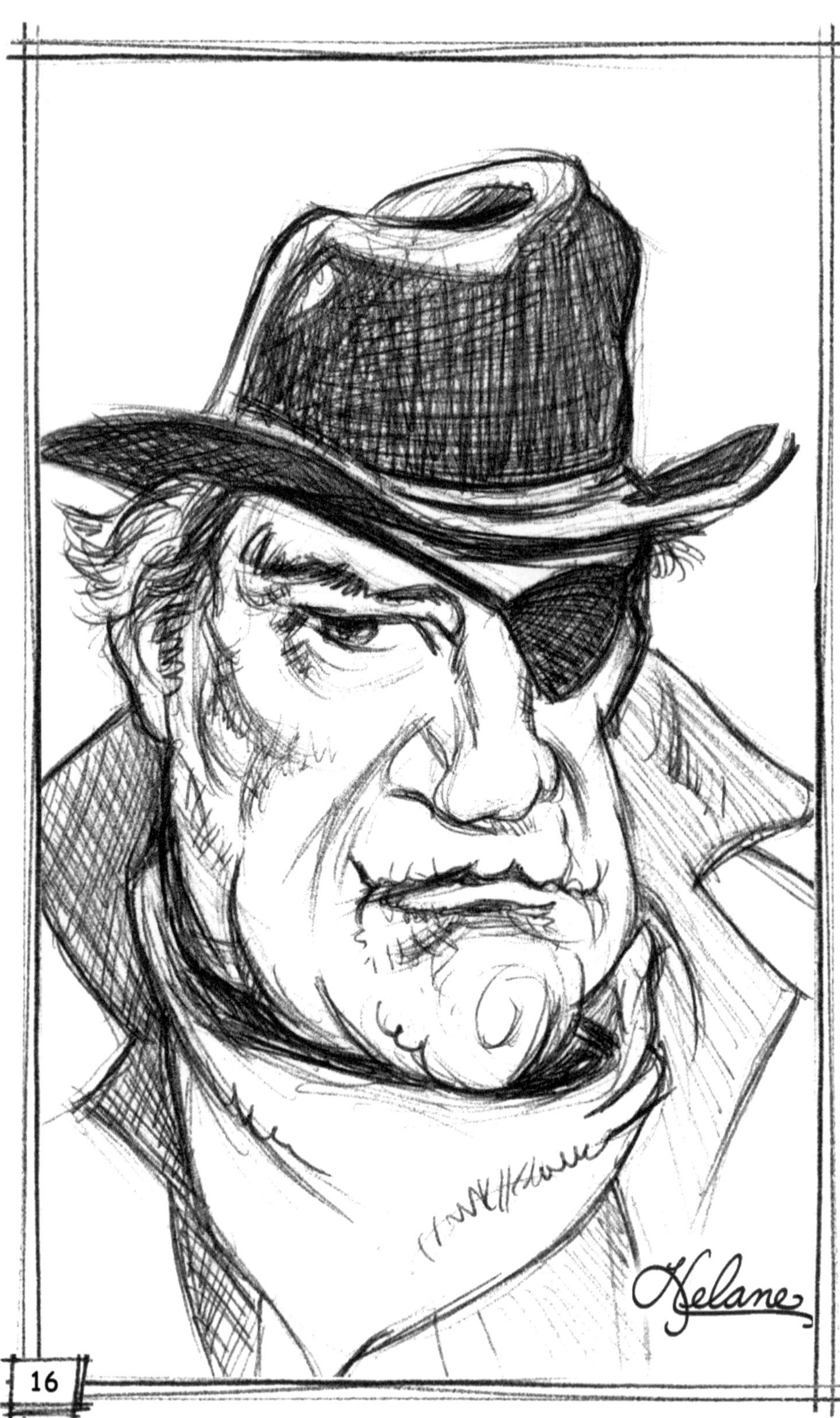

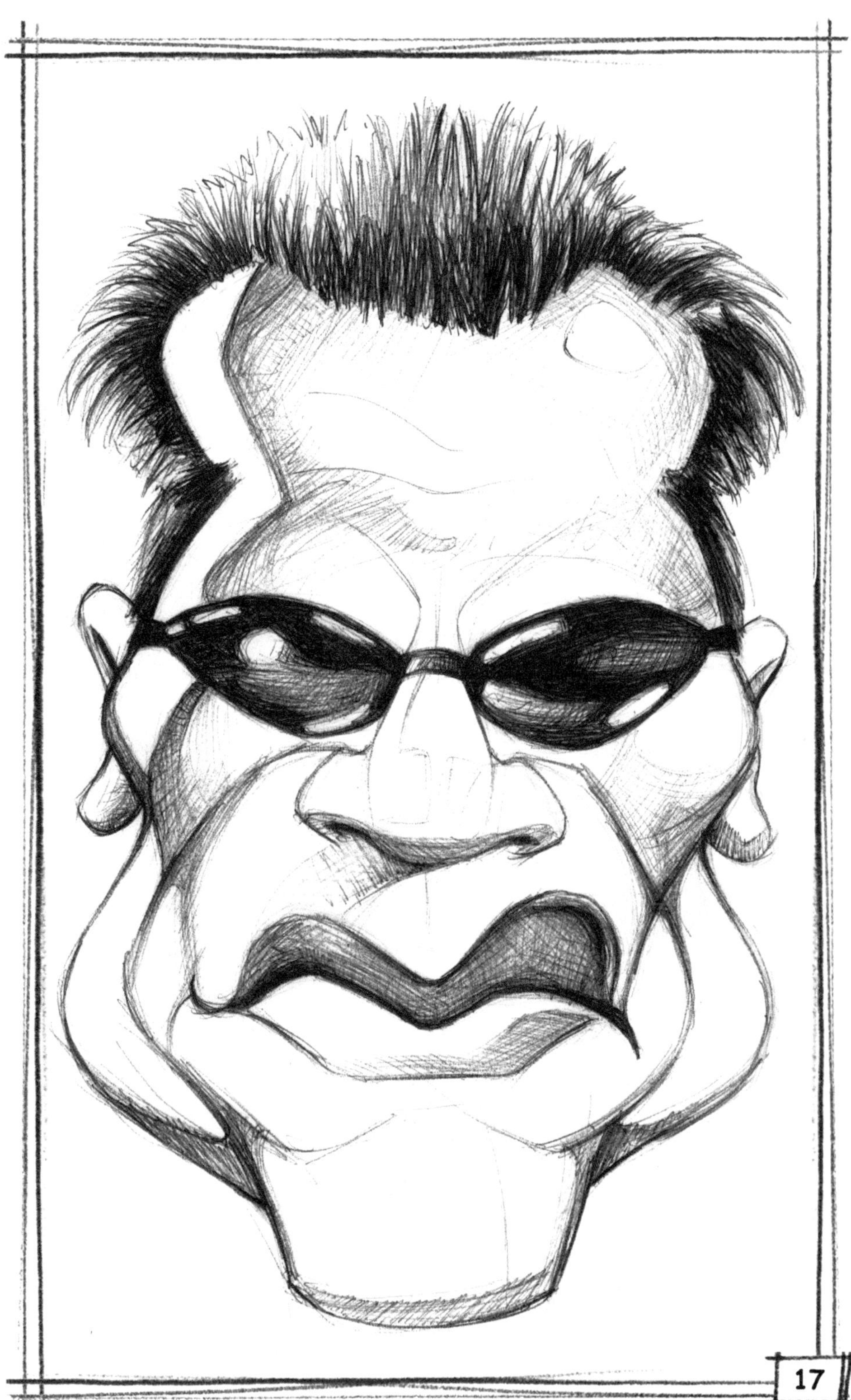

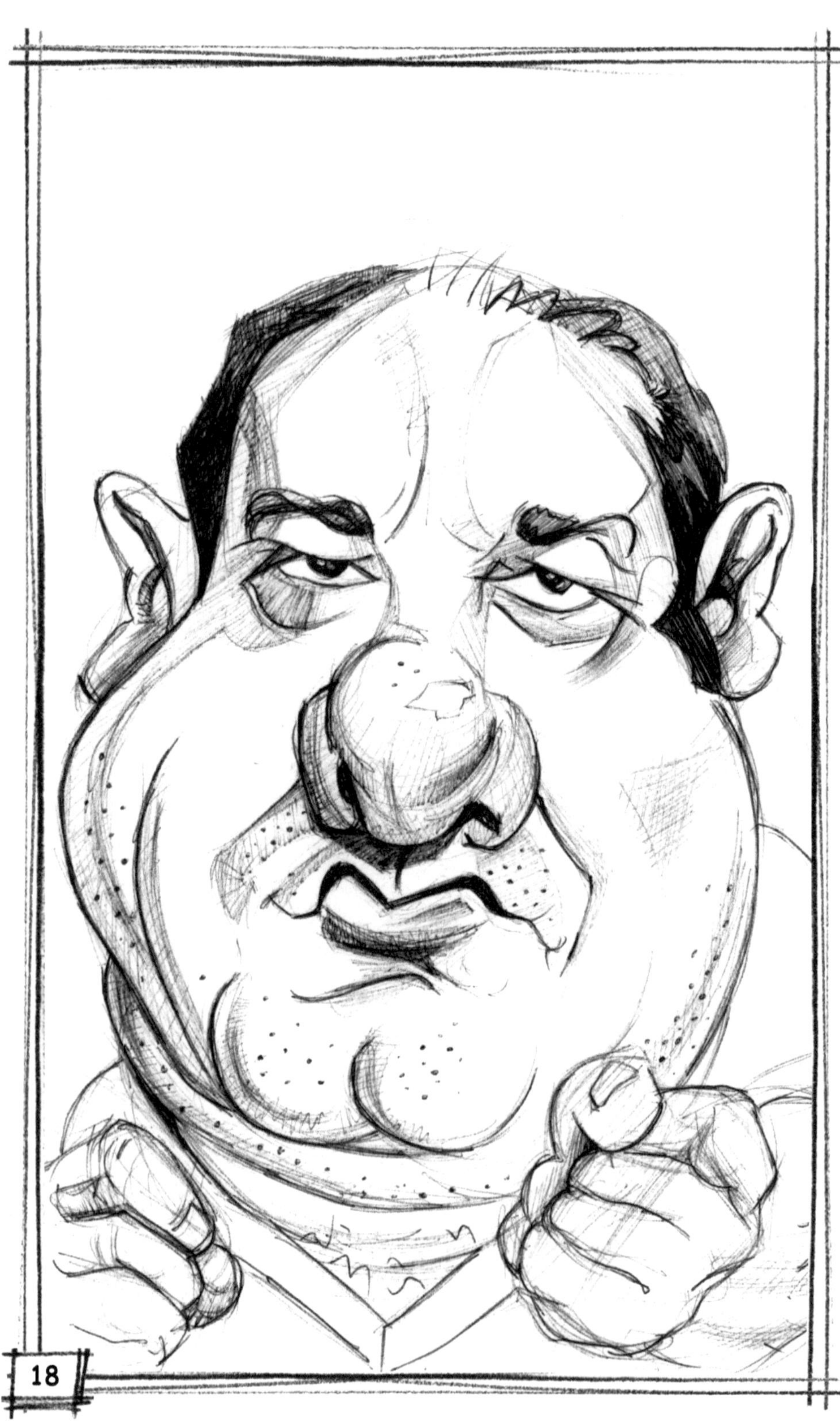

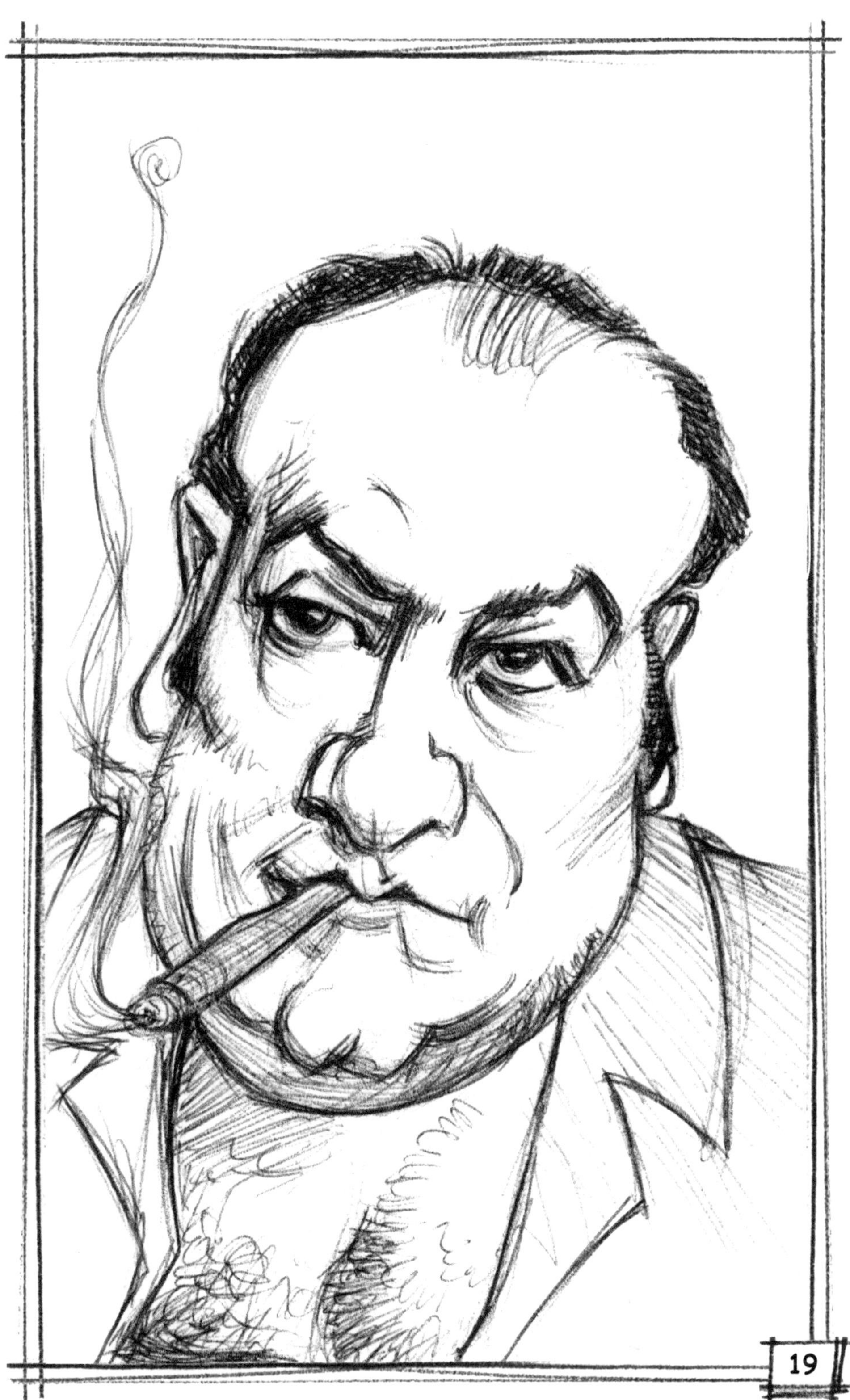

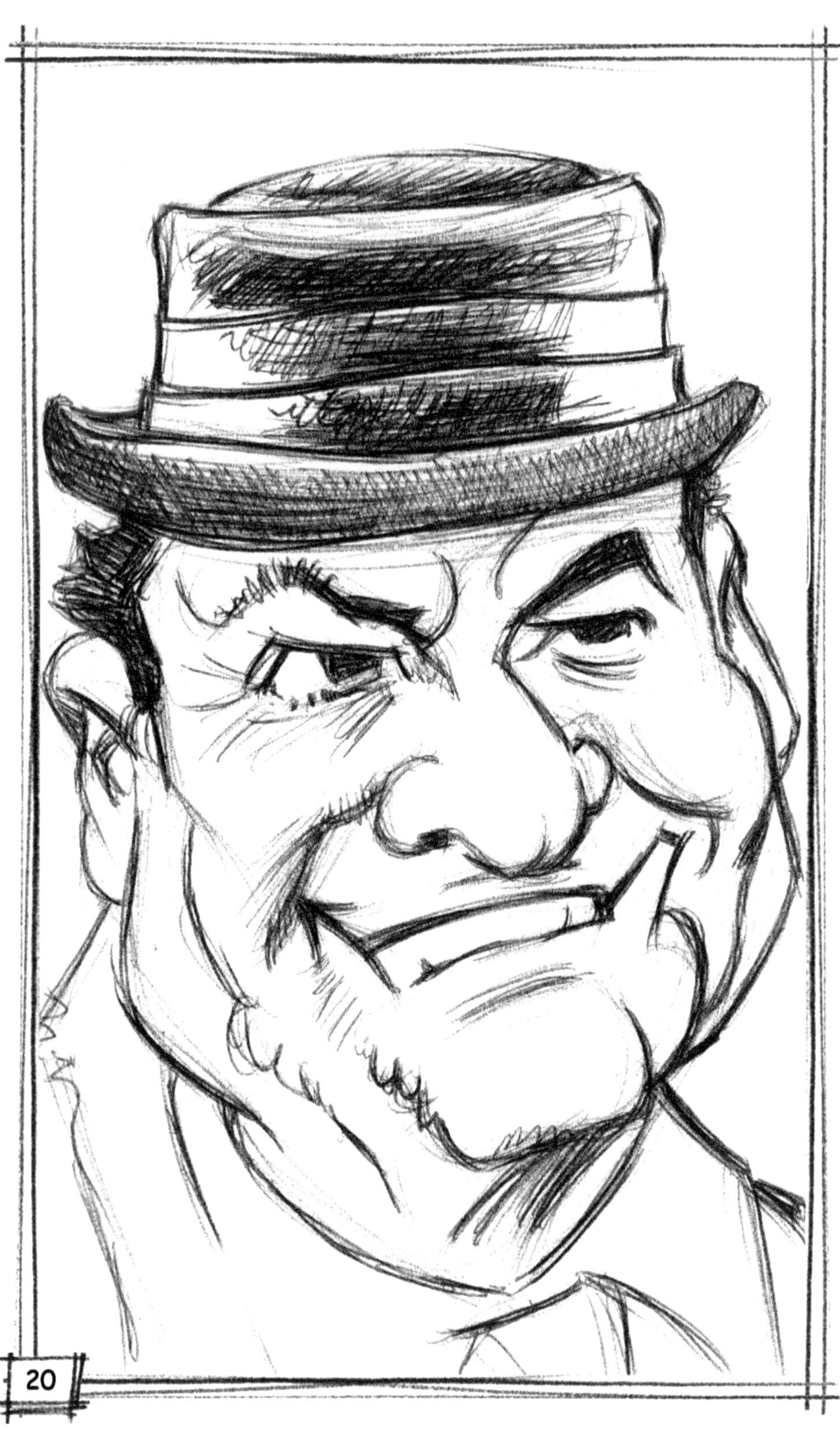

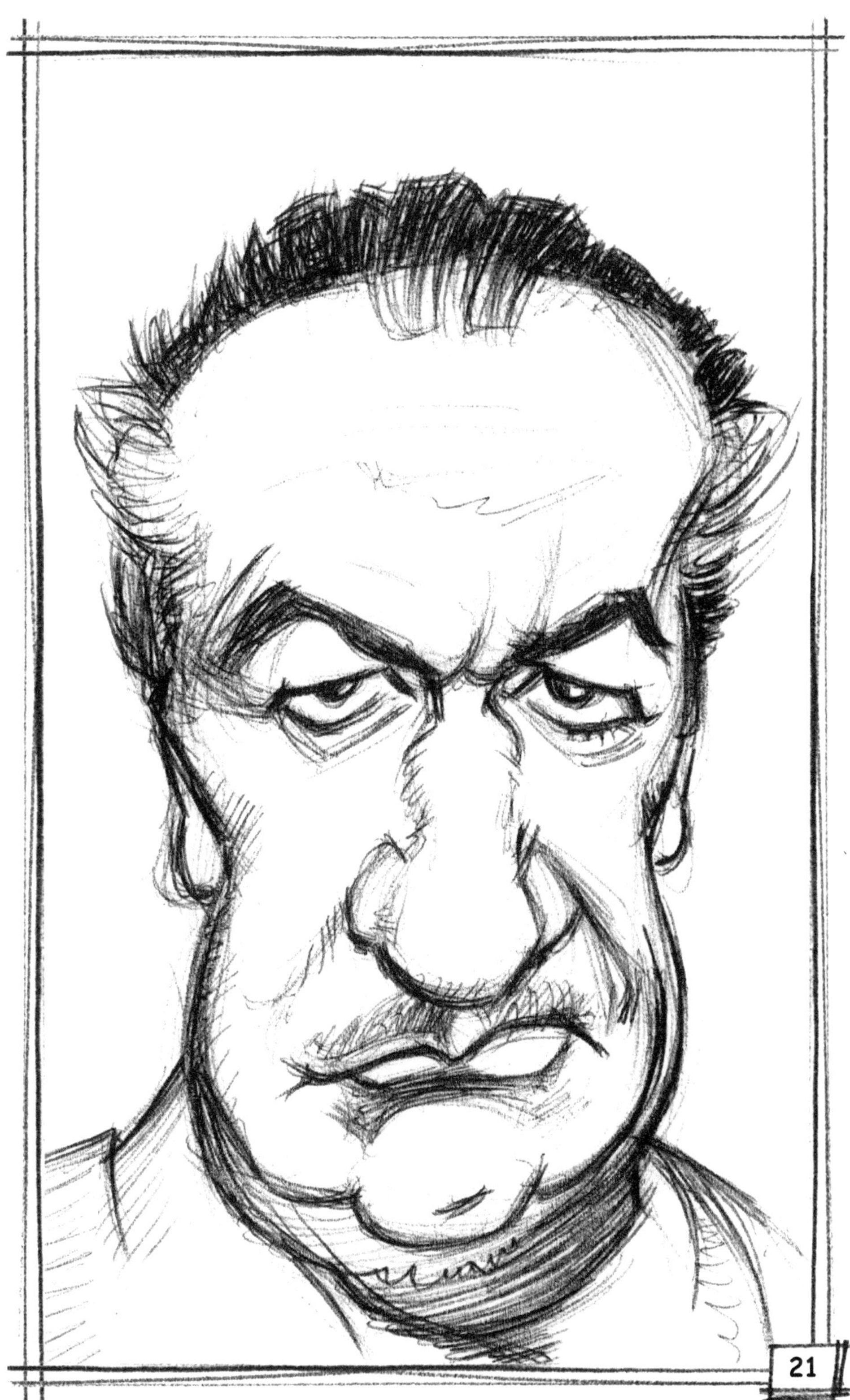

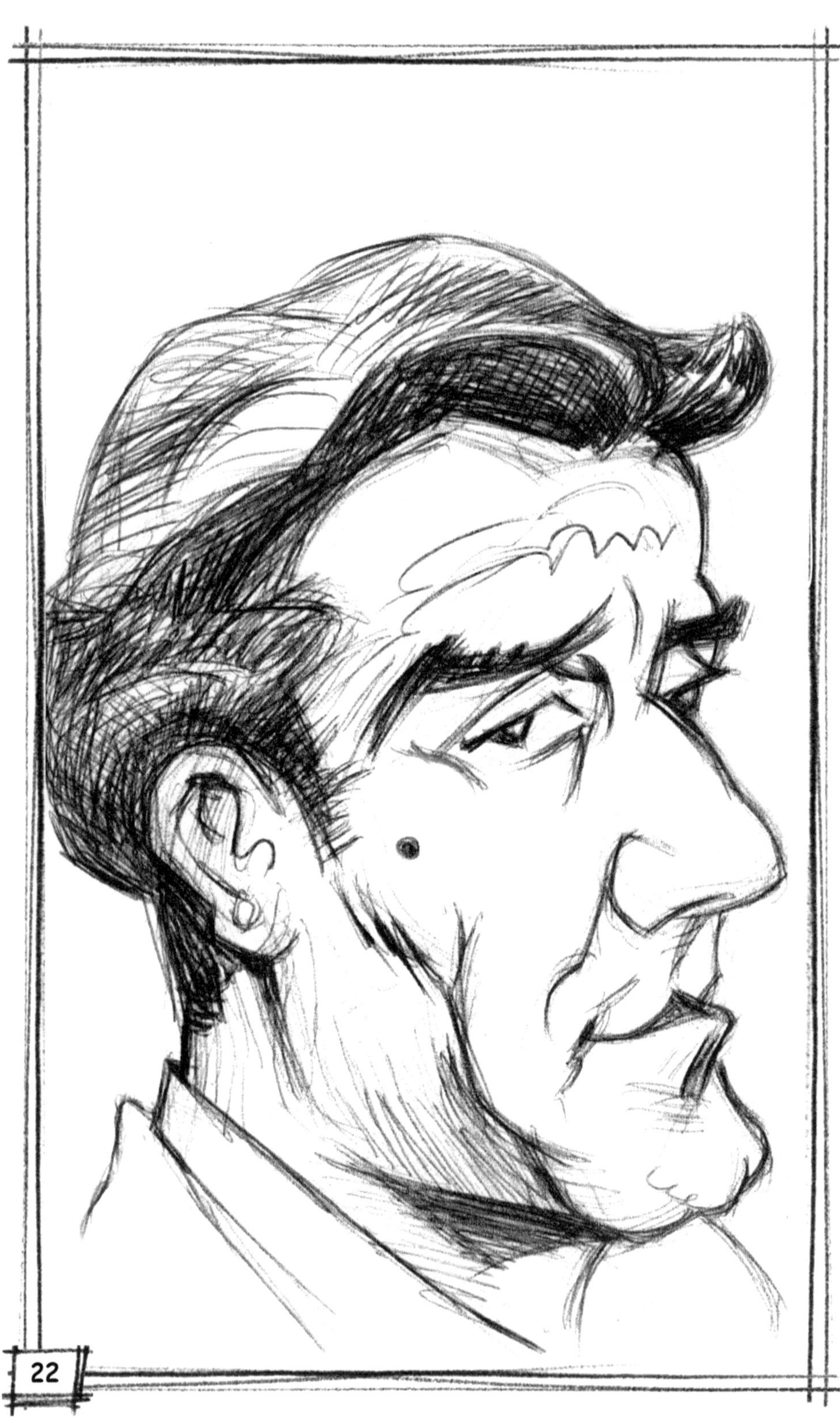

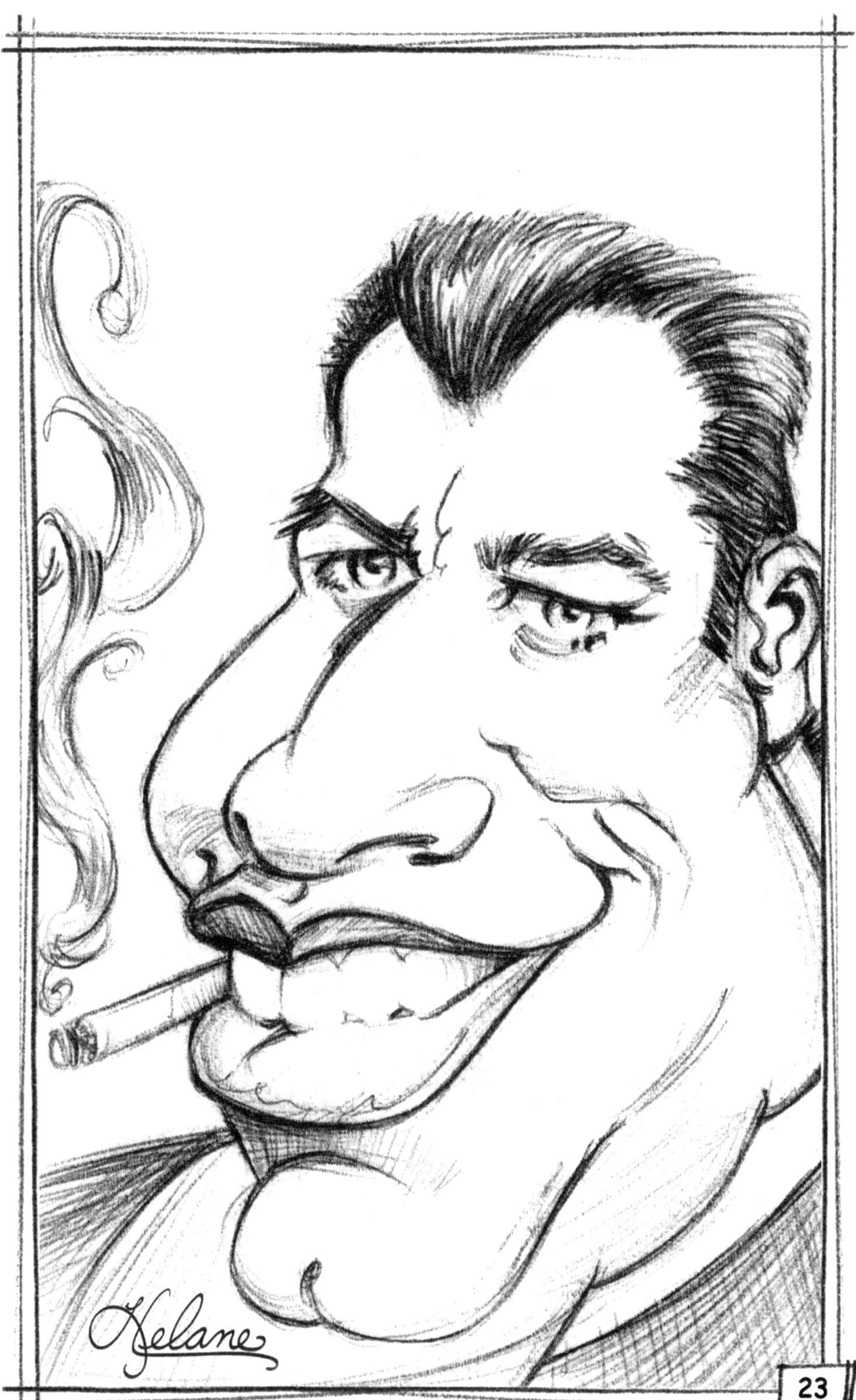

Kelane

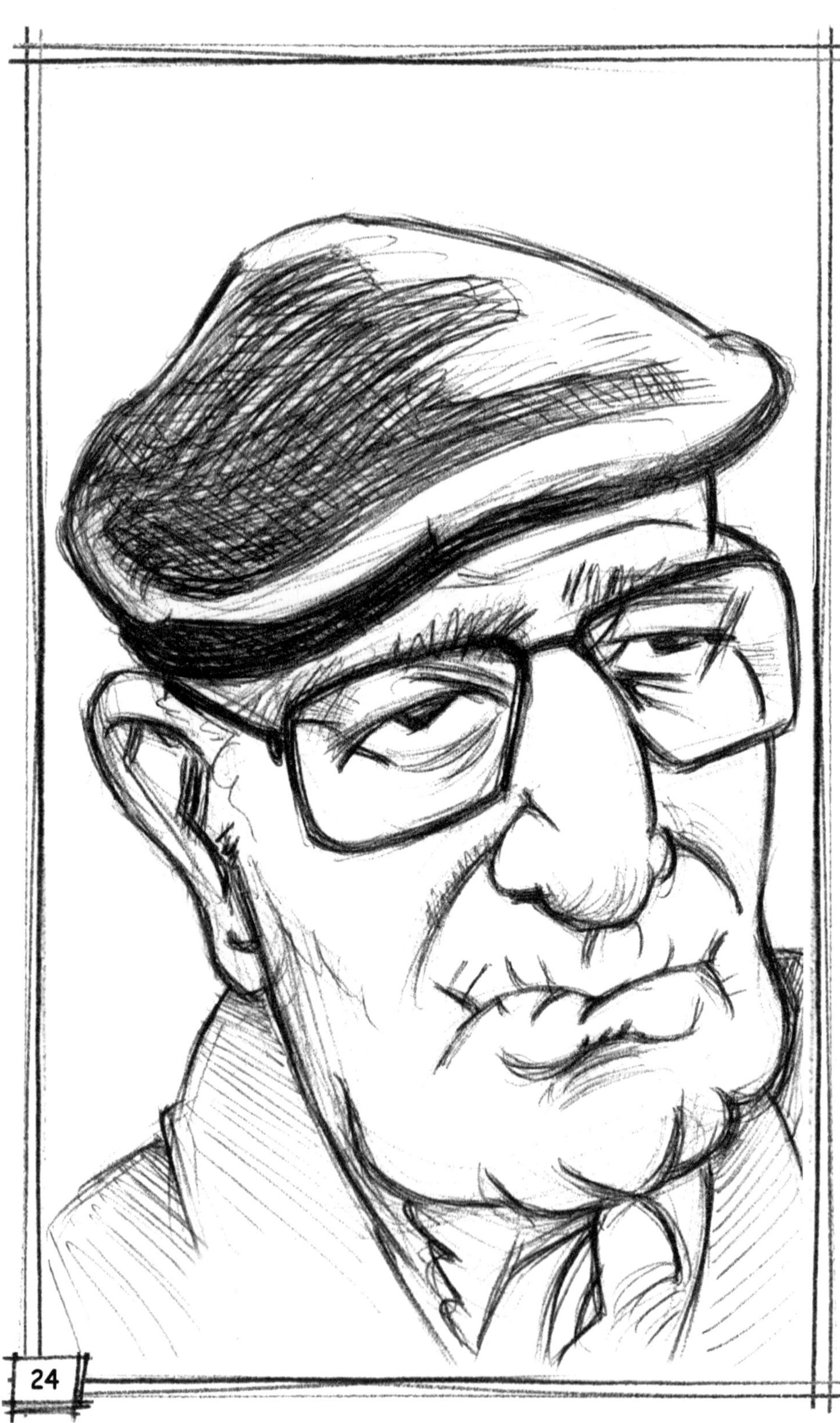

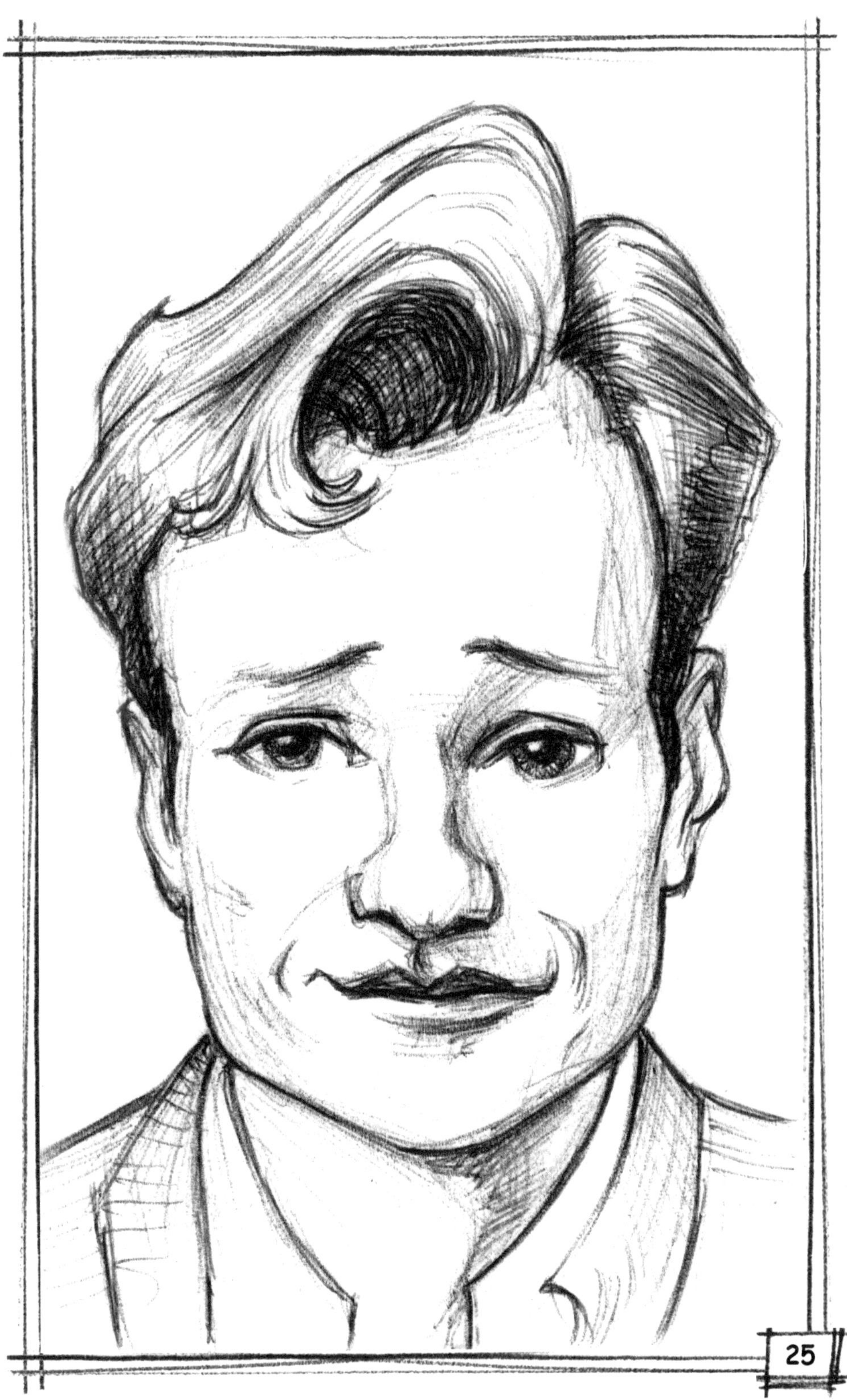

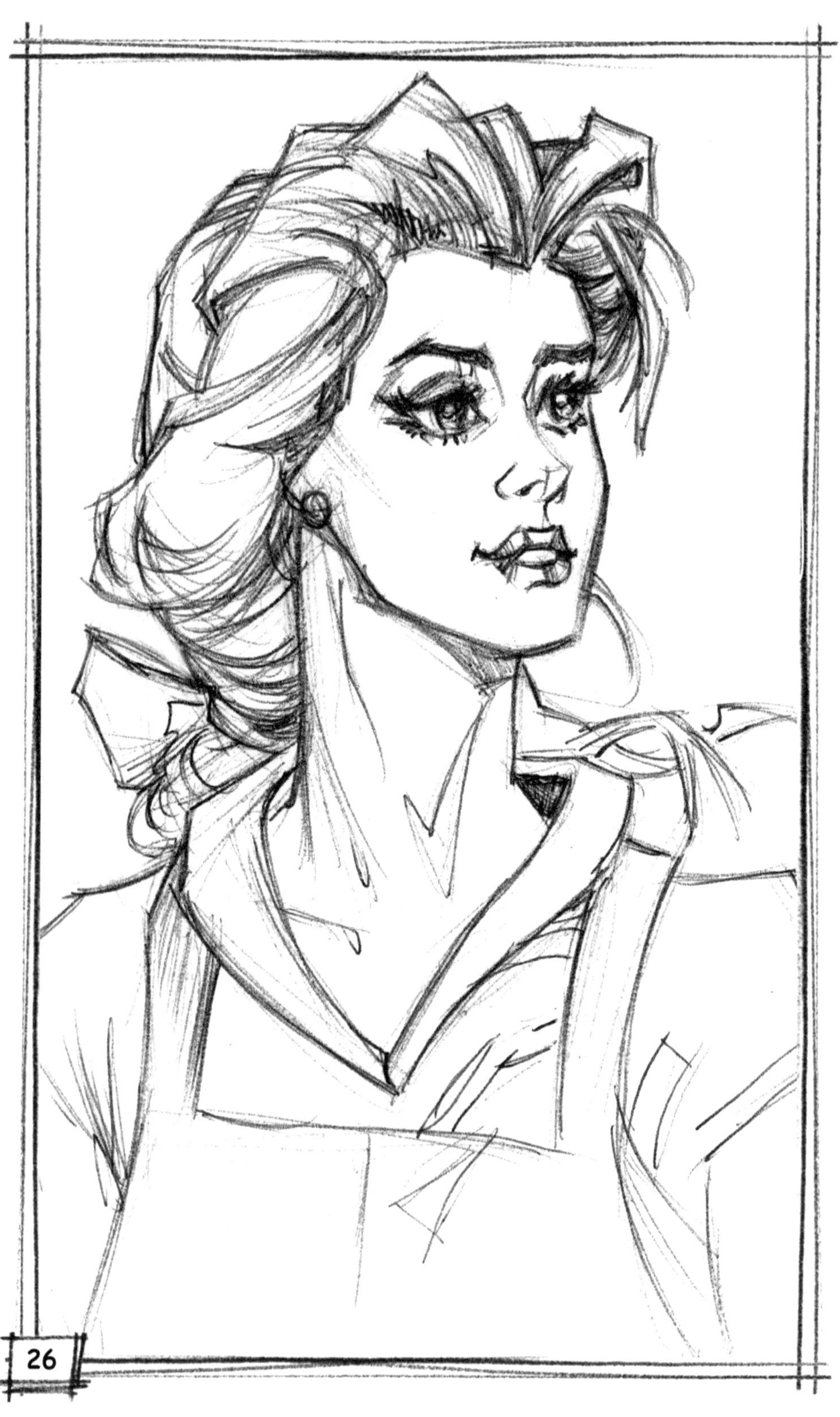

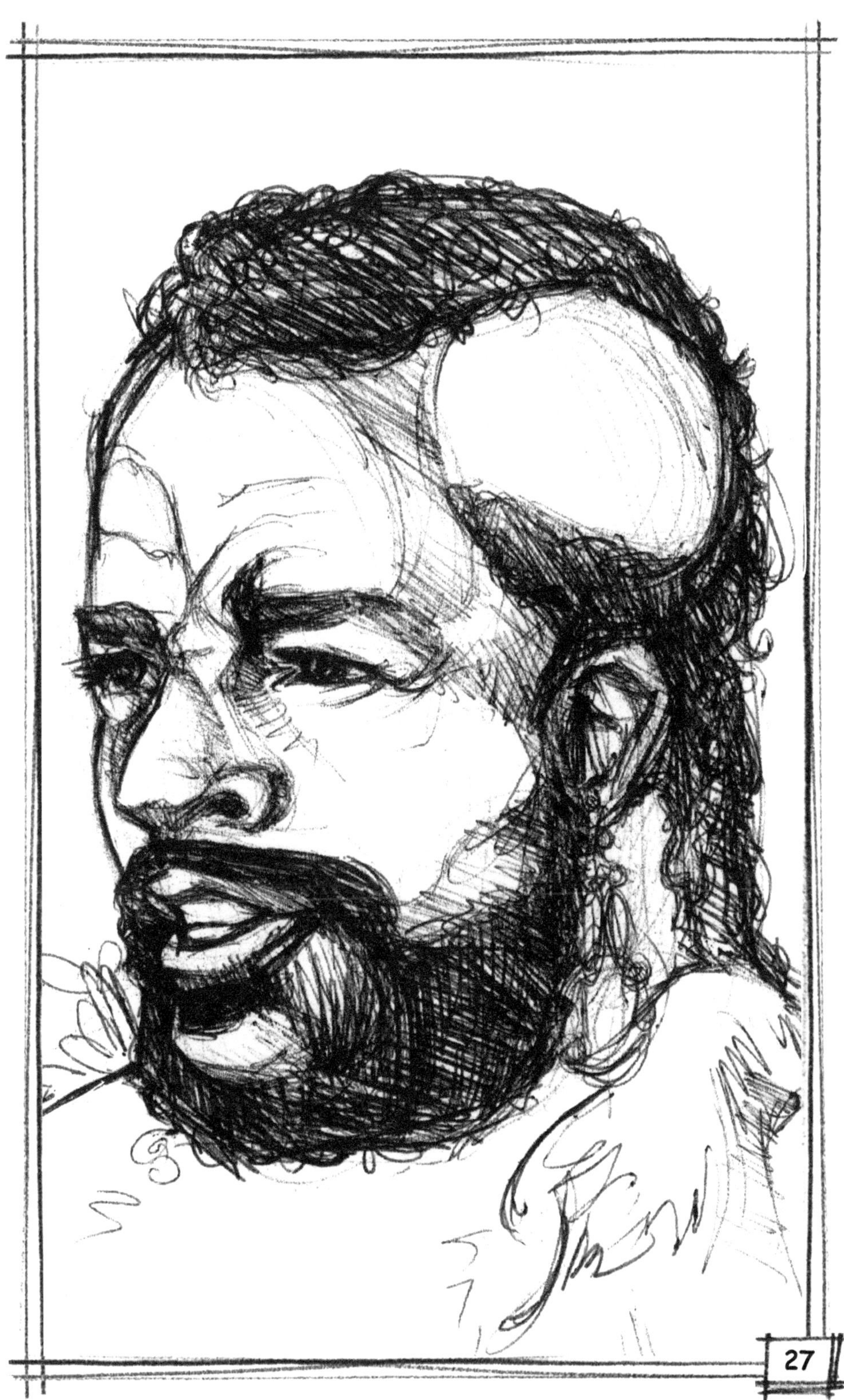

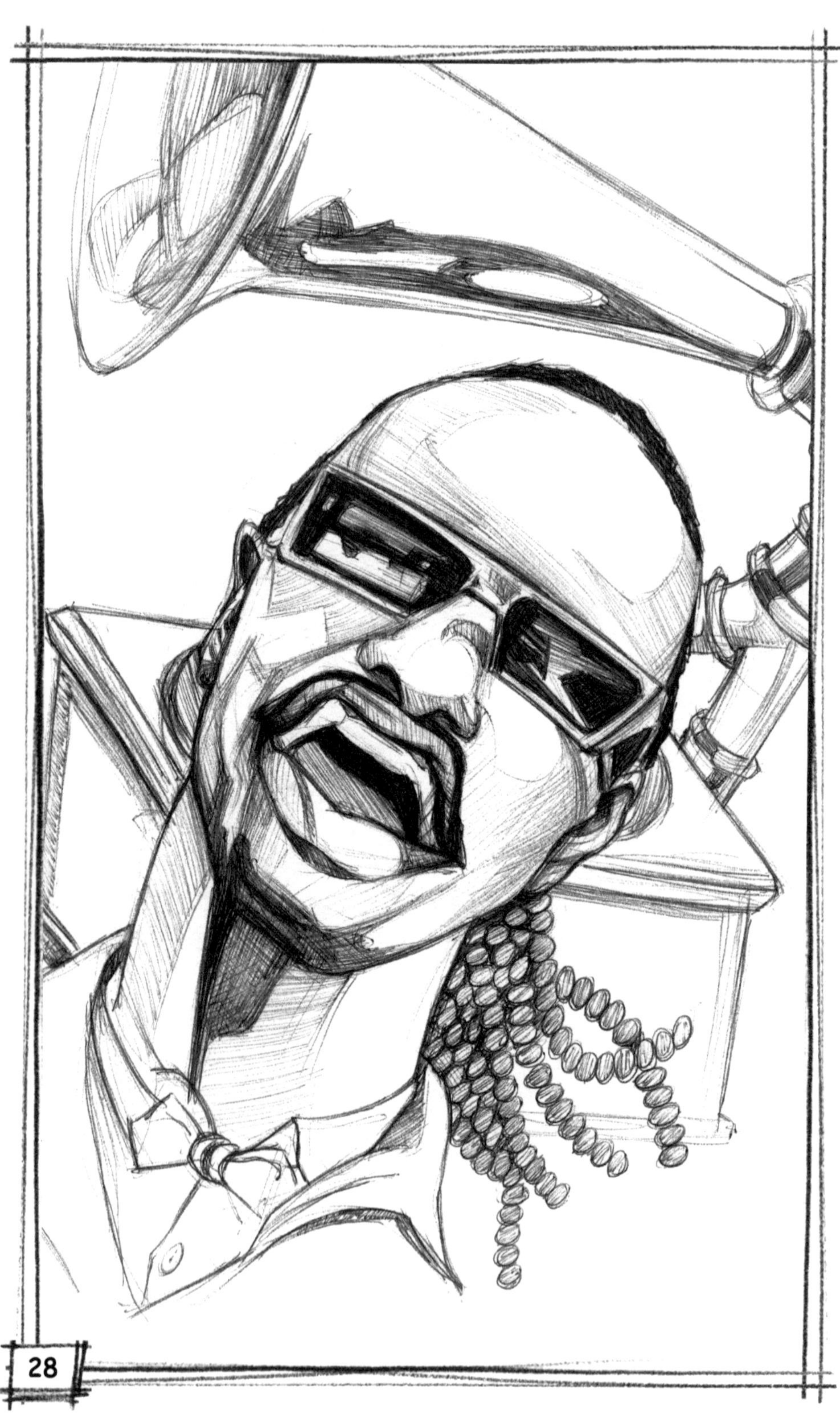

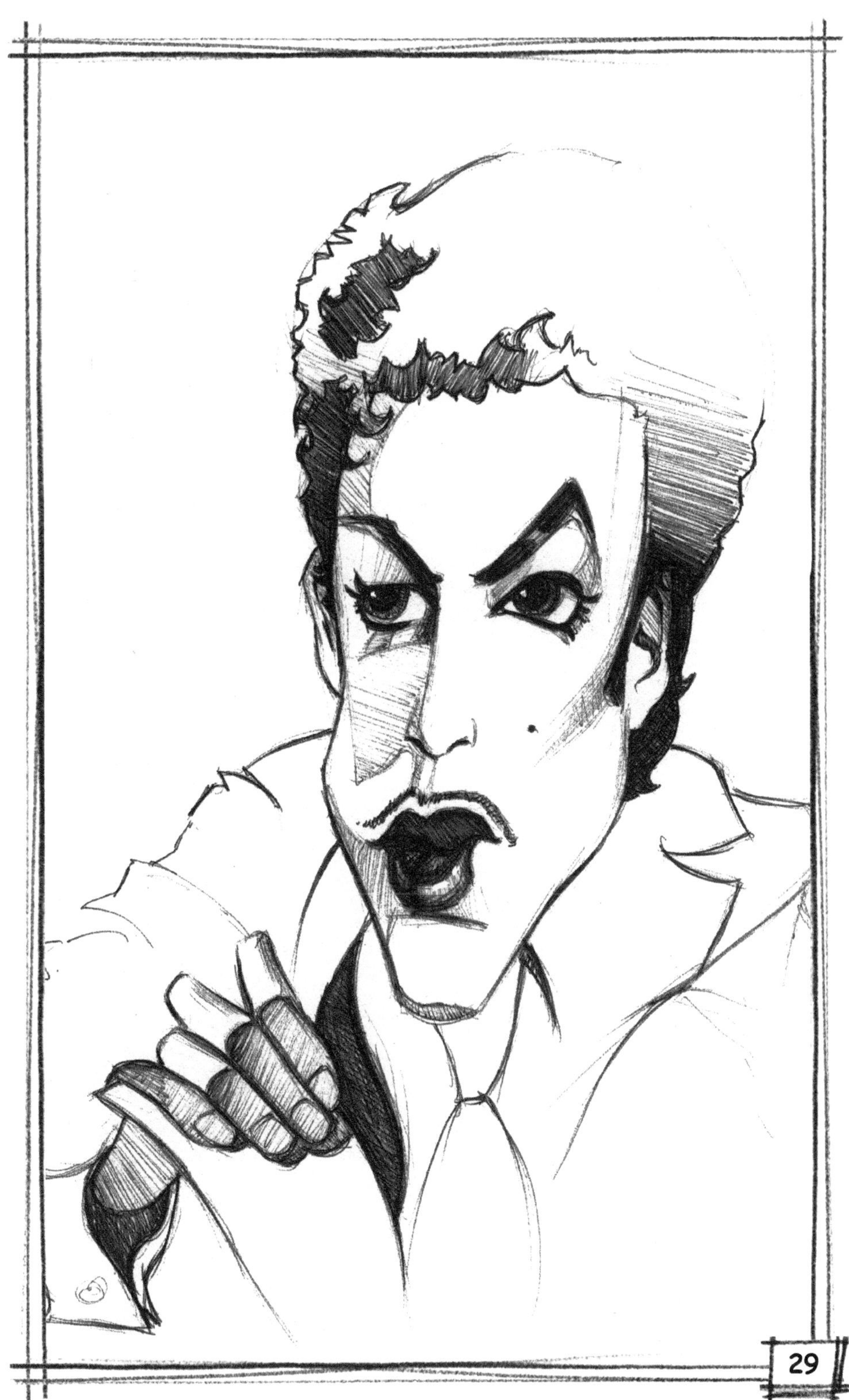

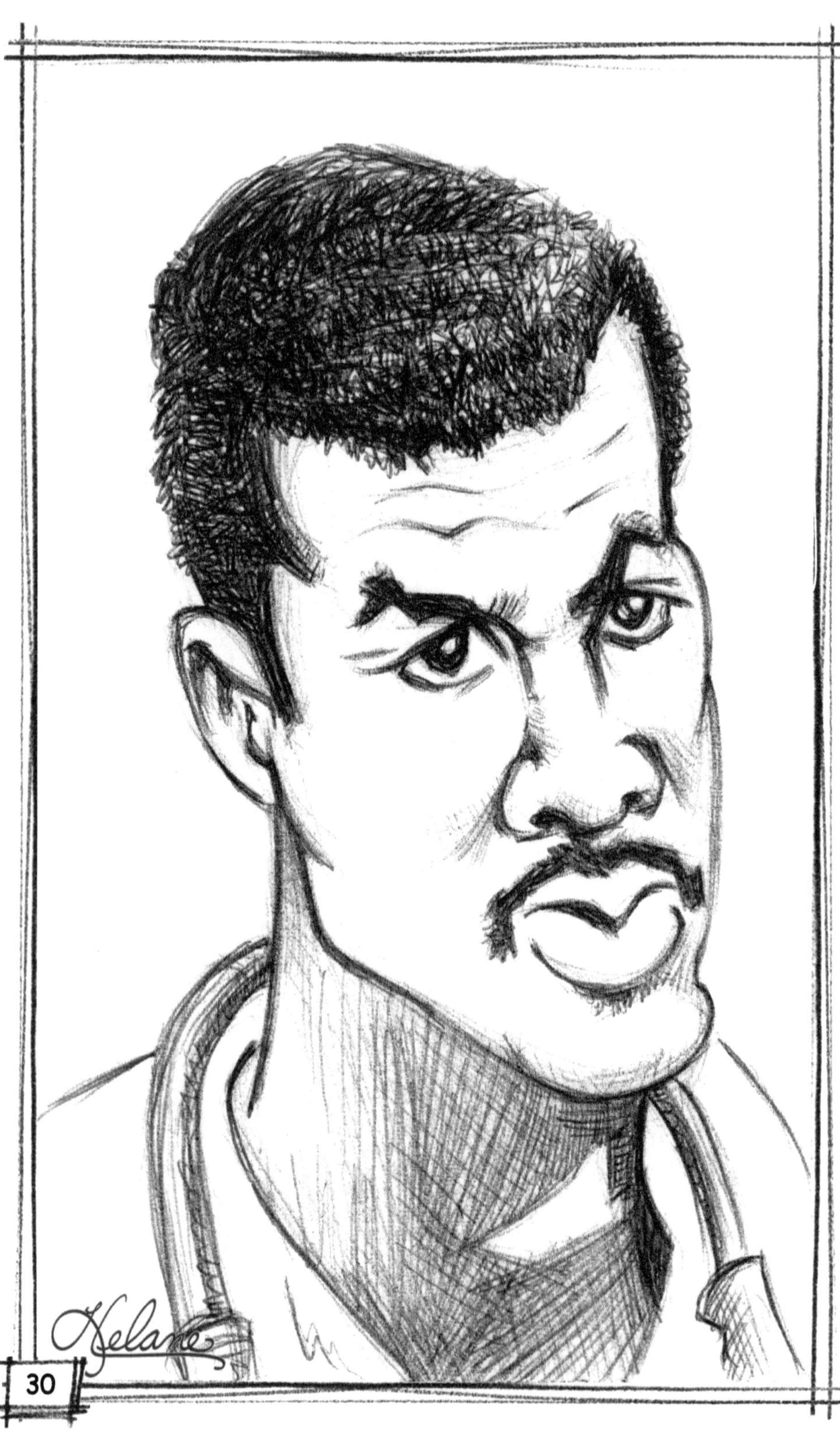

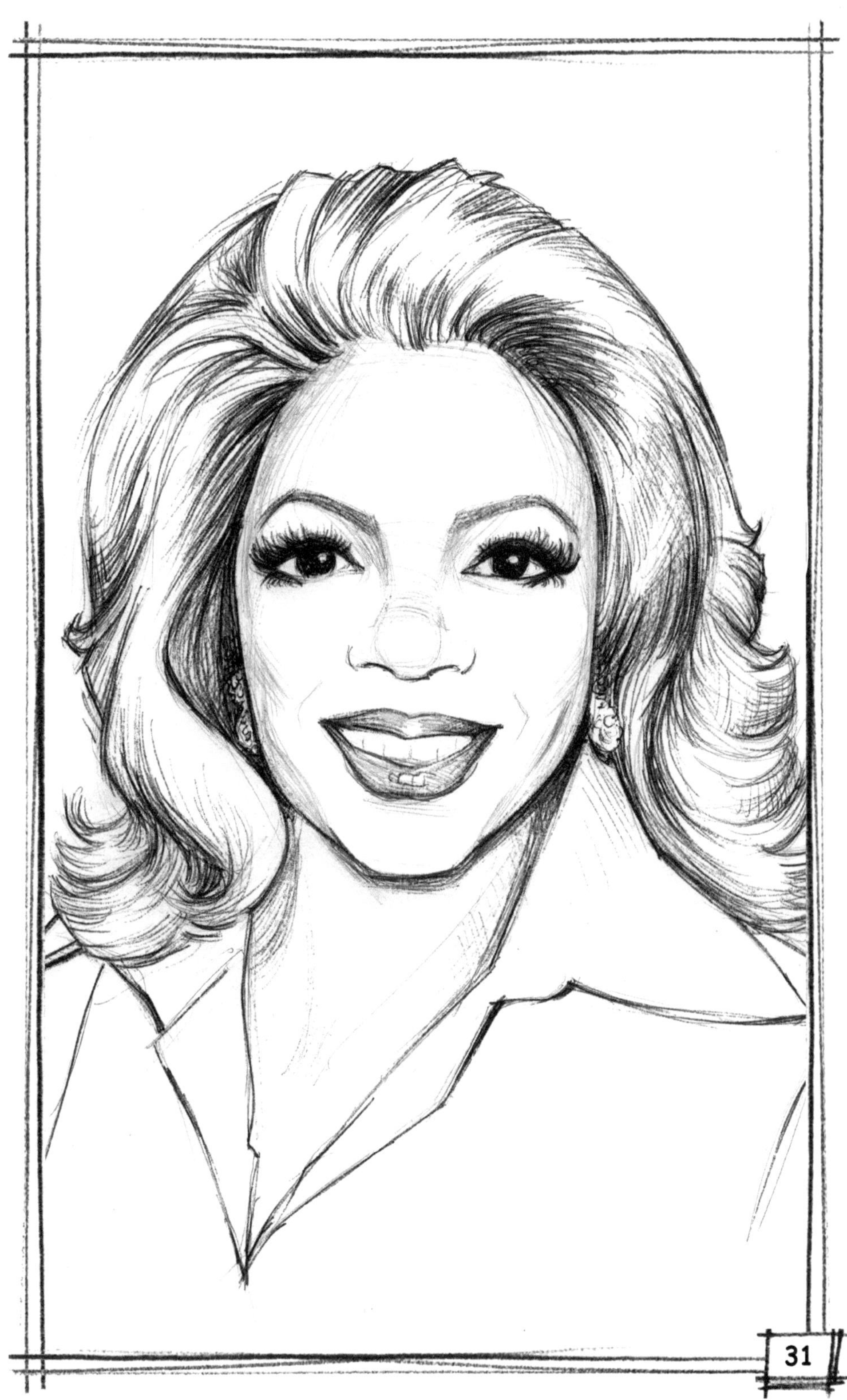

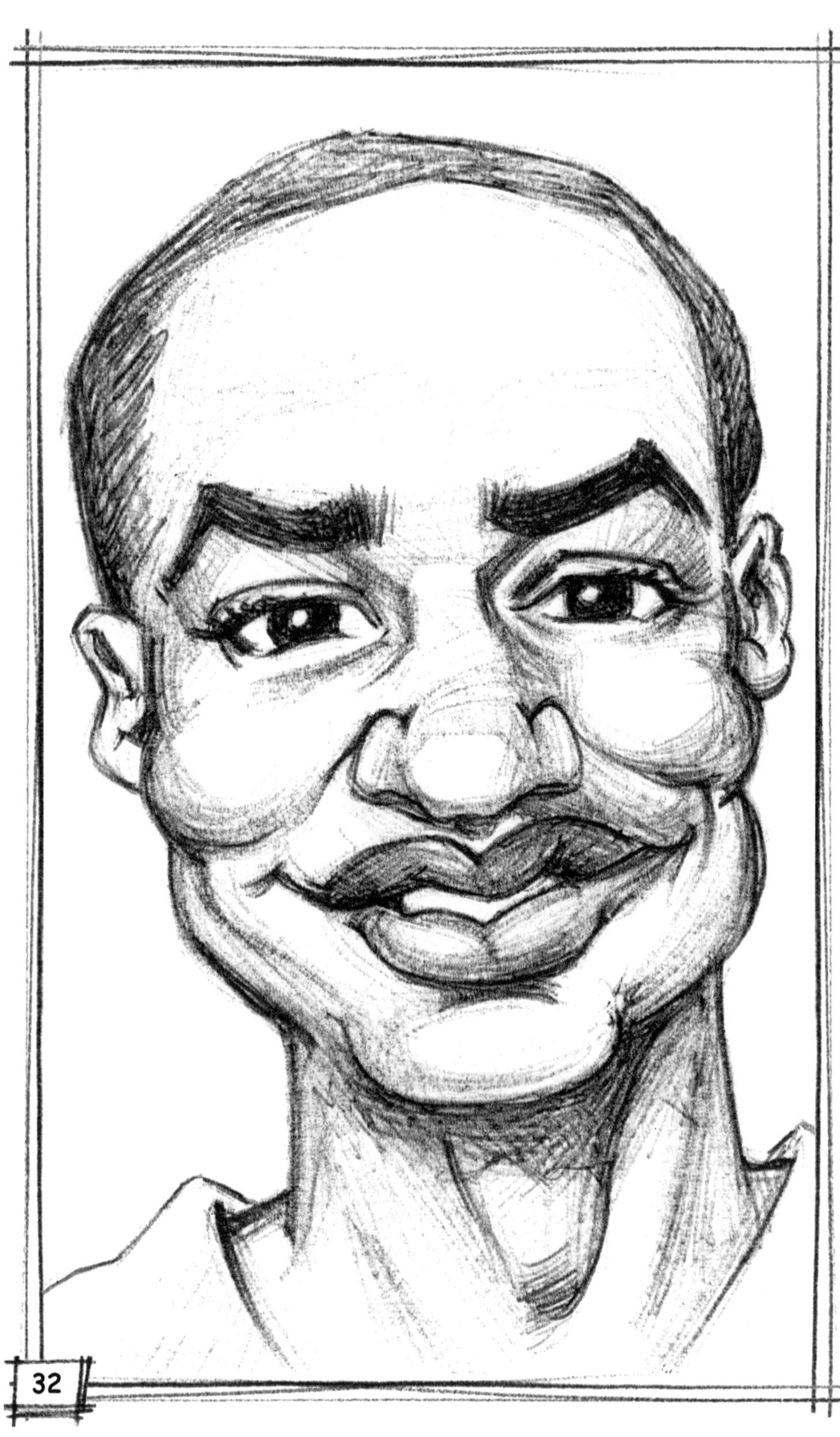

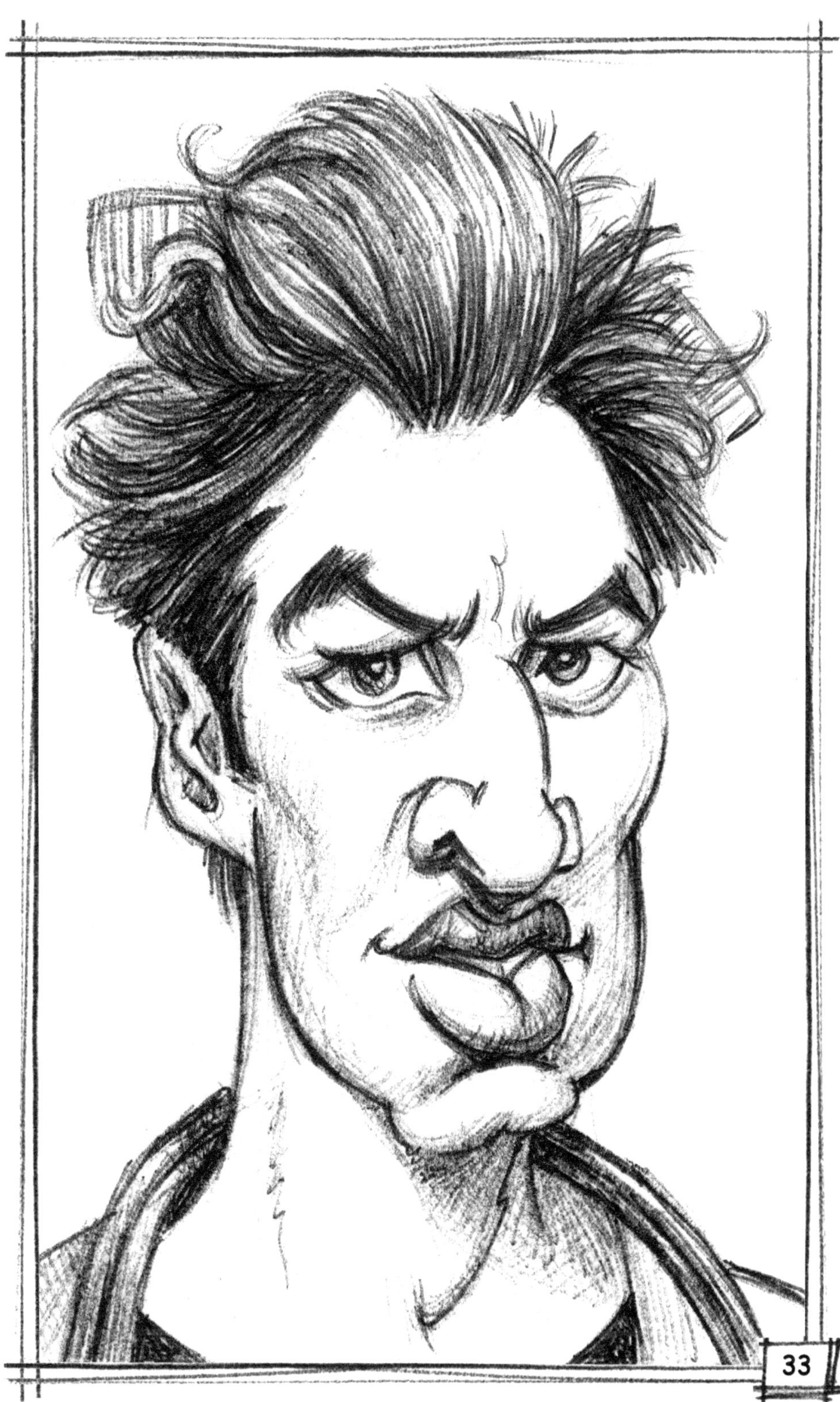

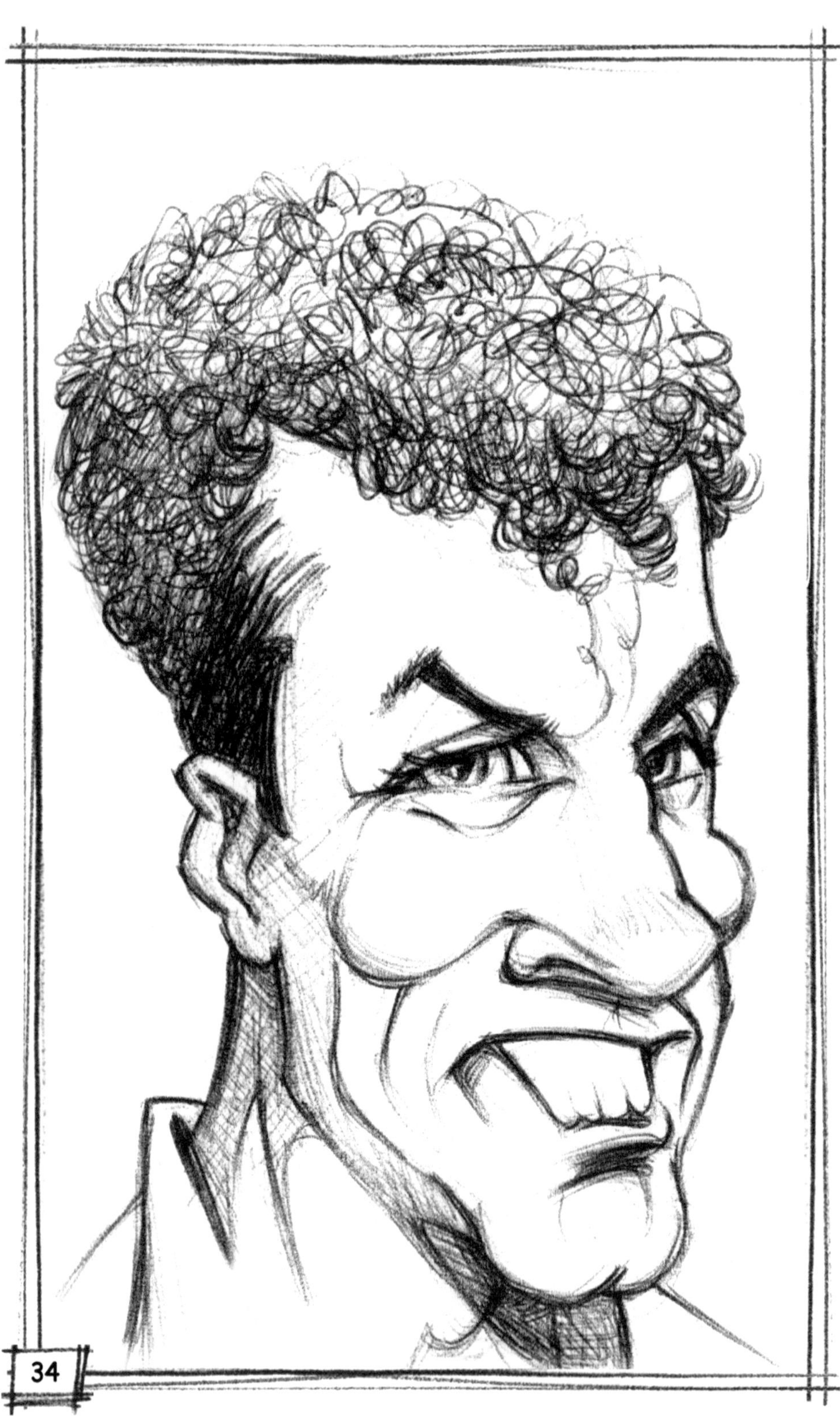

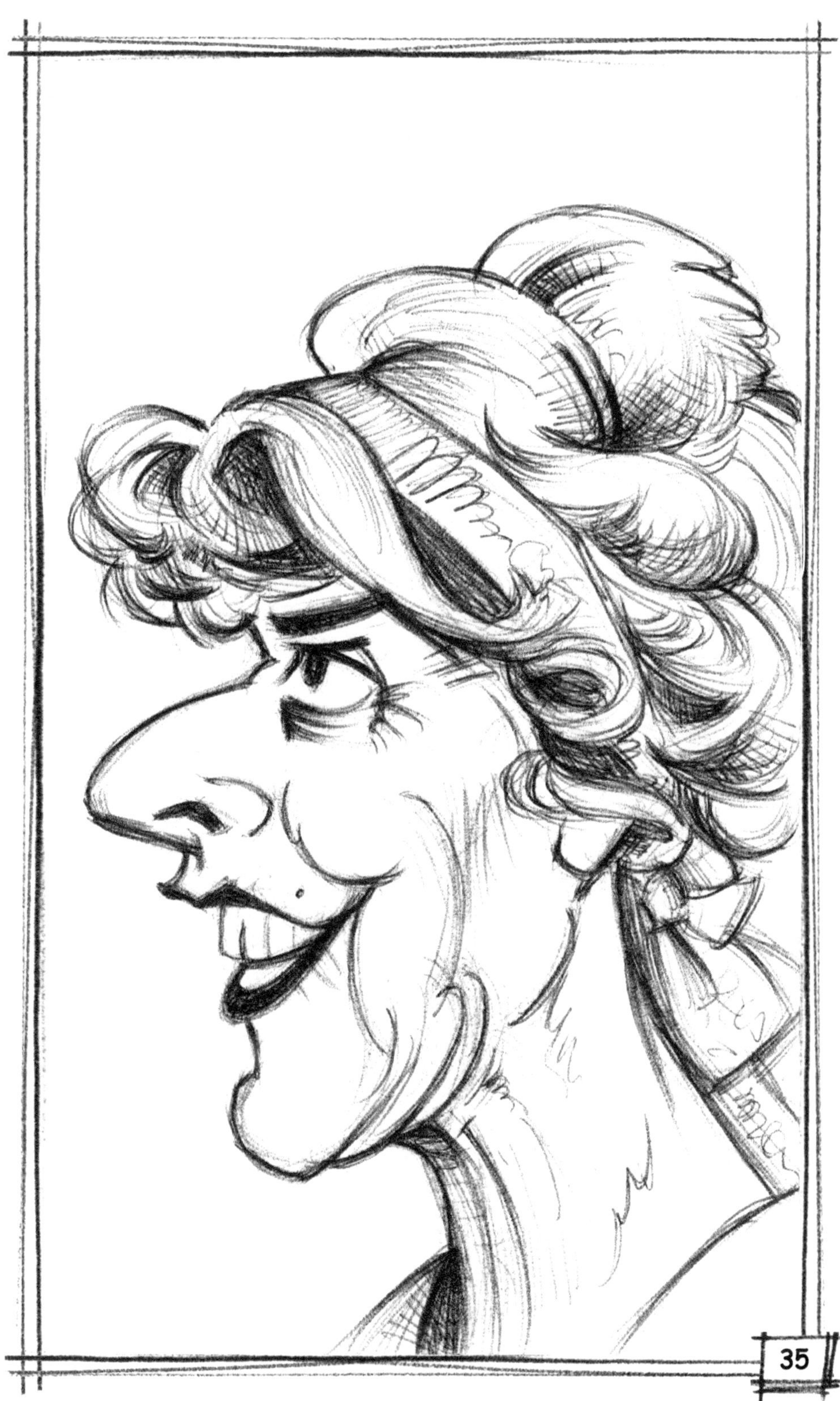

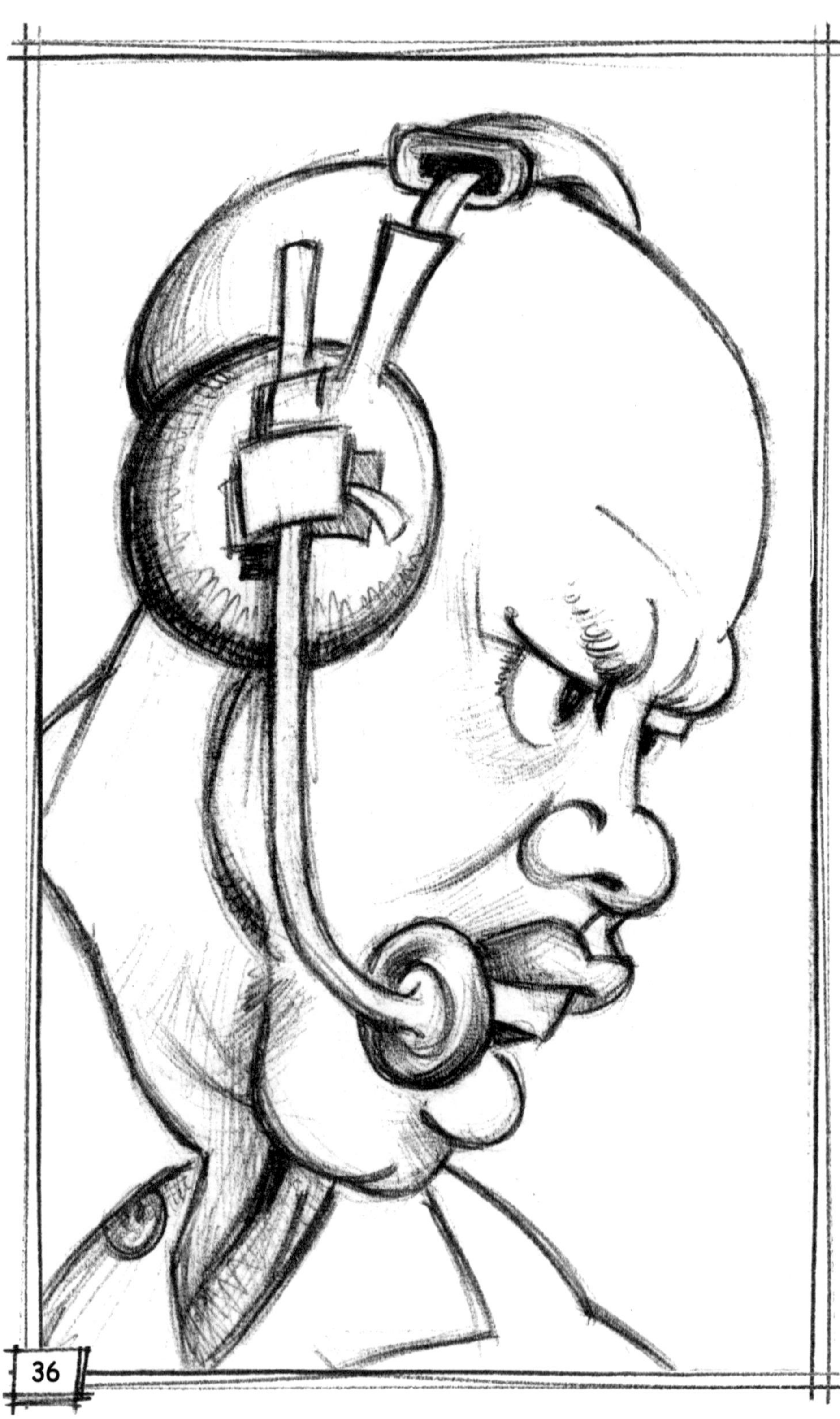

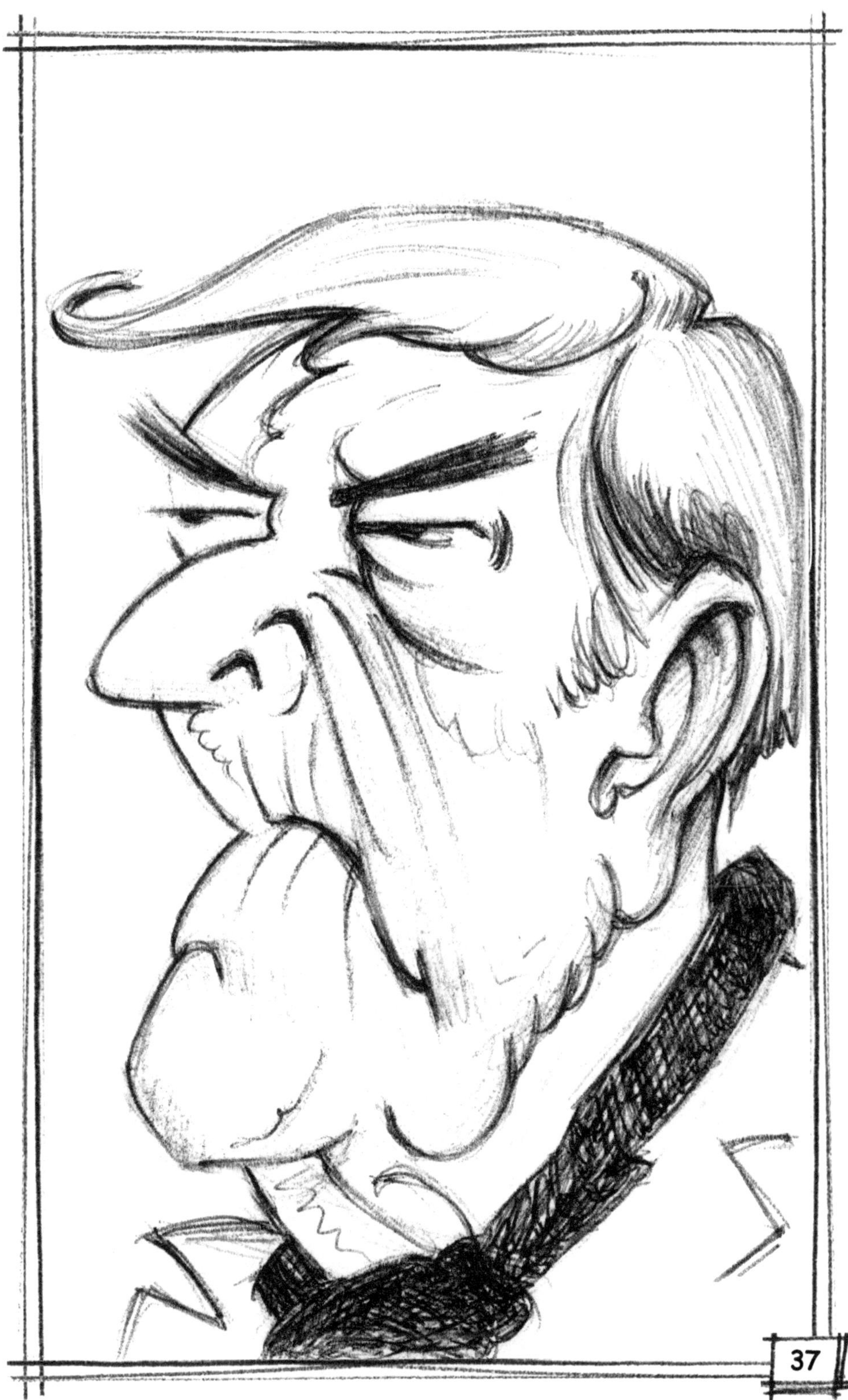

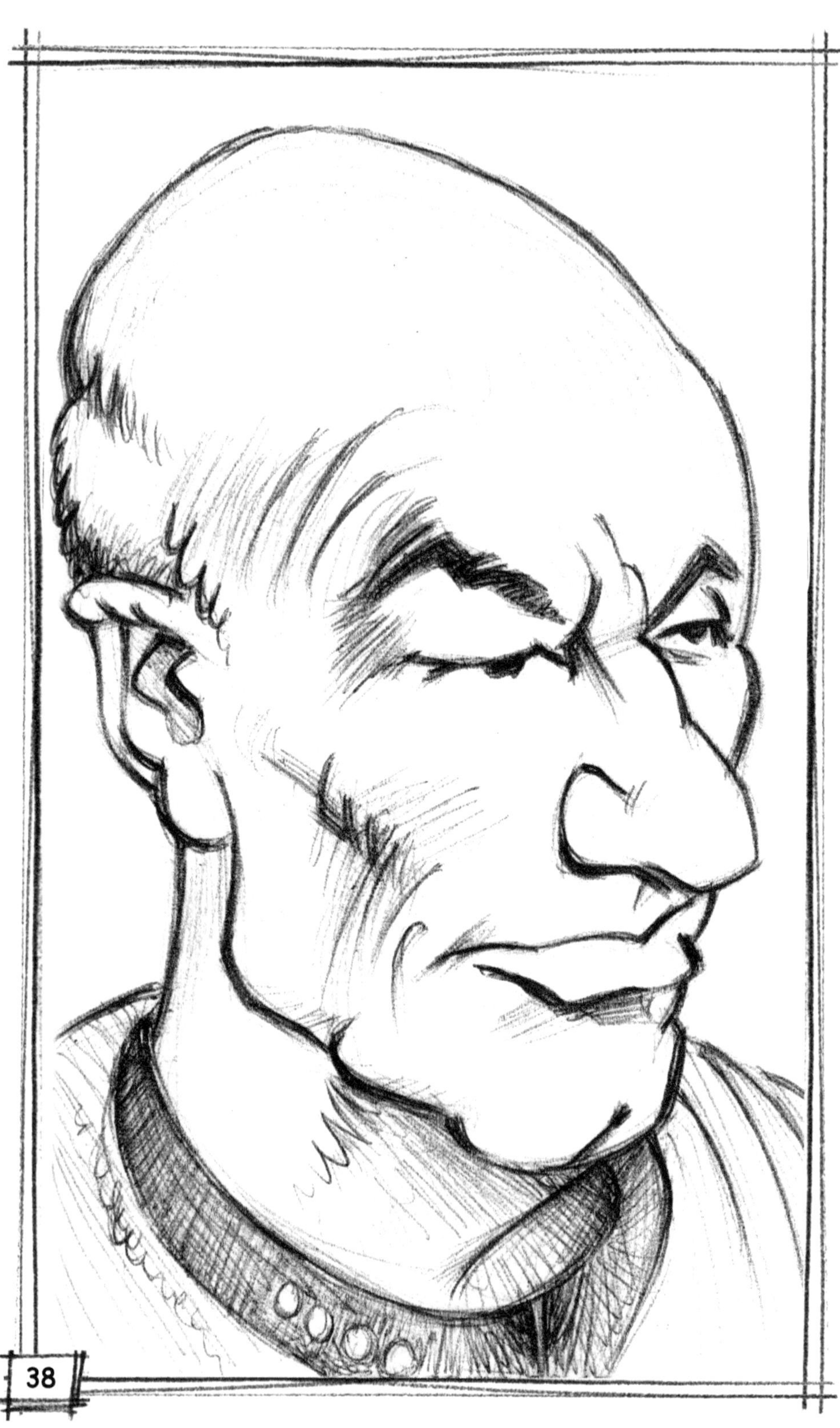

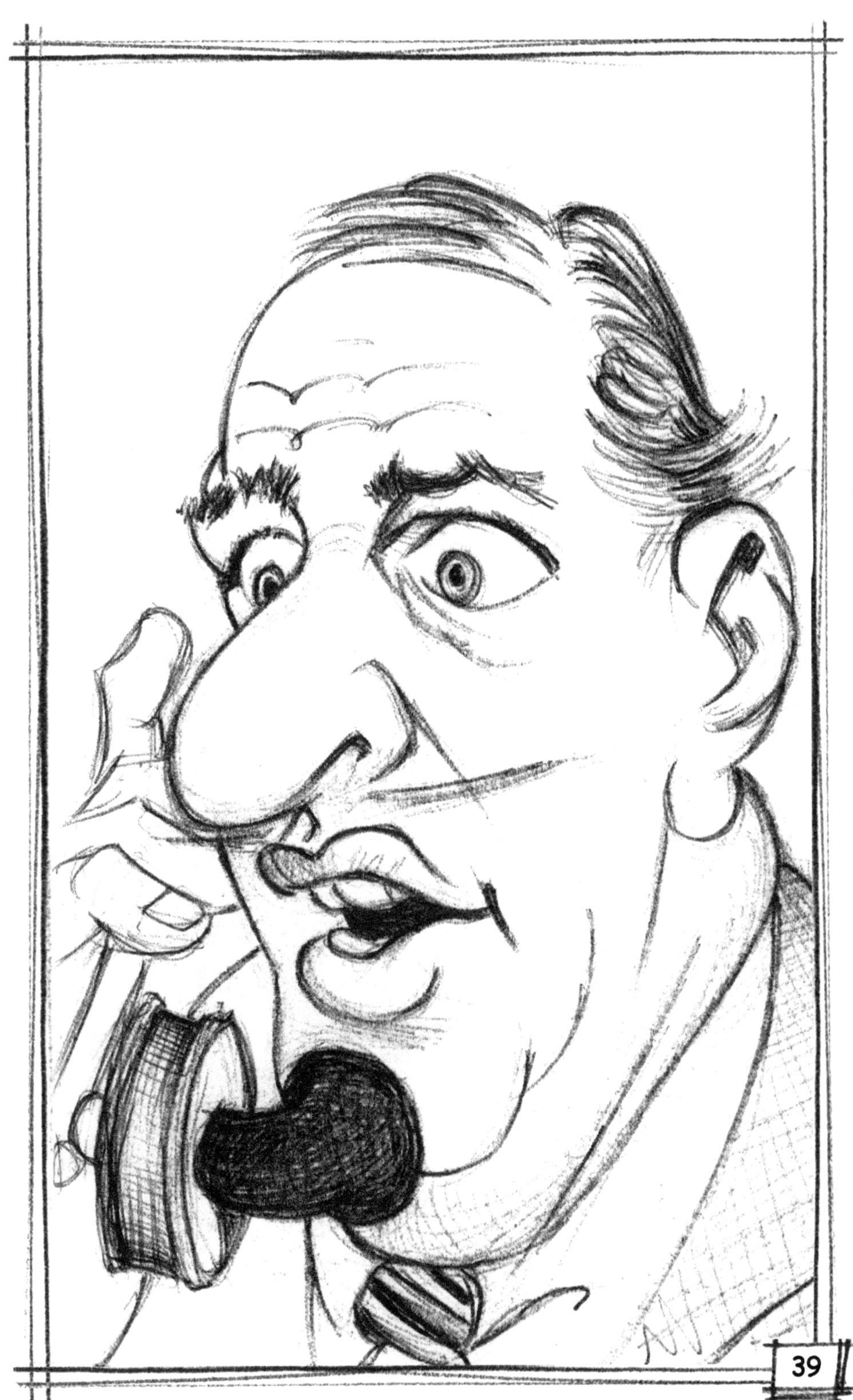

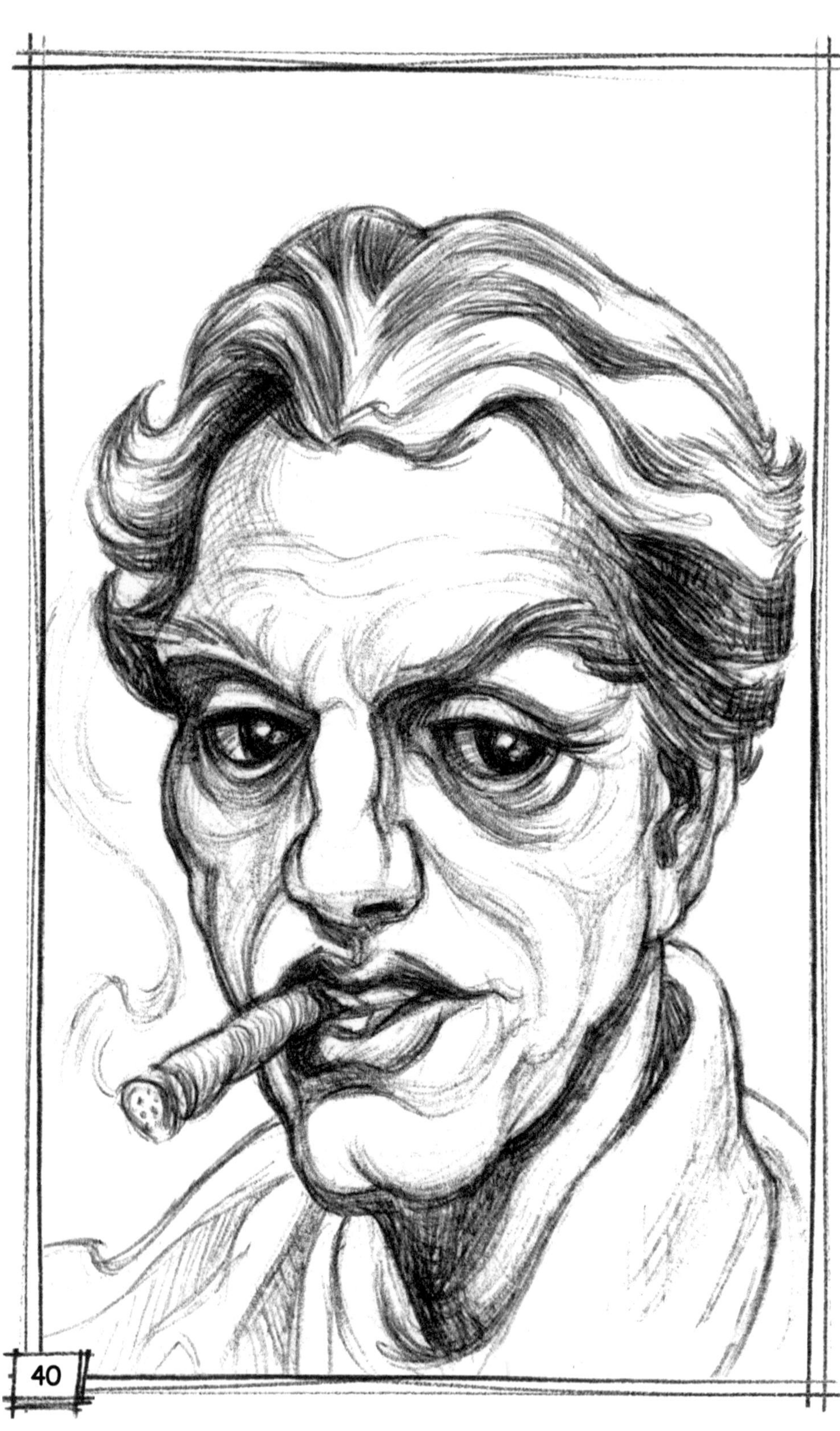

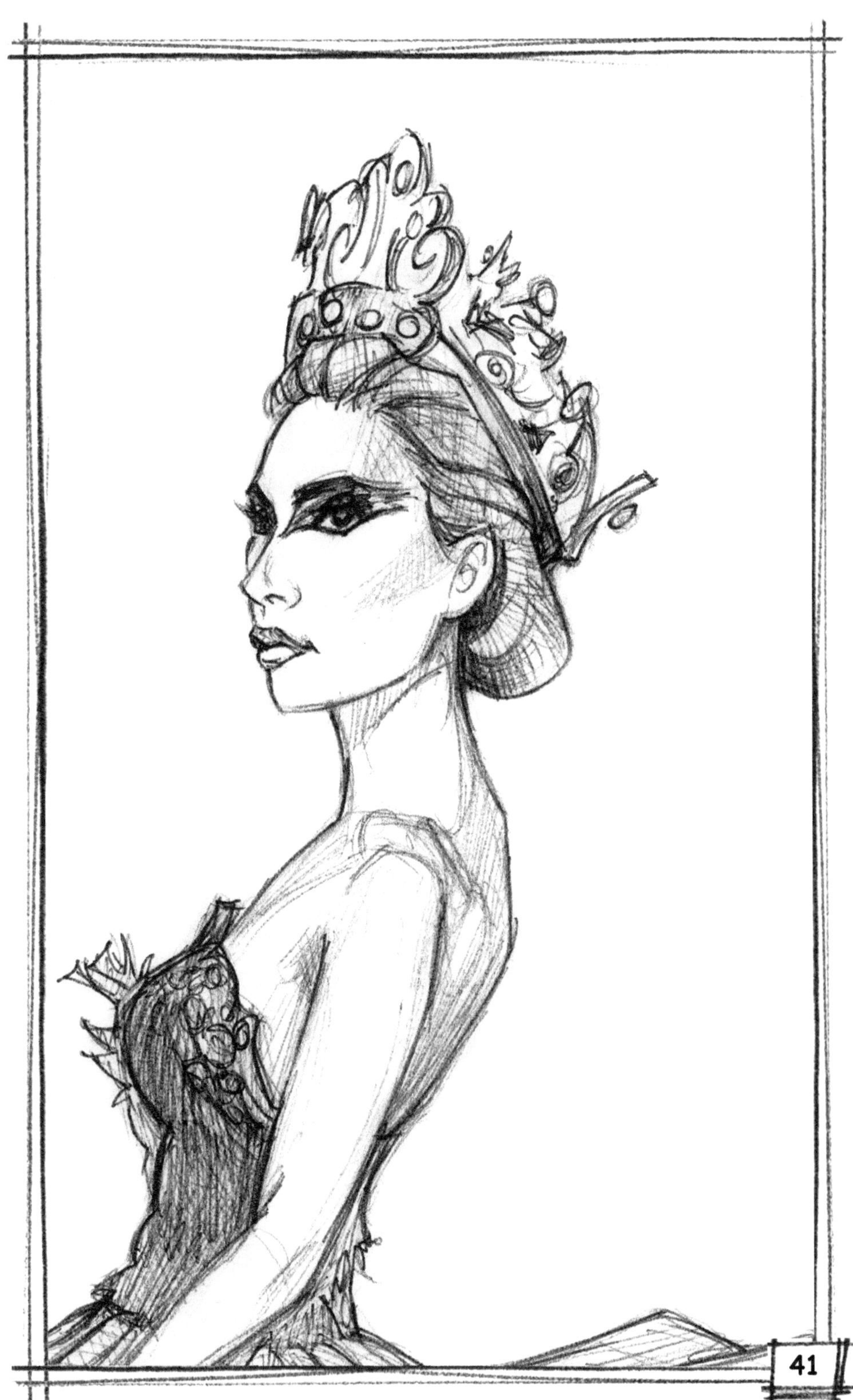

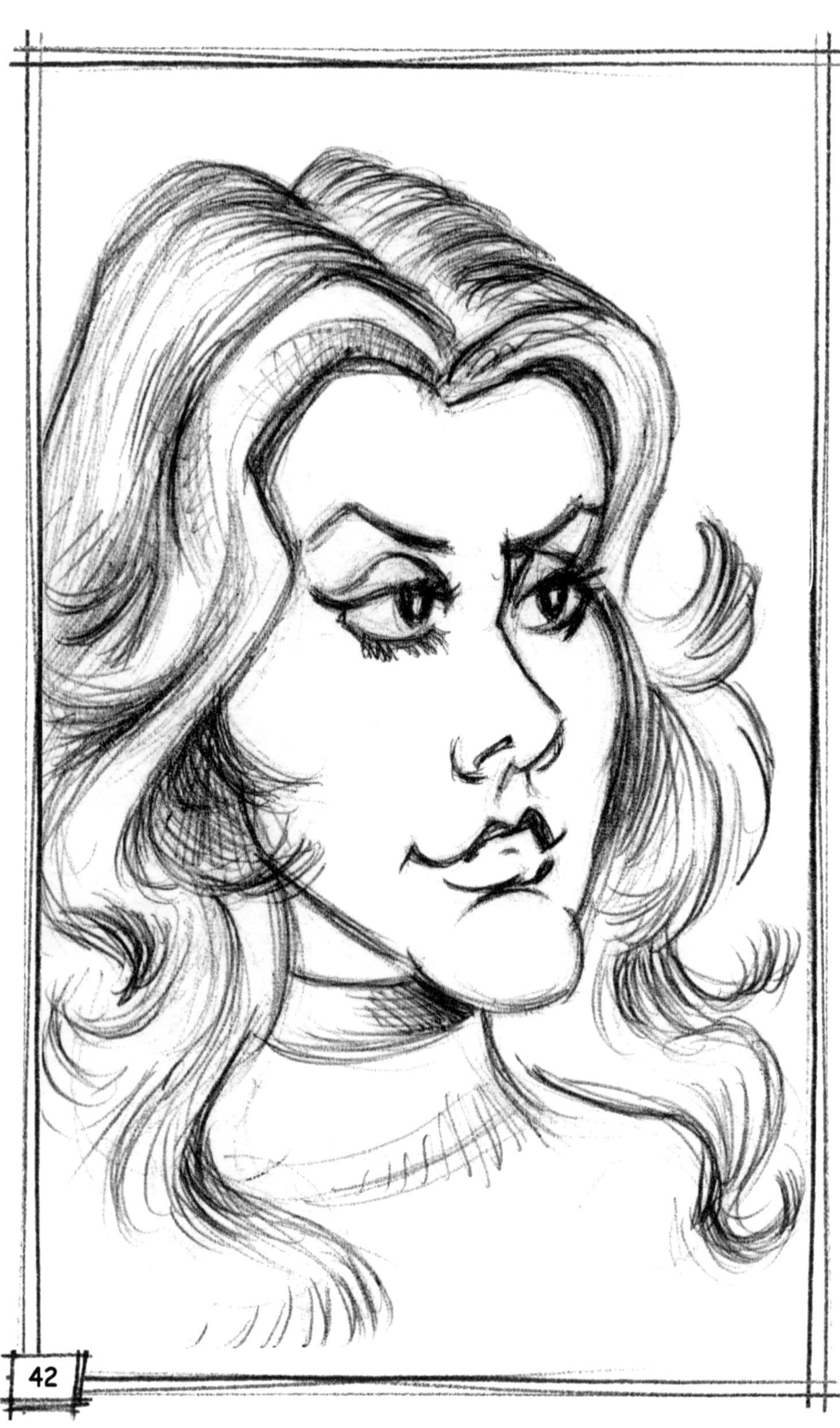

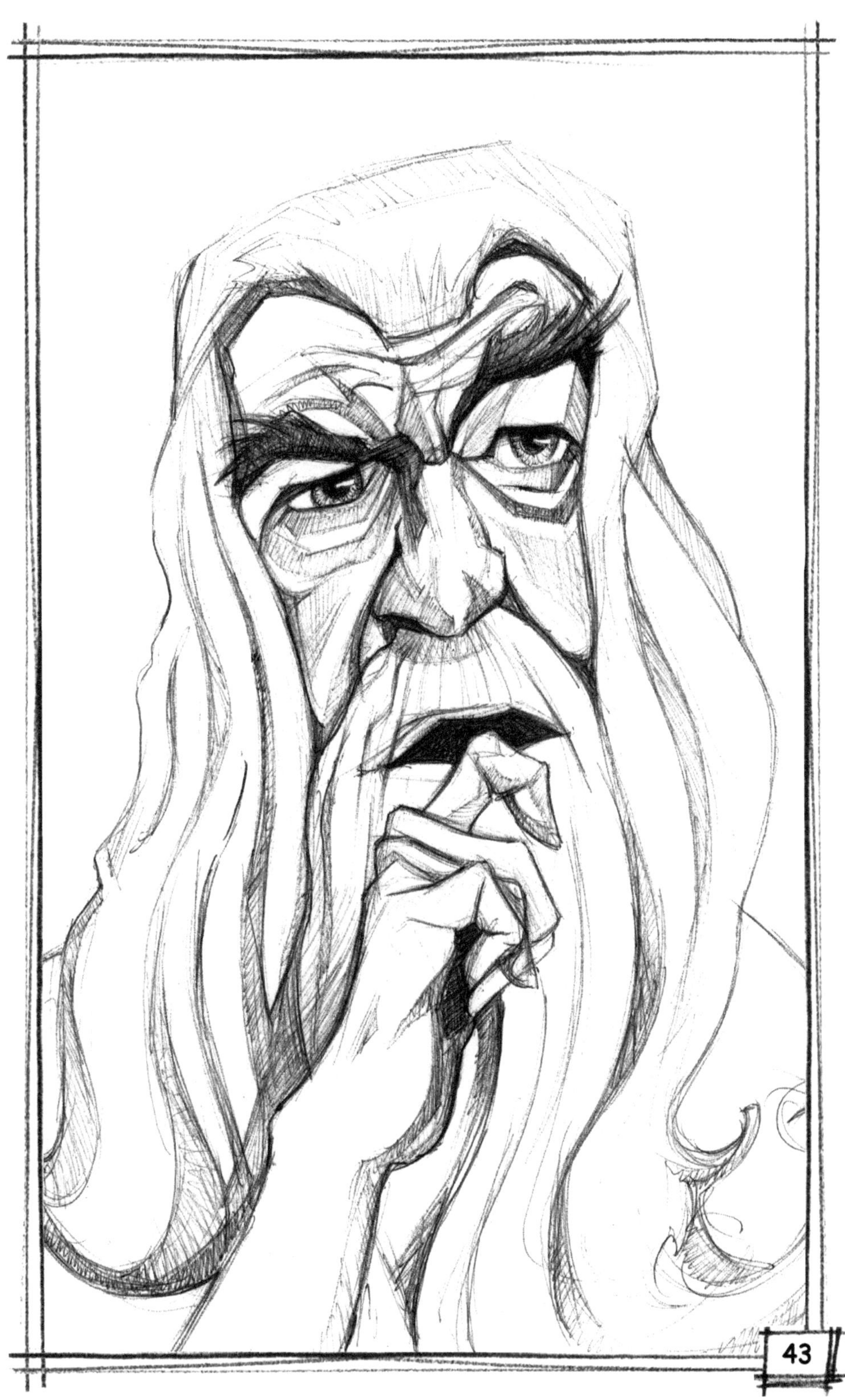

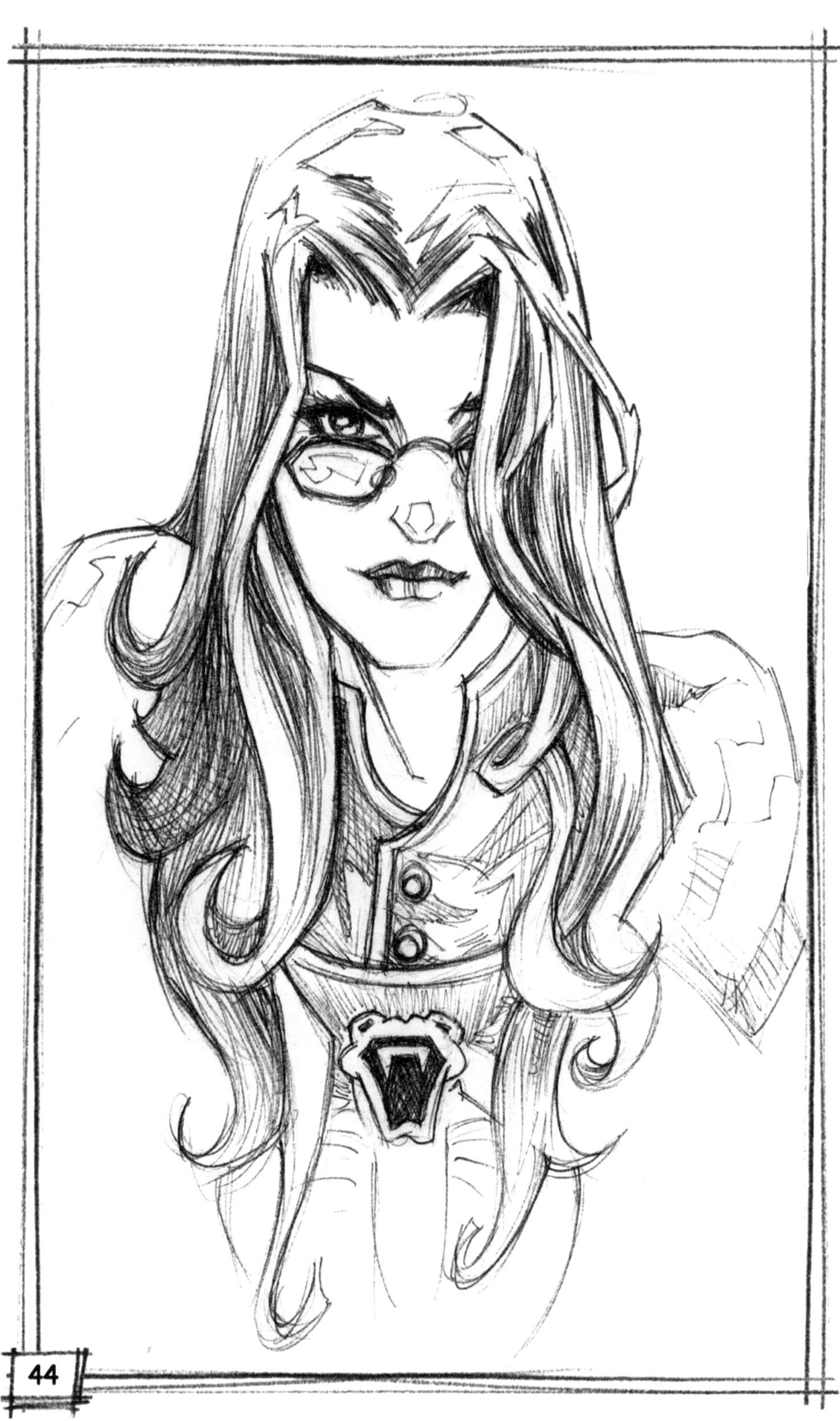

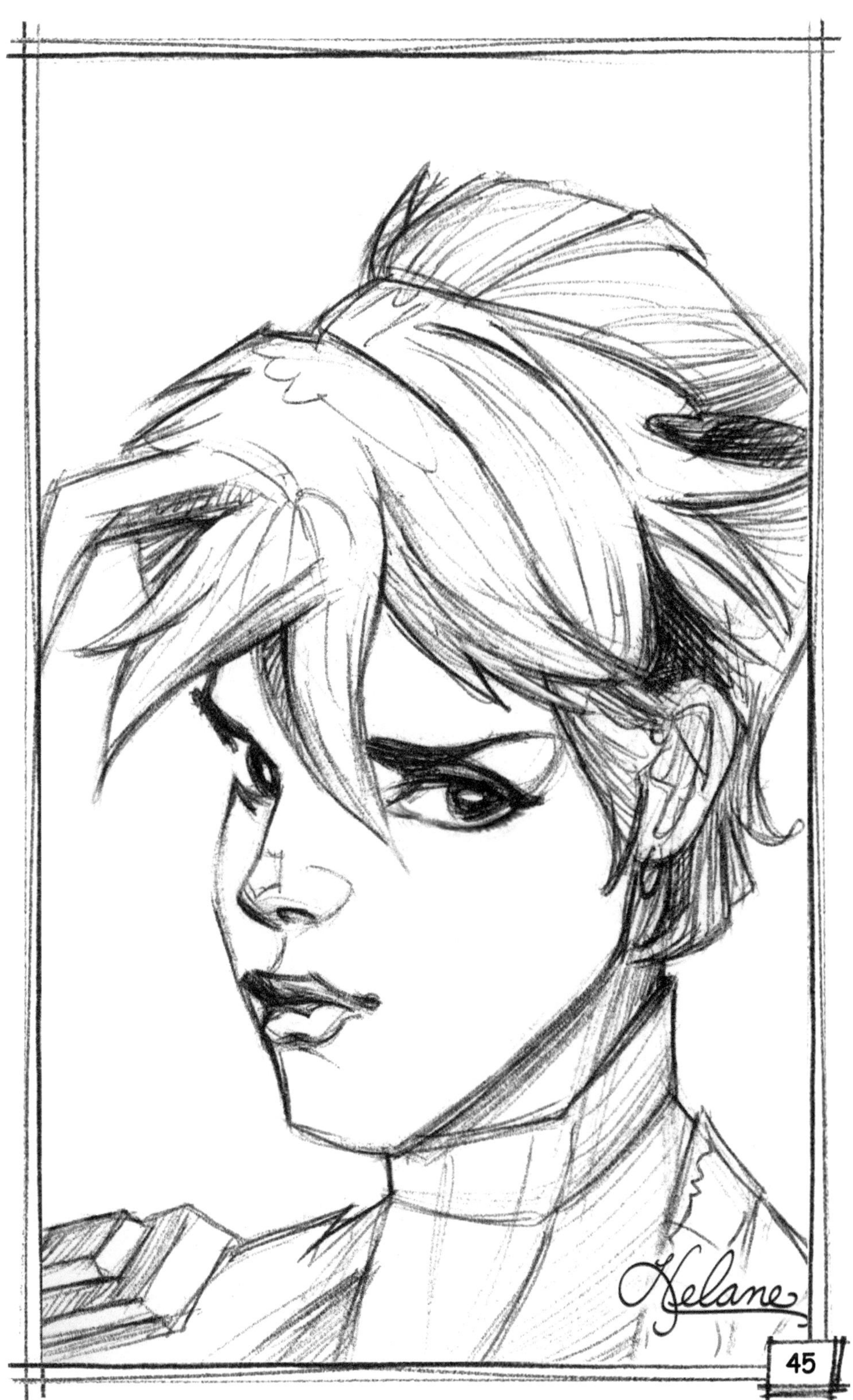

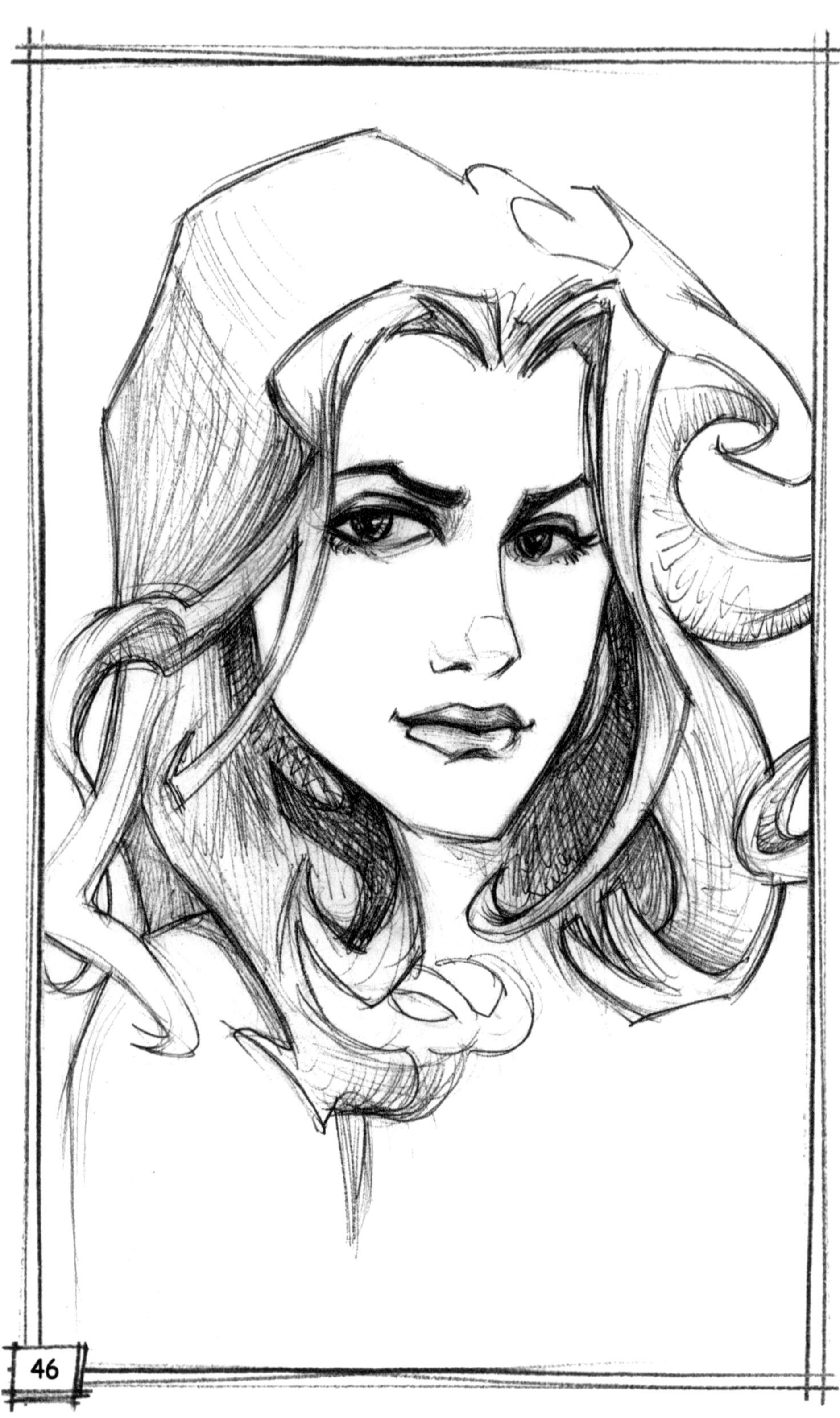

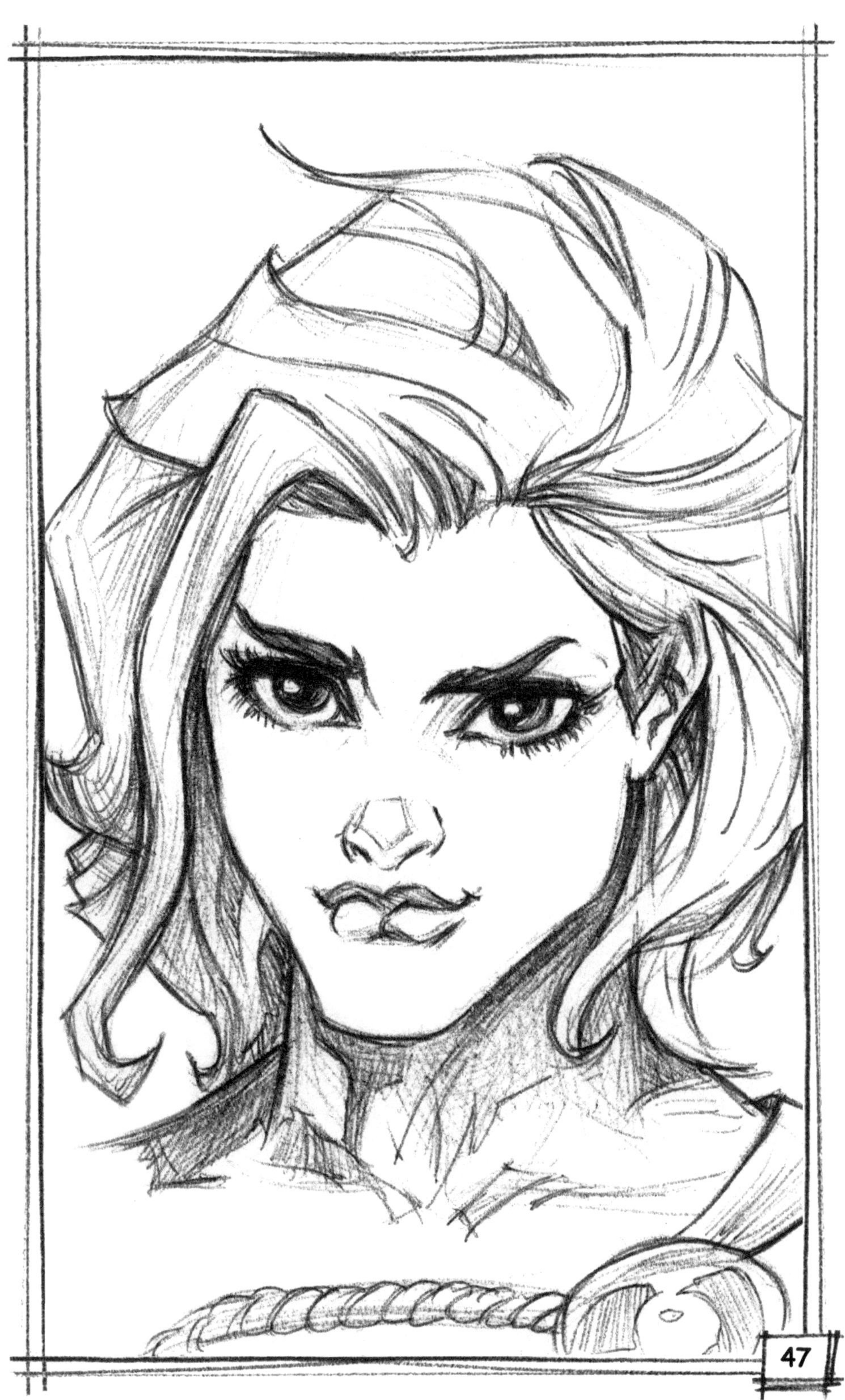

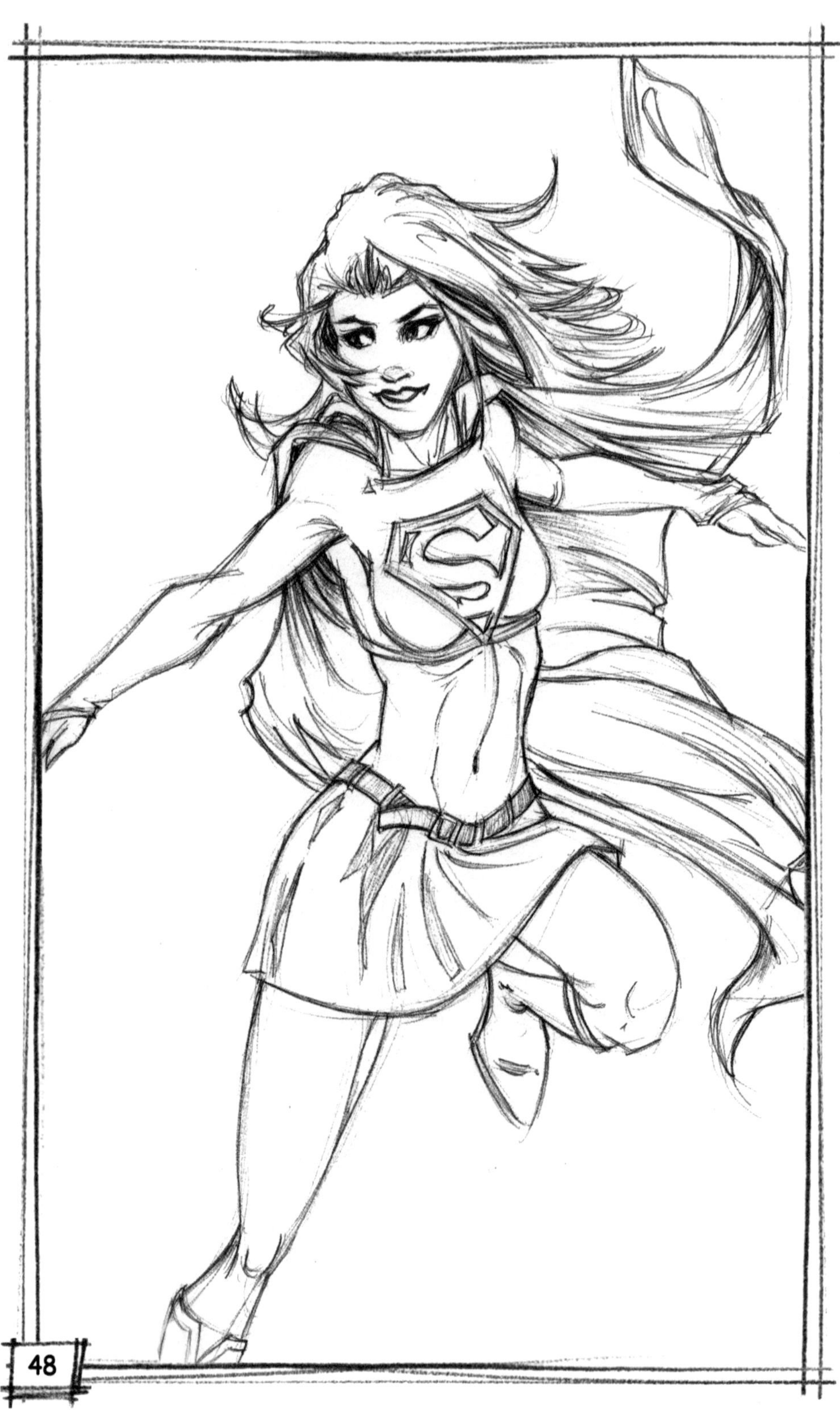

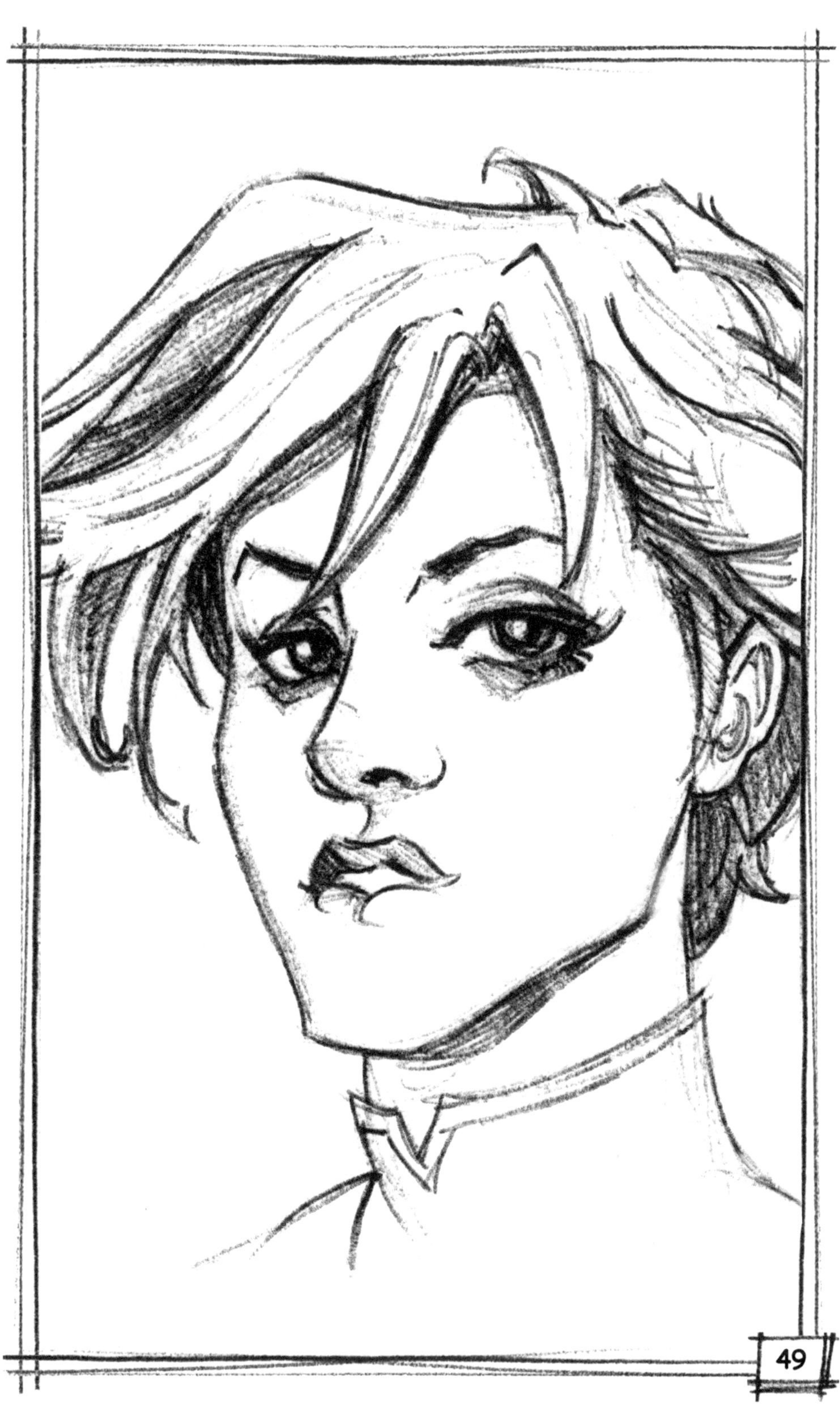

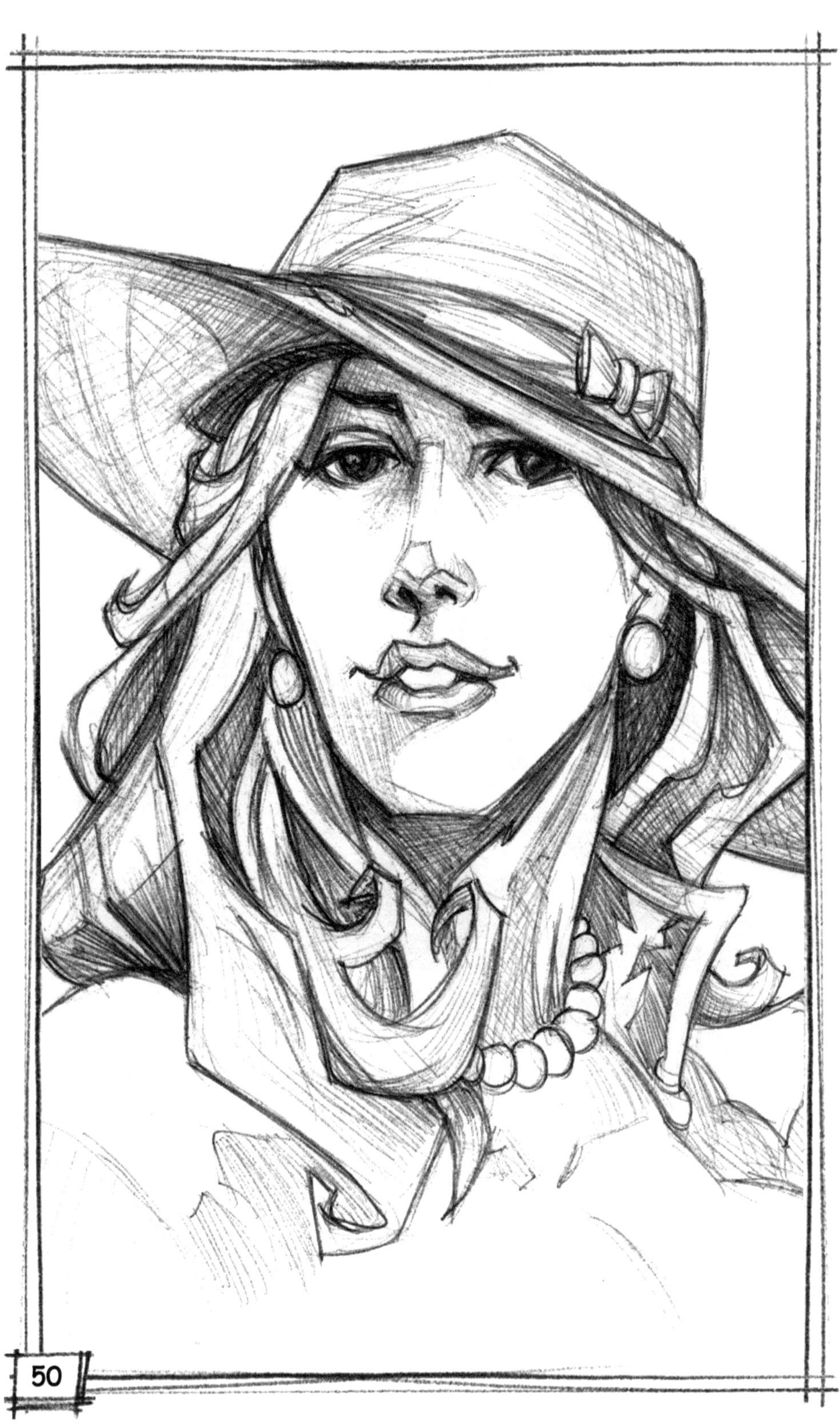

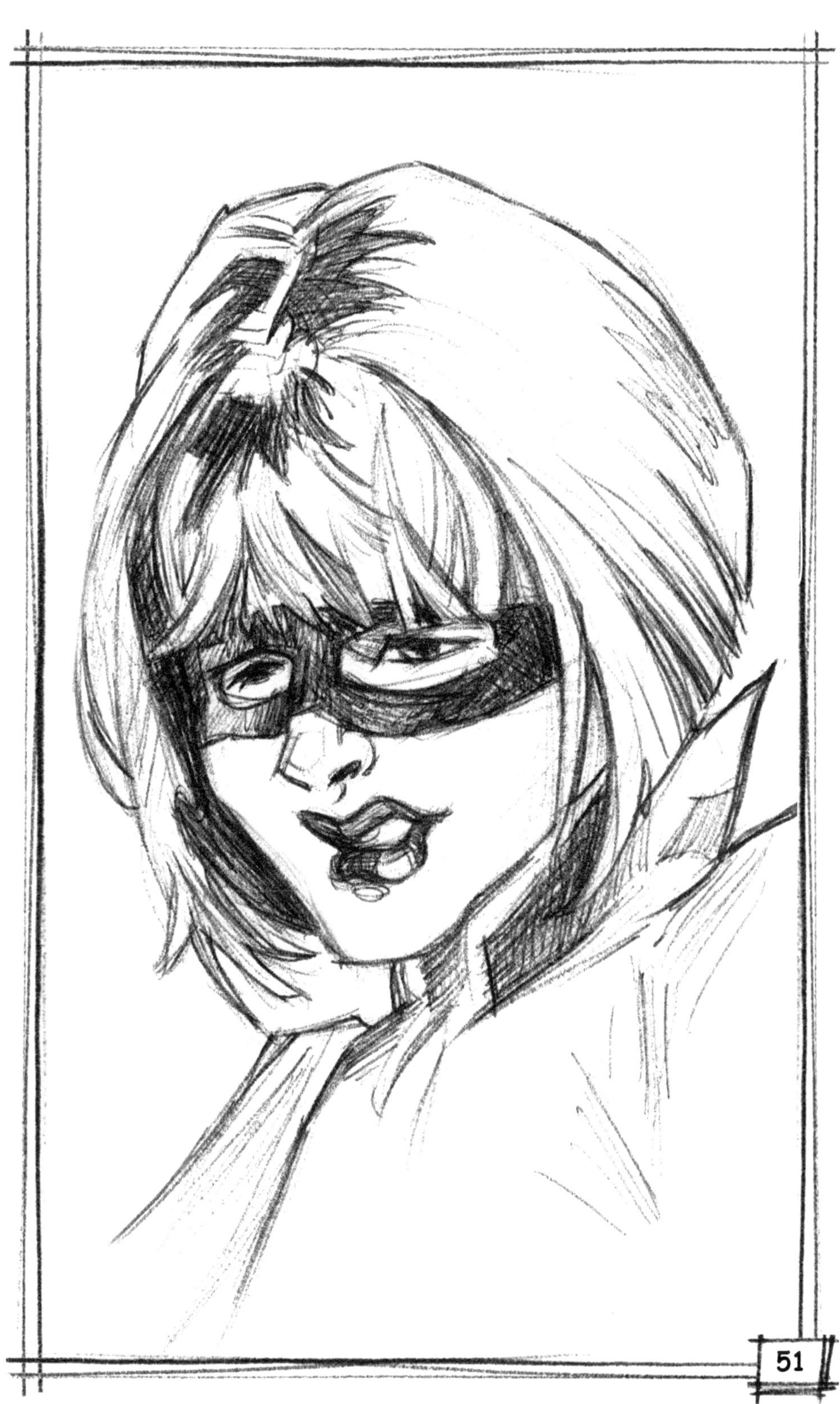

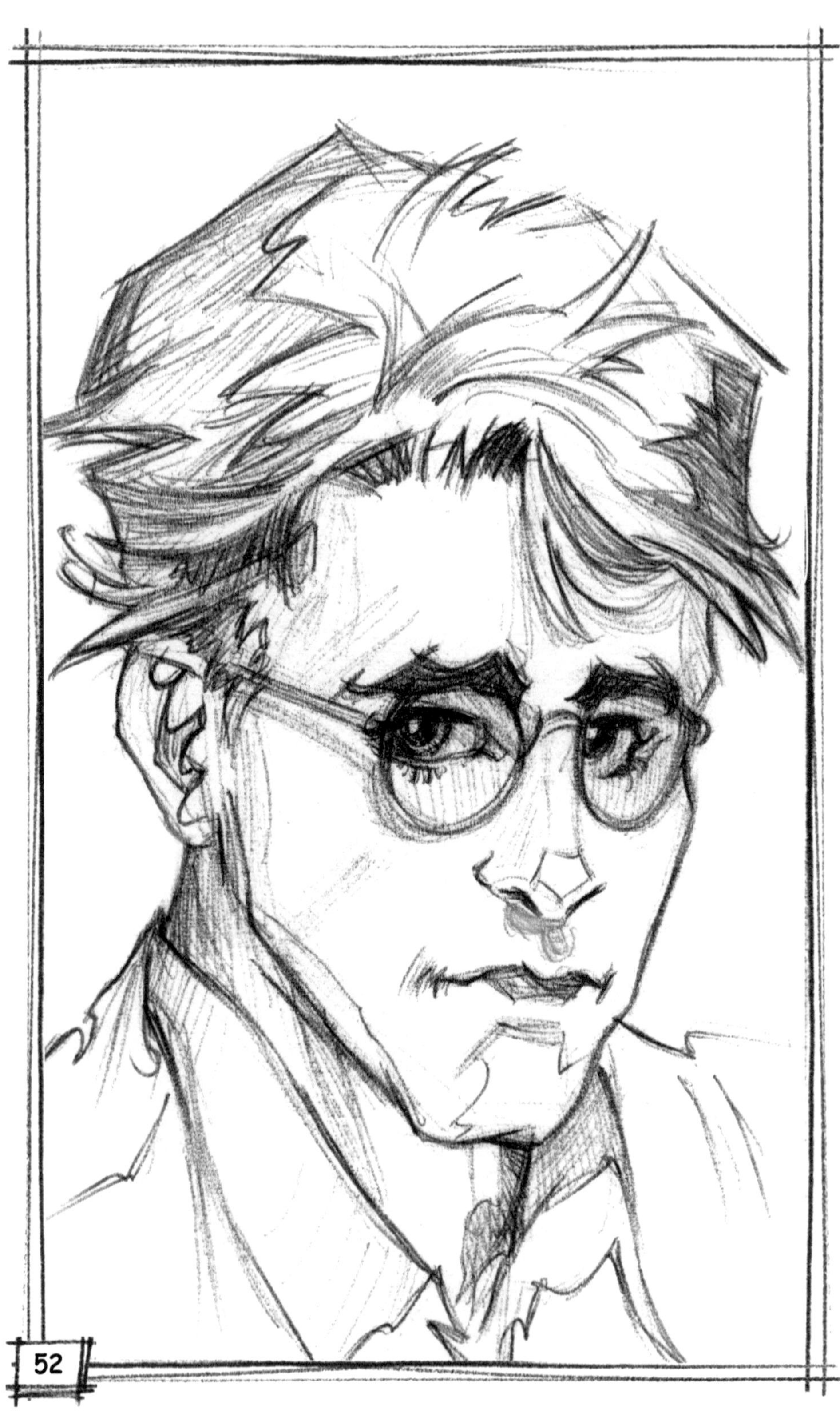

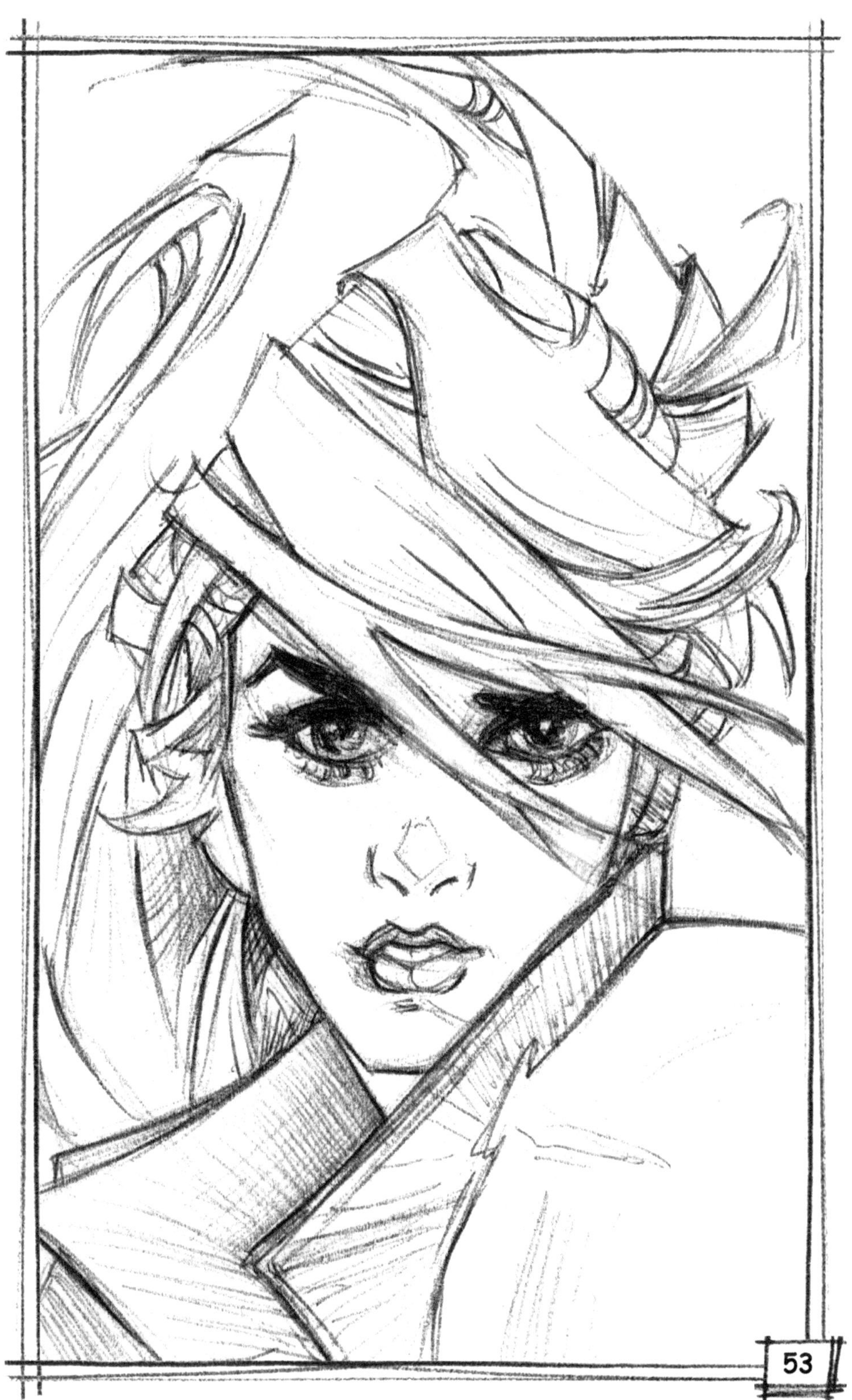

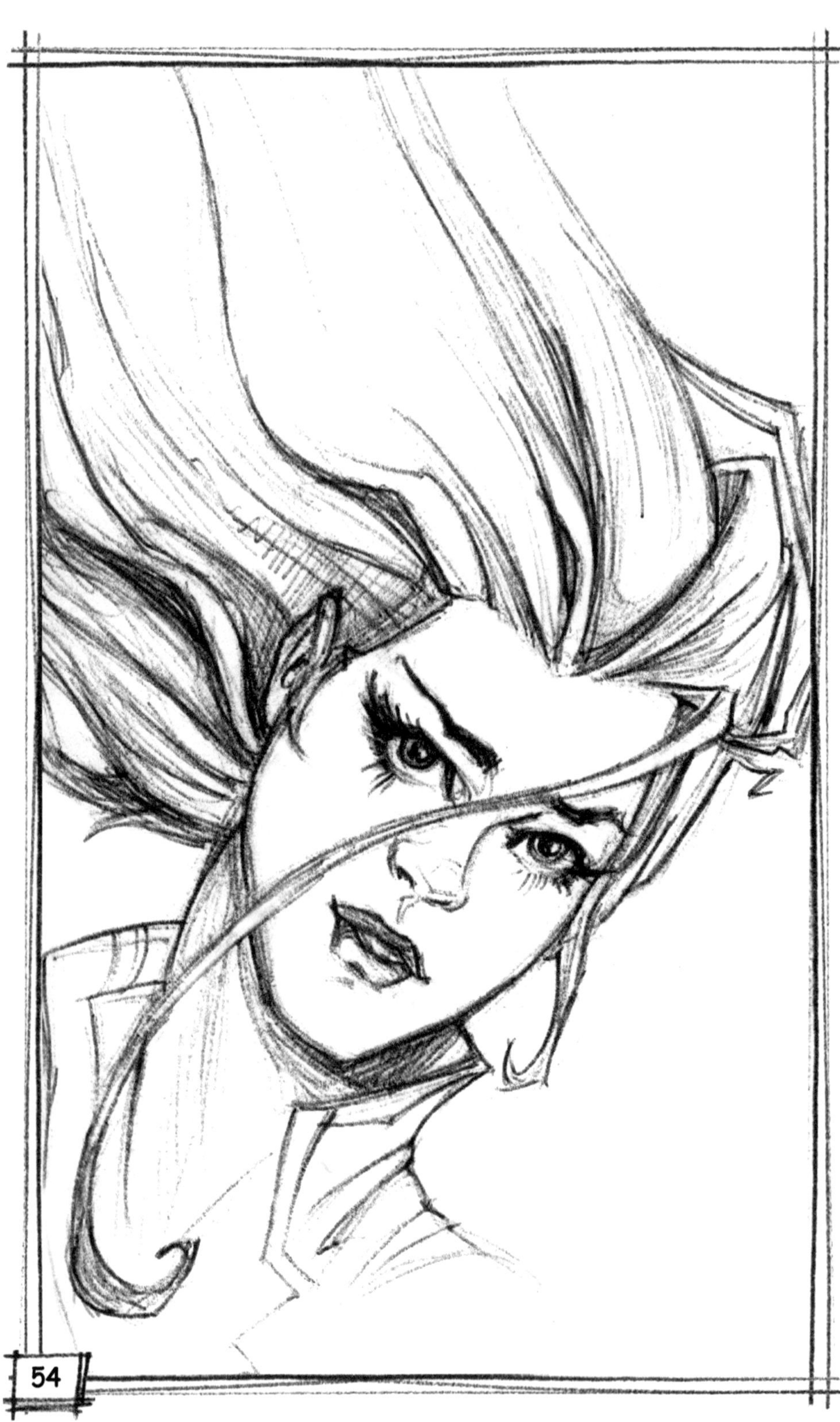

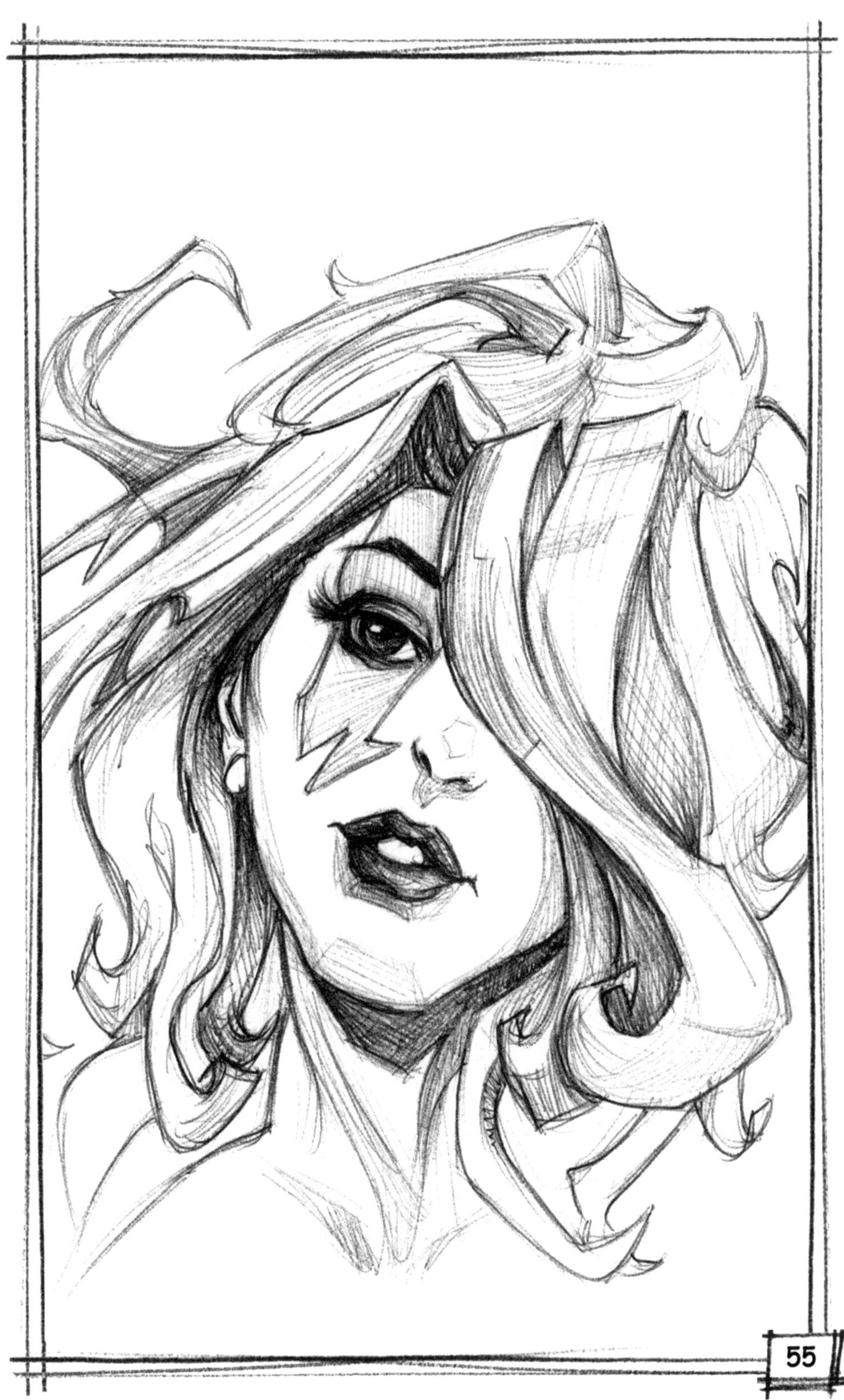

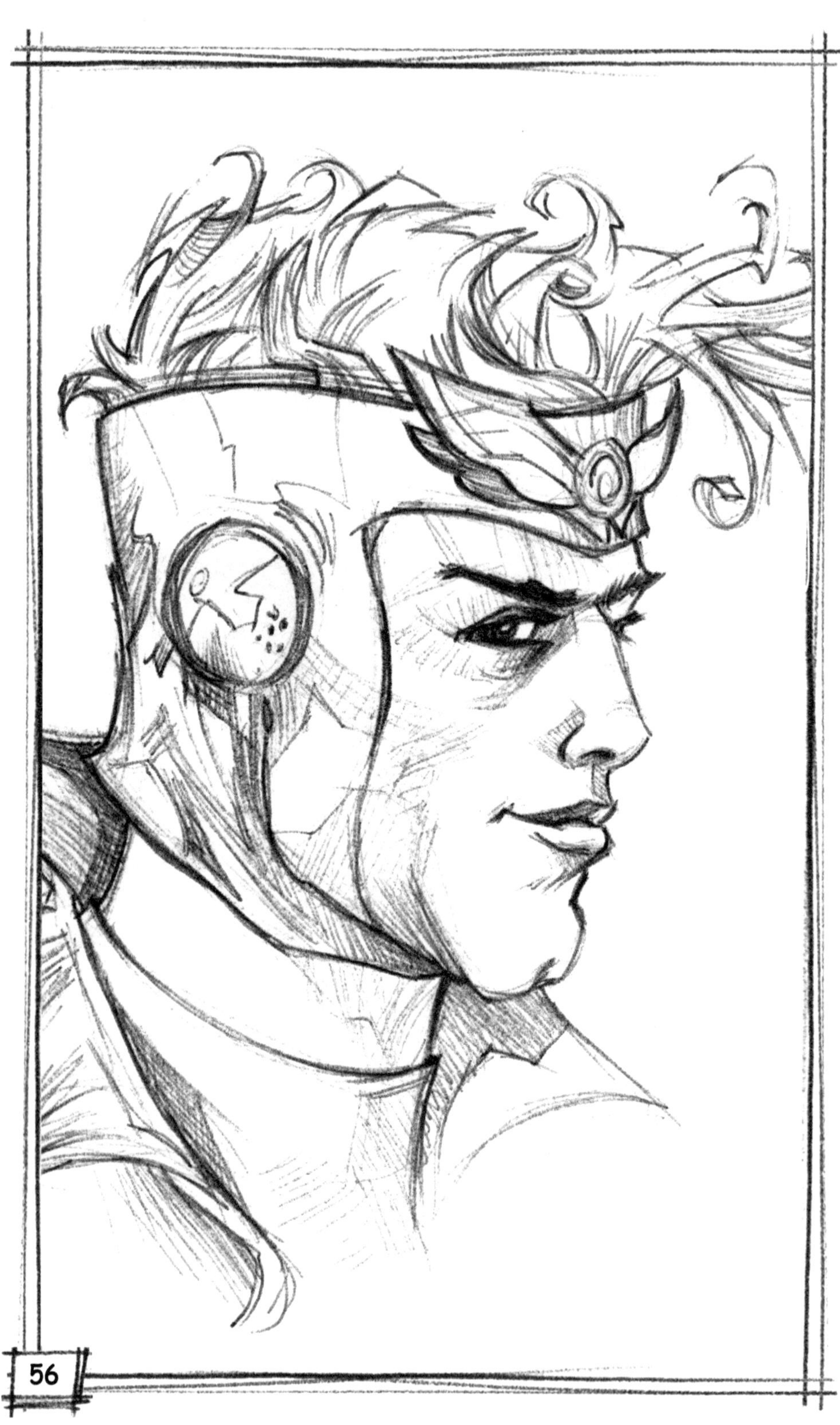

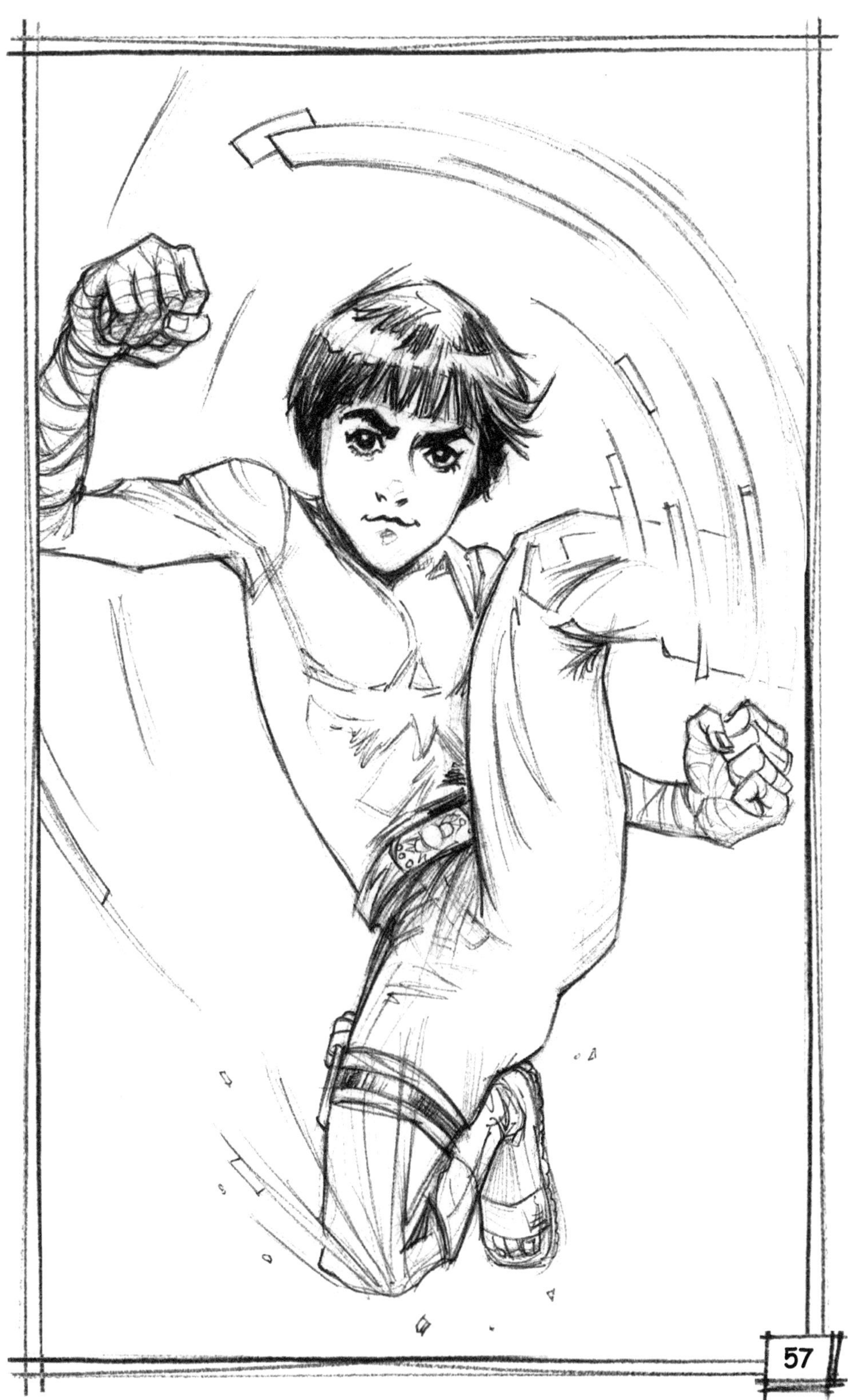

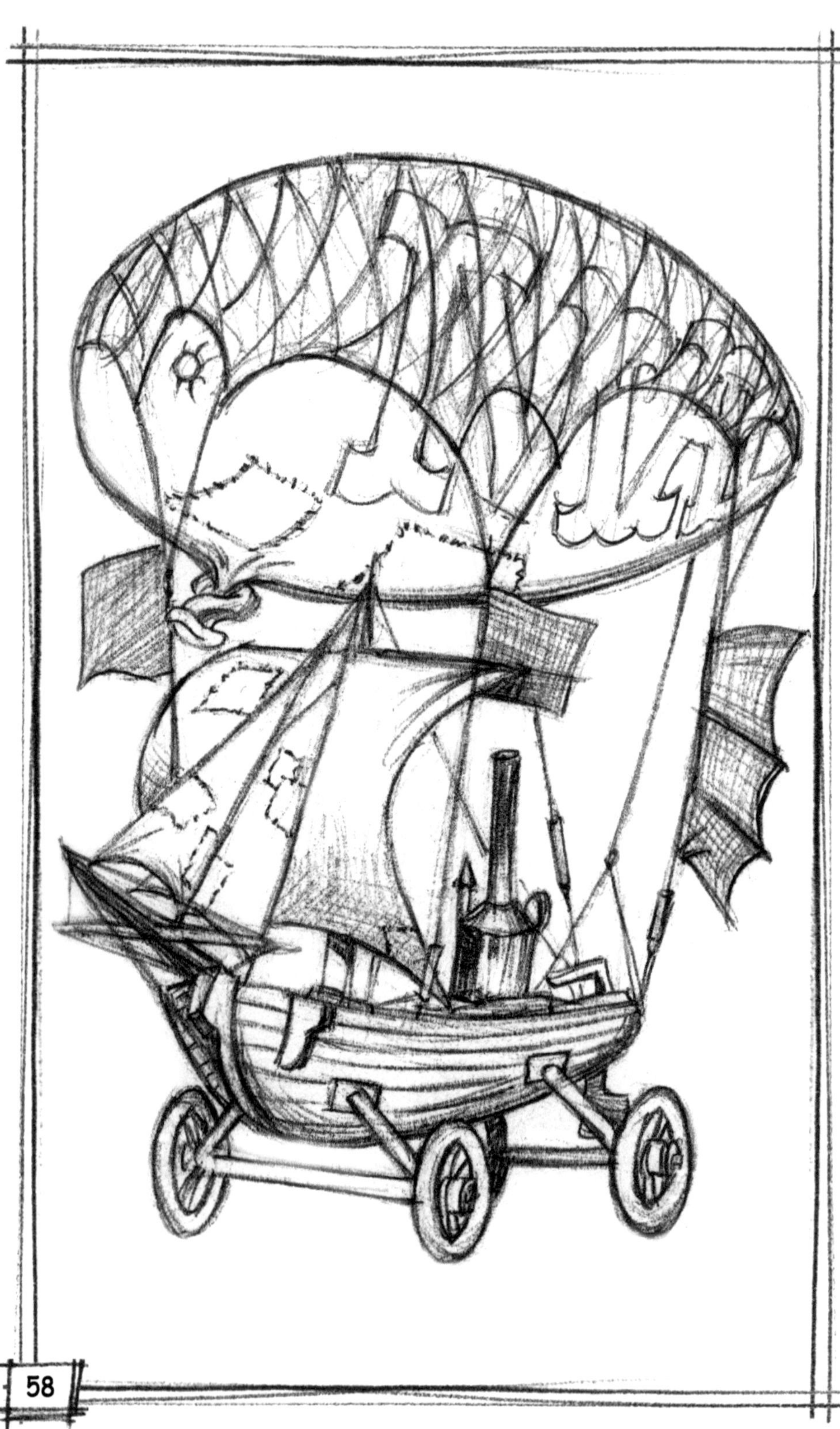

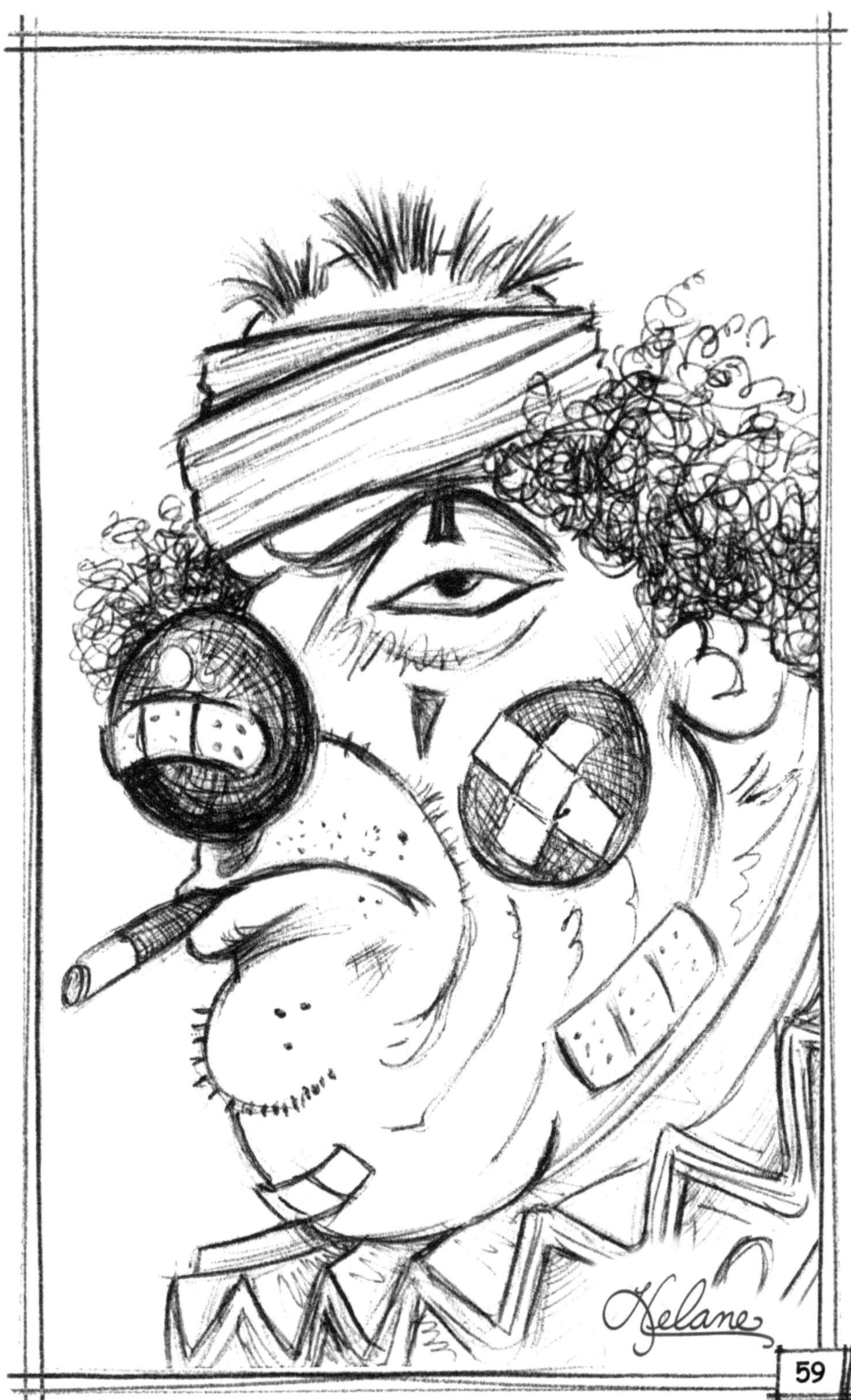

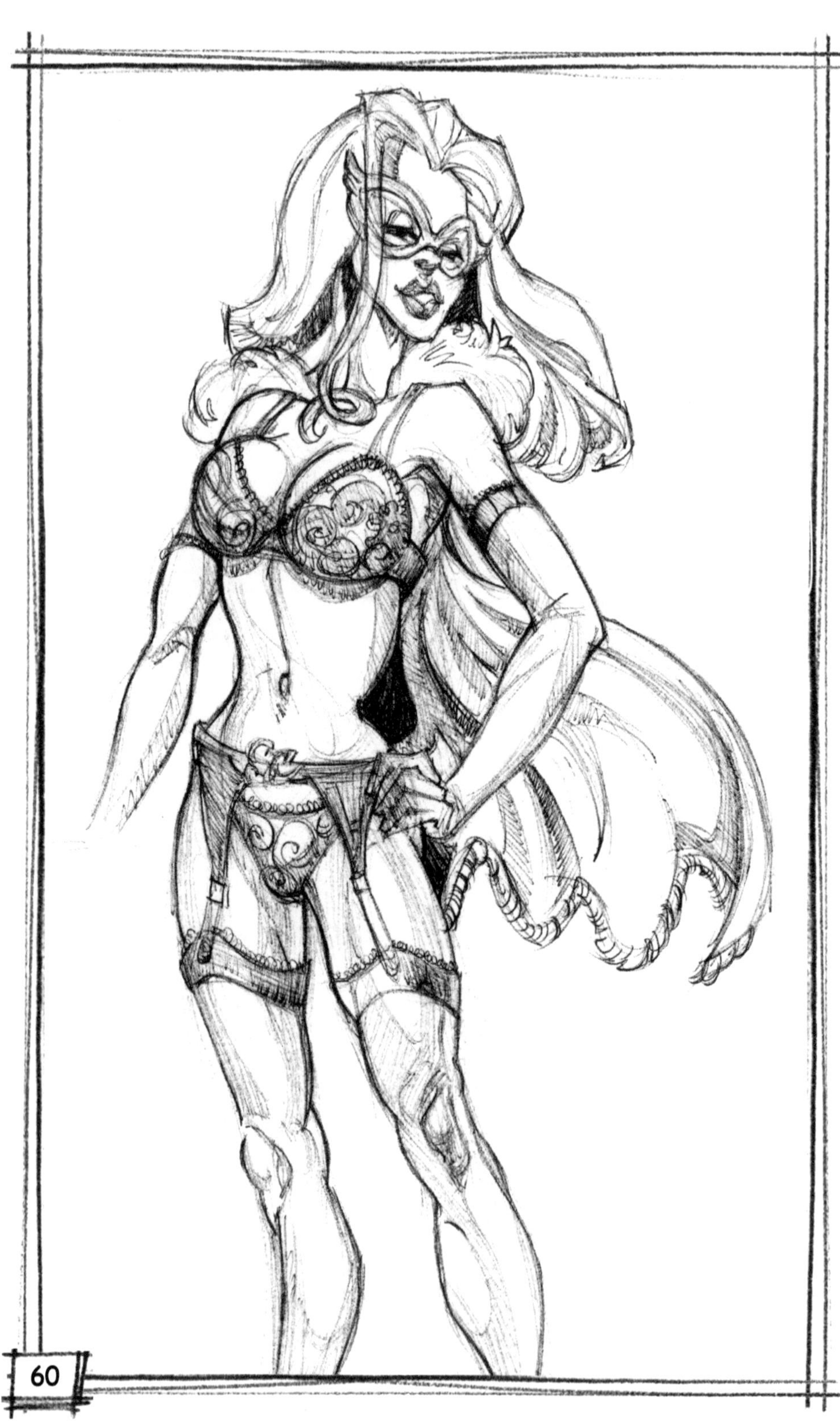

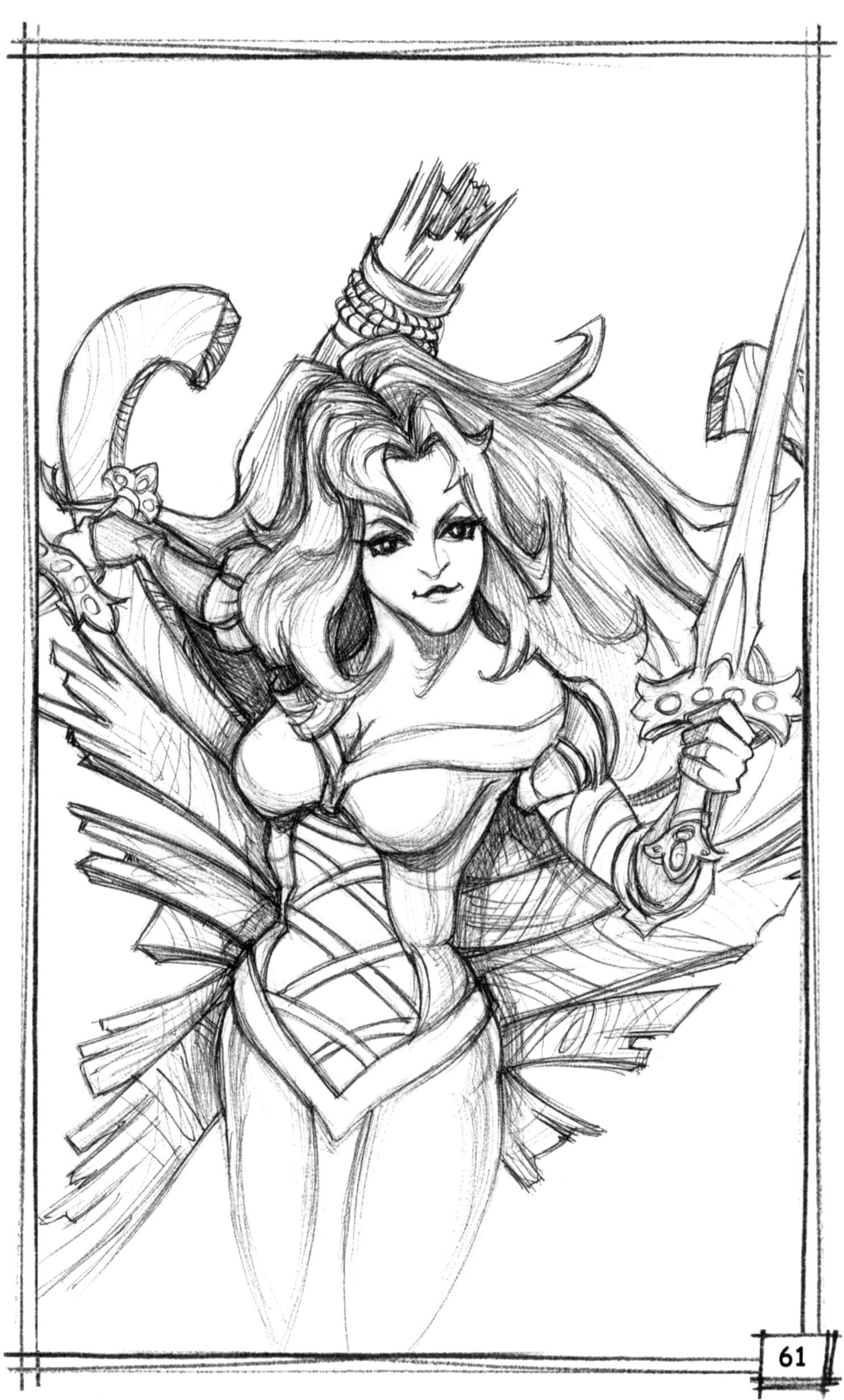

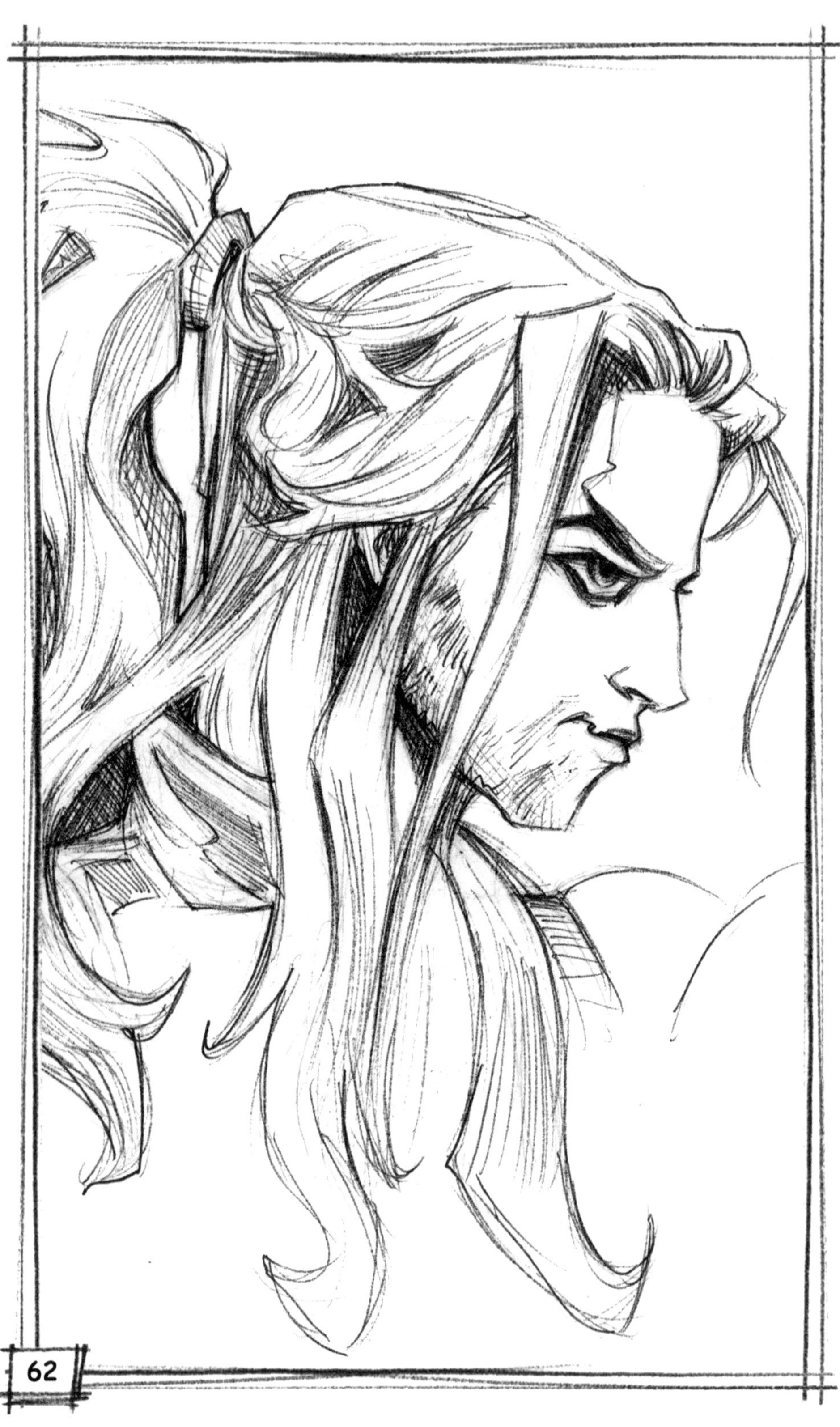

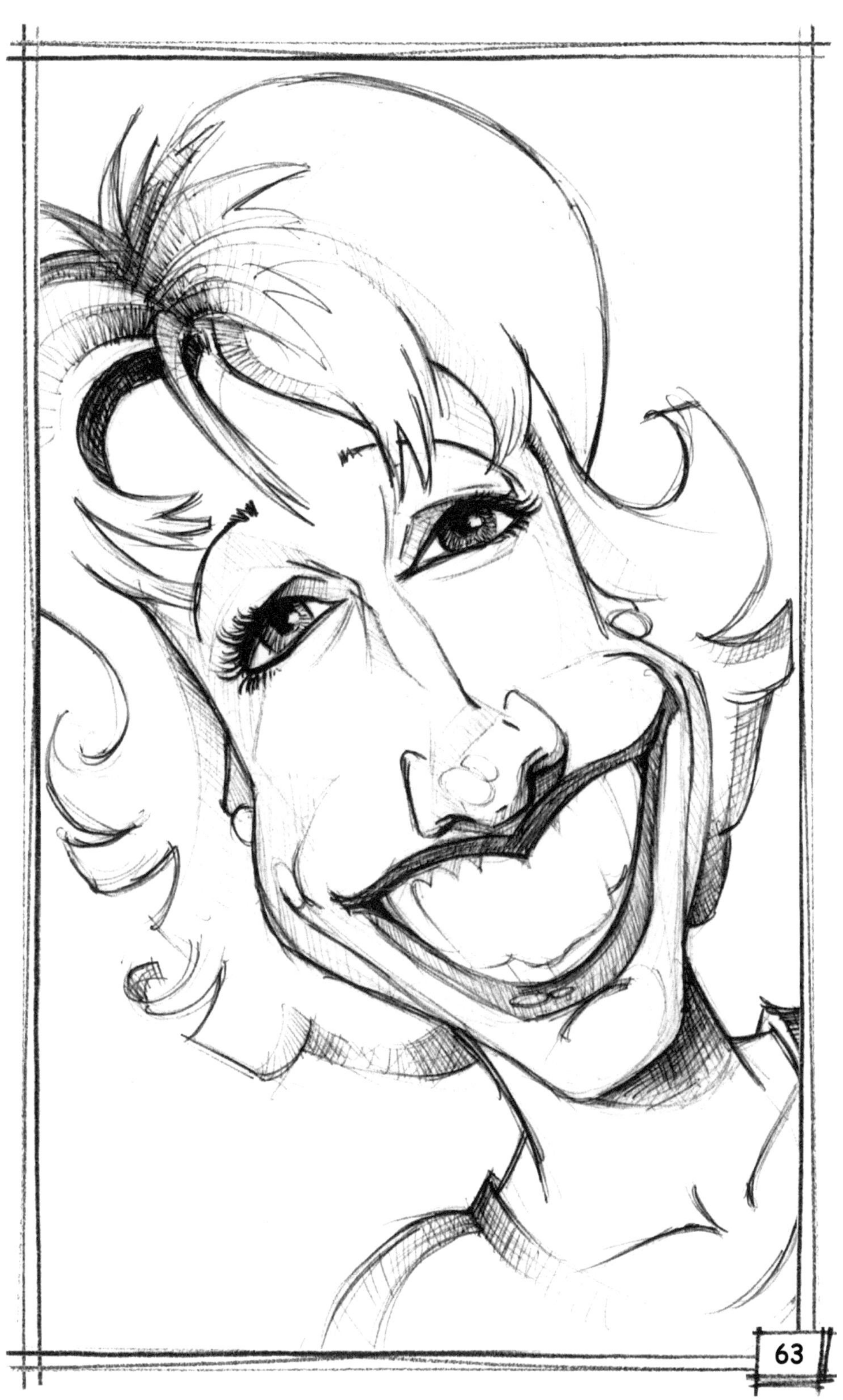

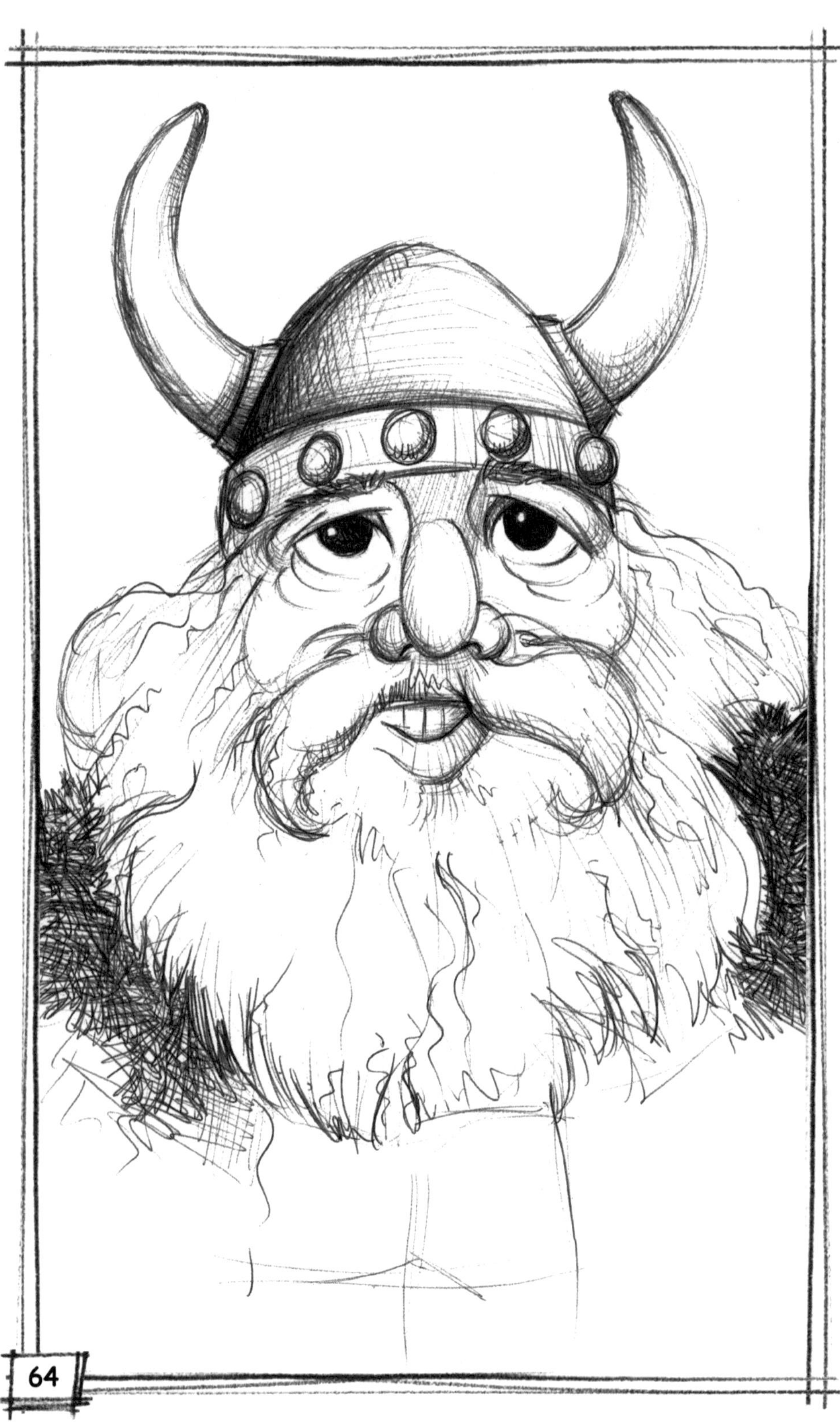

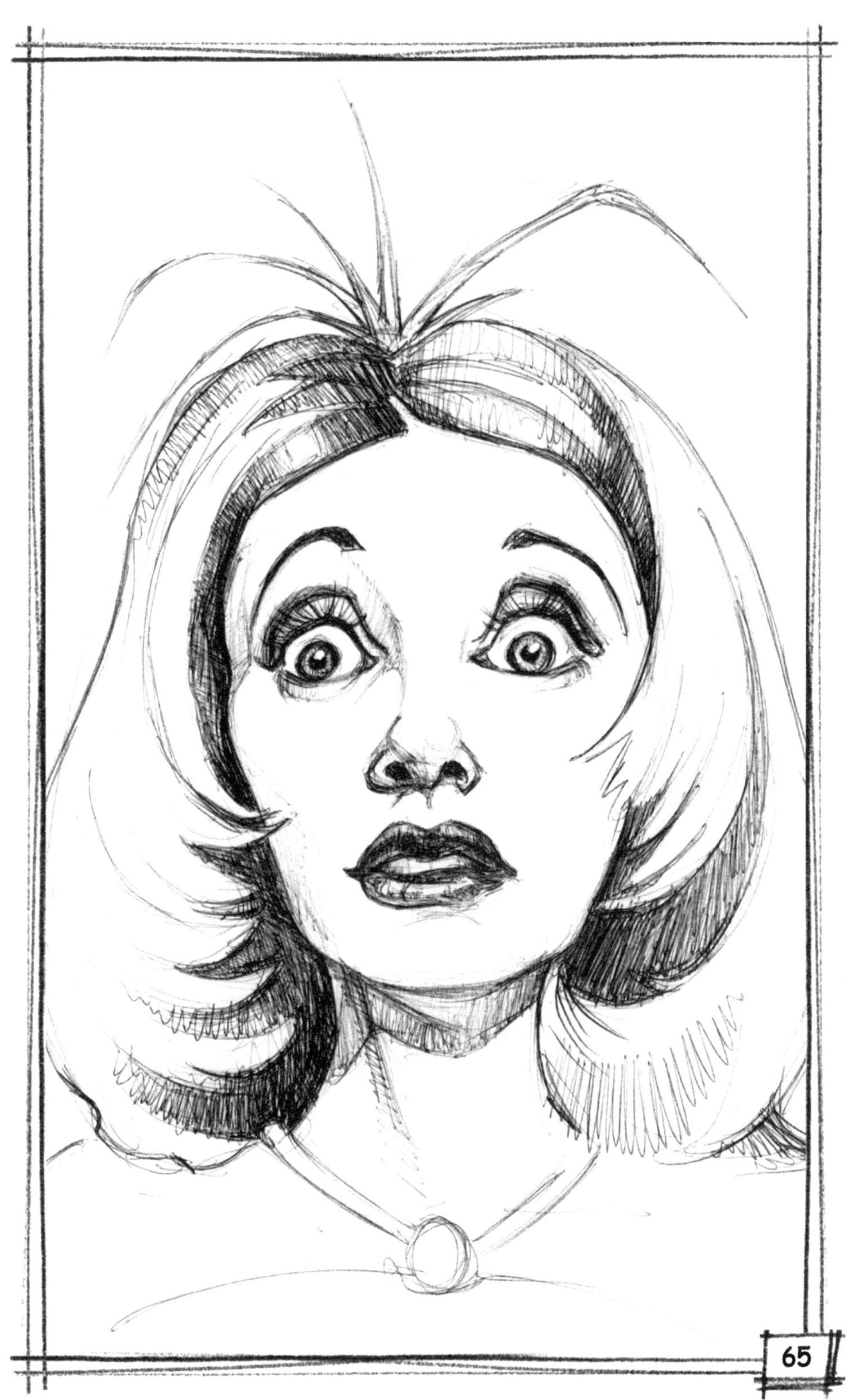

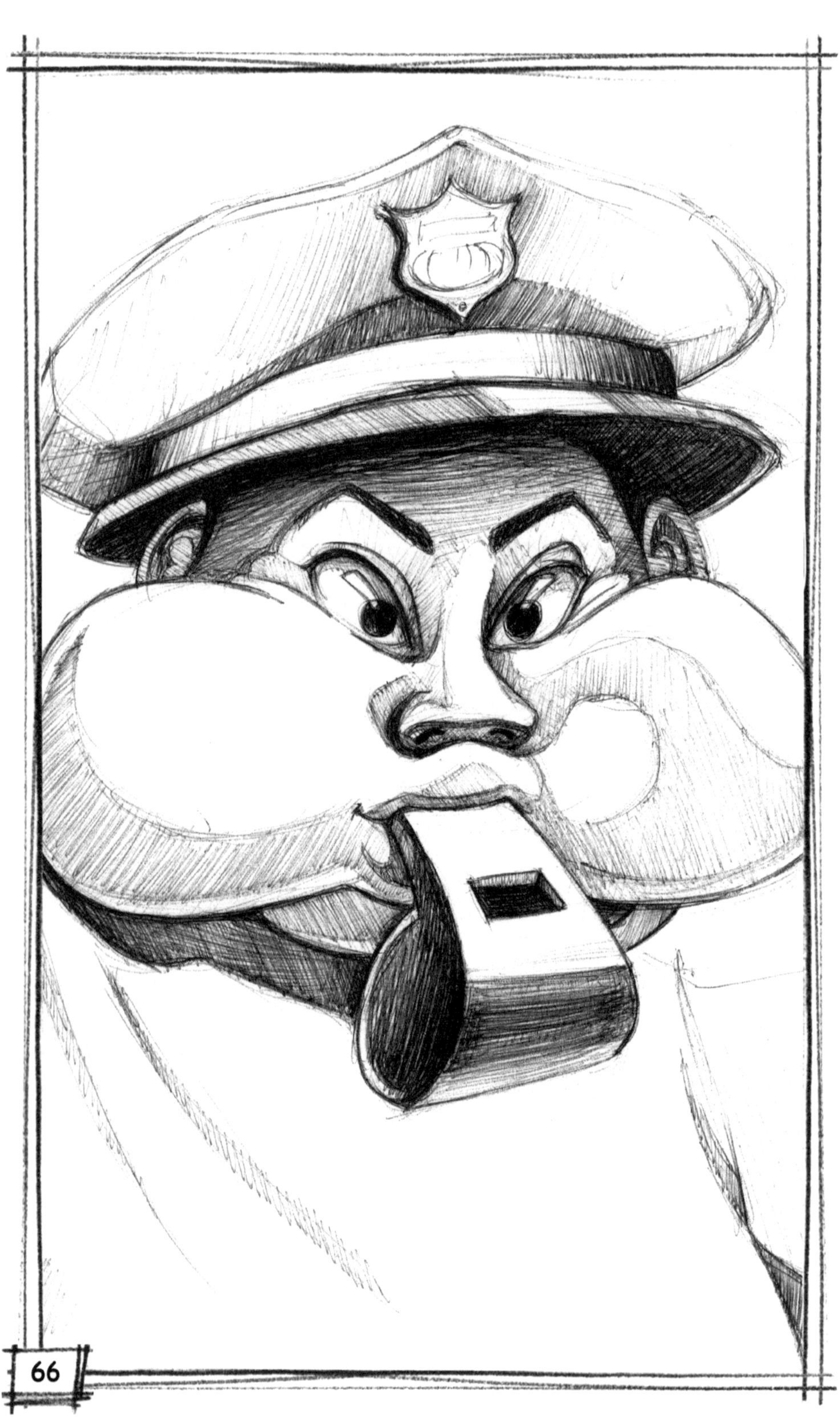

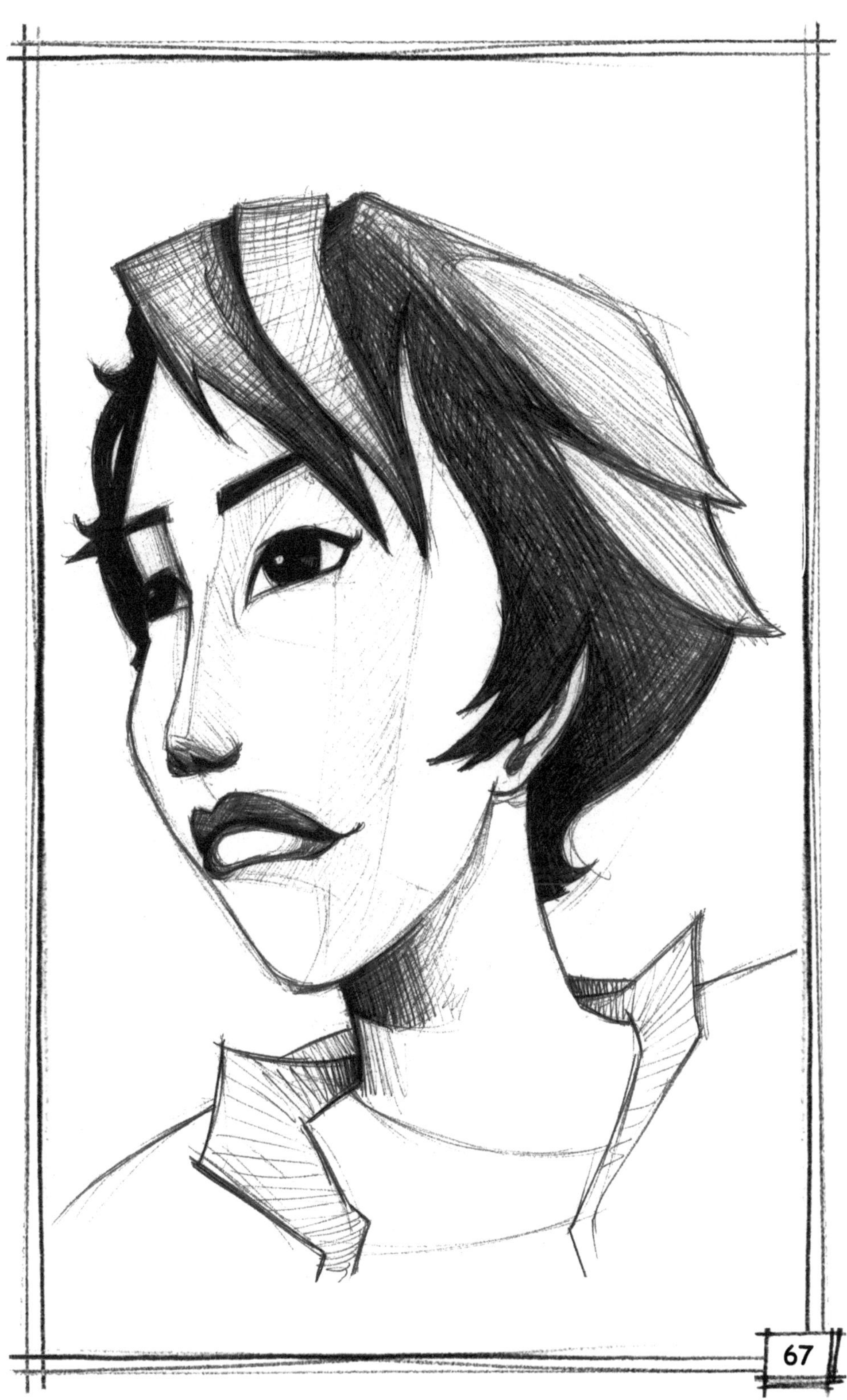

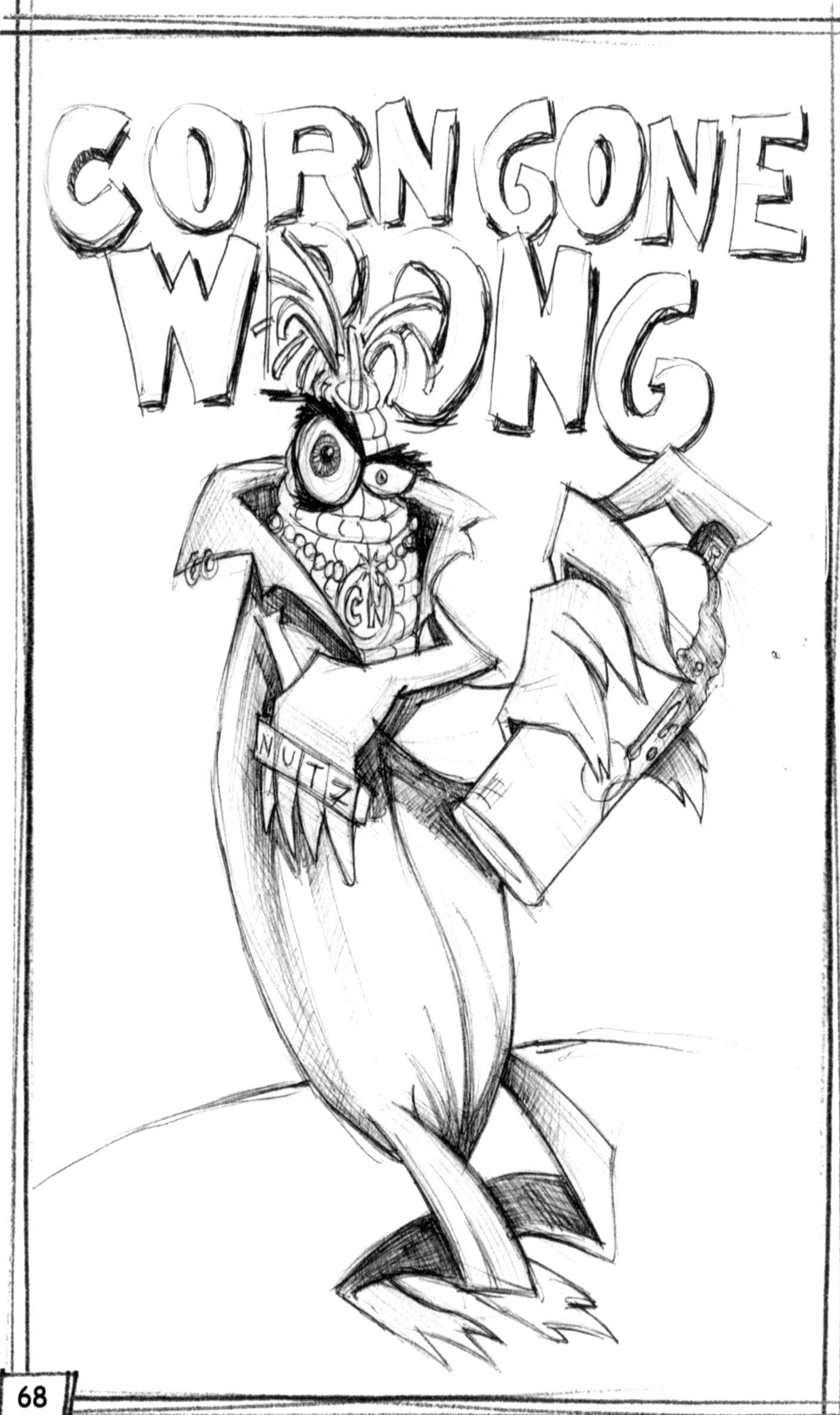

CORN GONE WRONG
CN
NUTZ

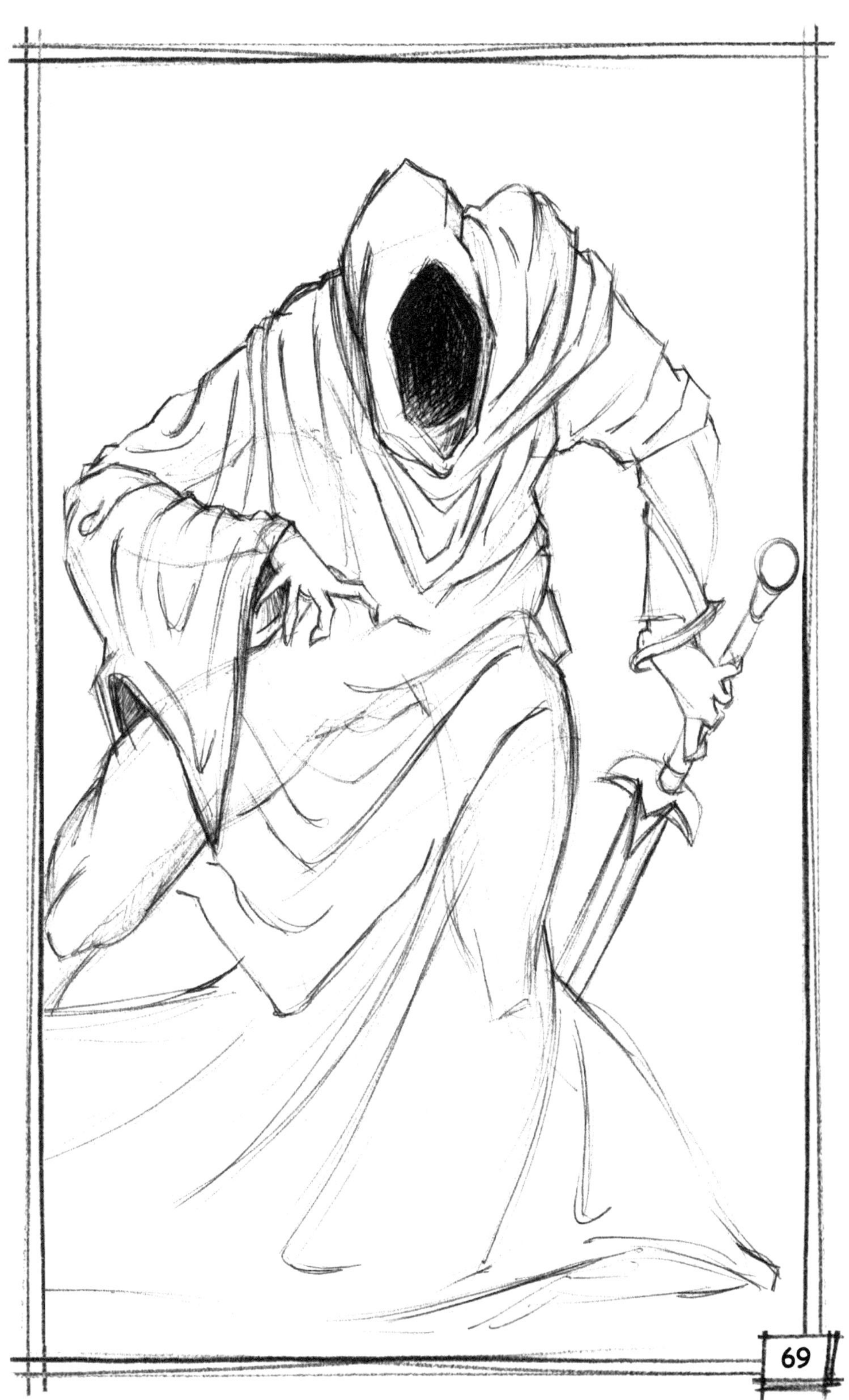

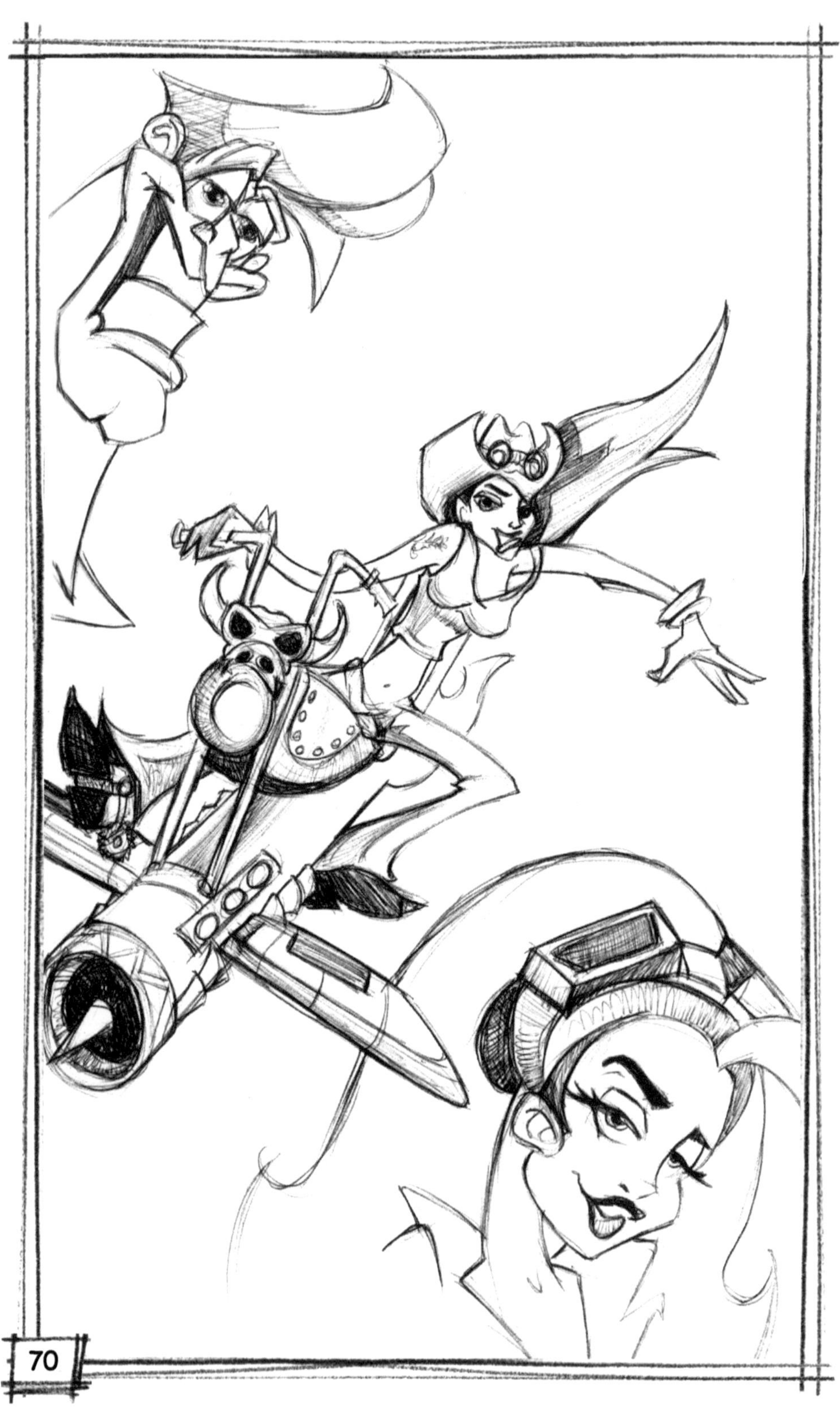

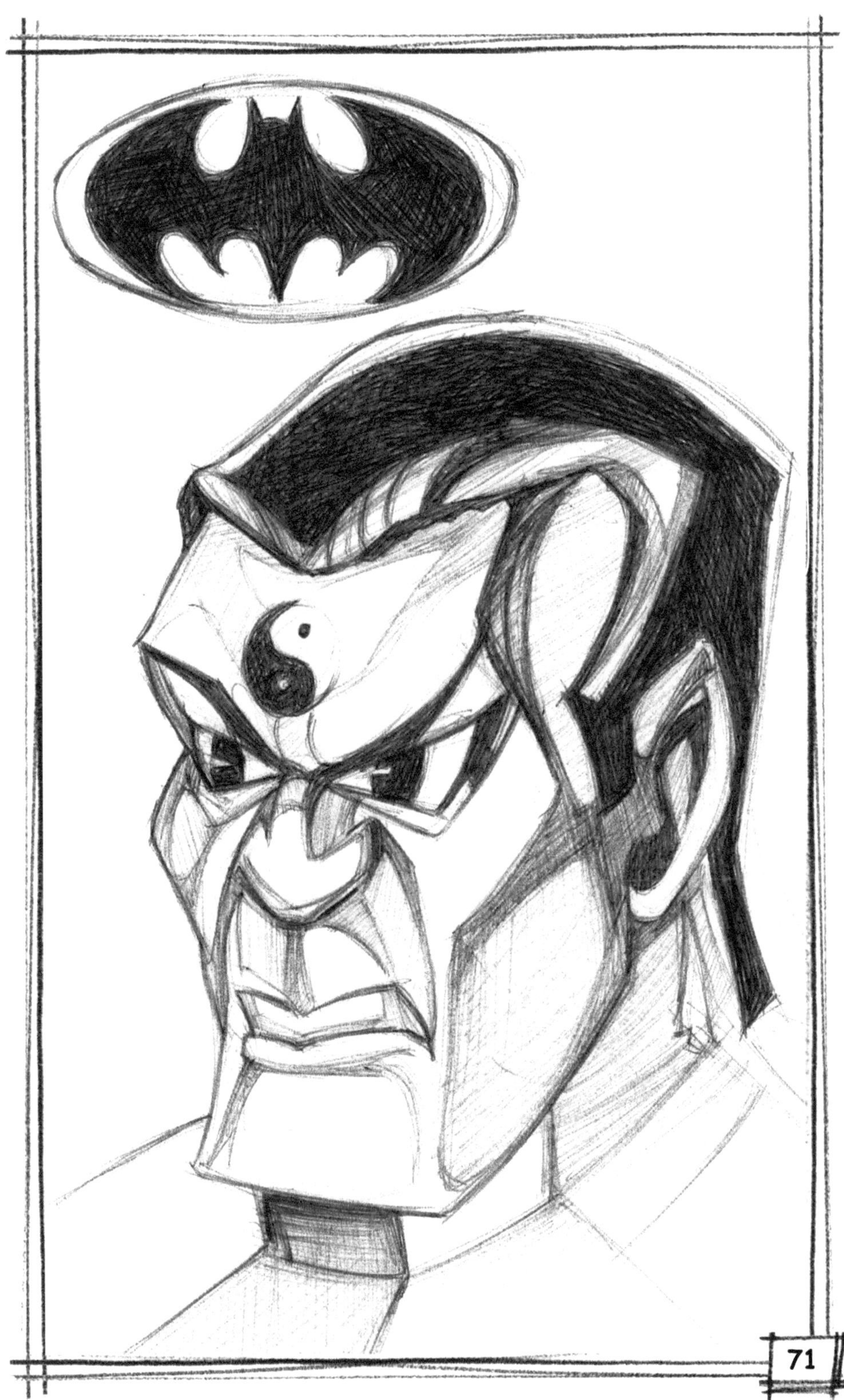

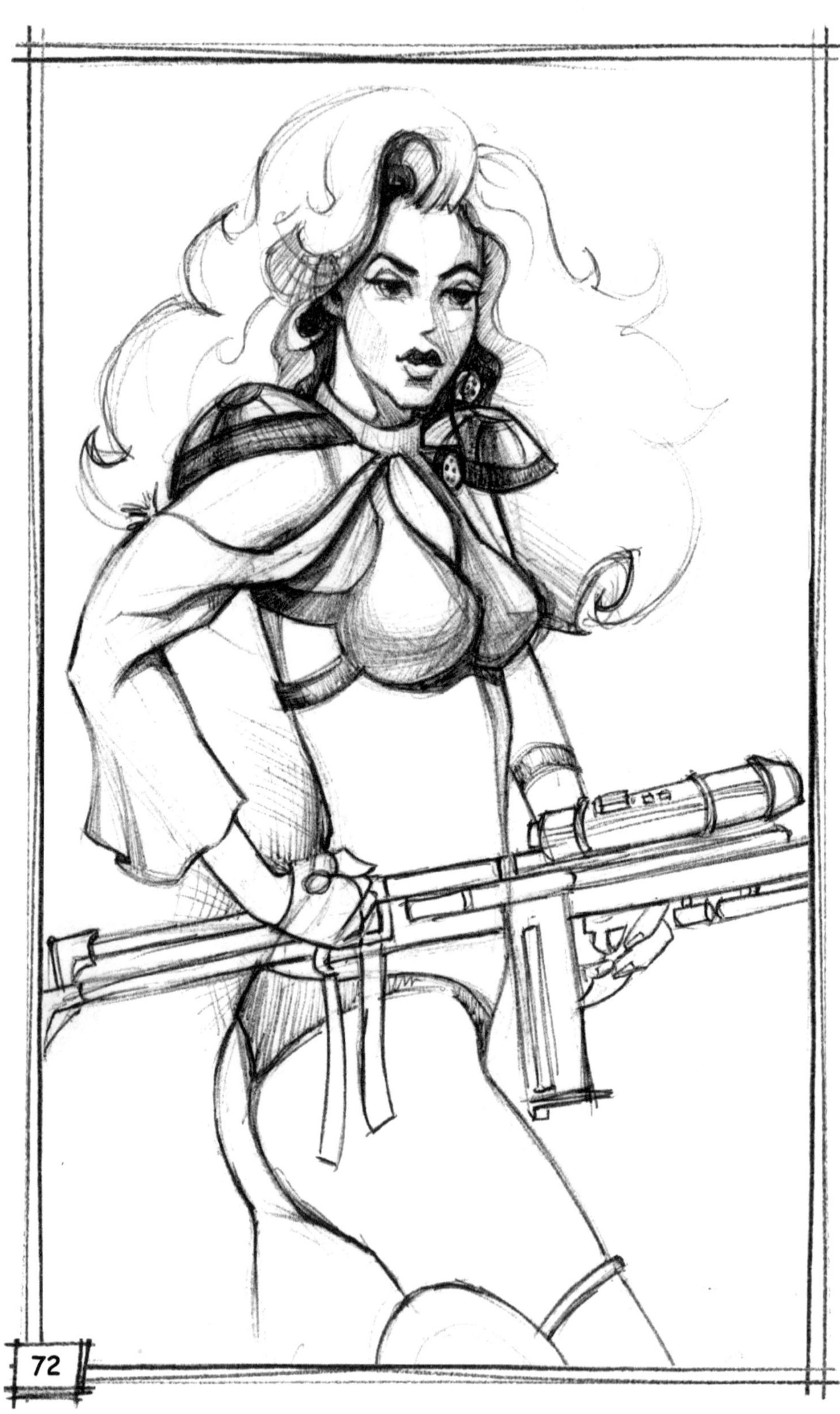

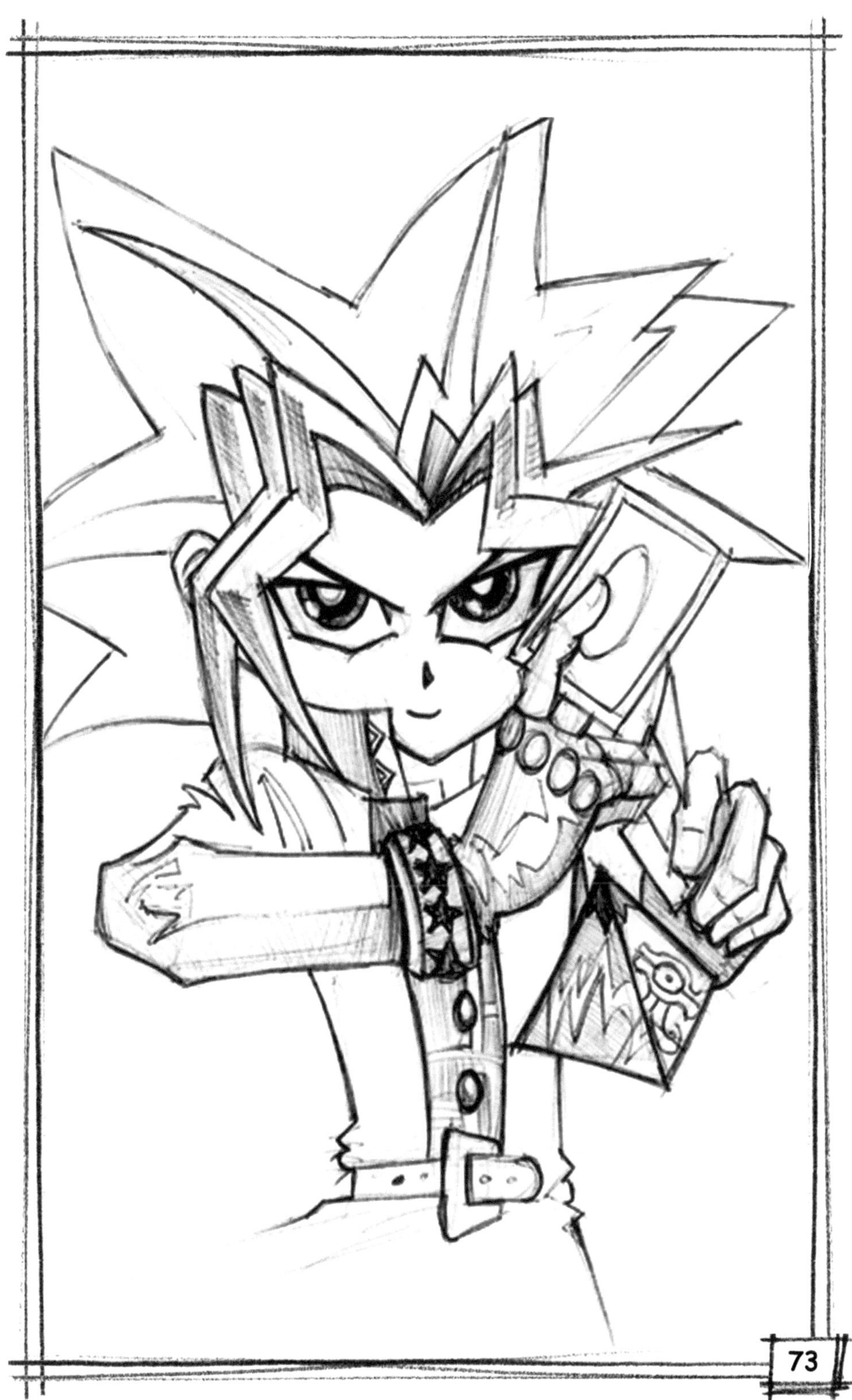

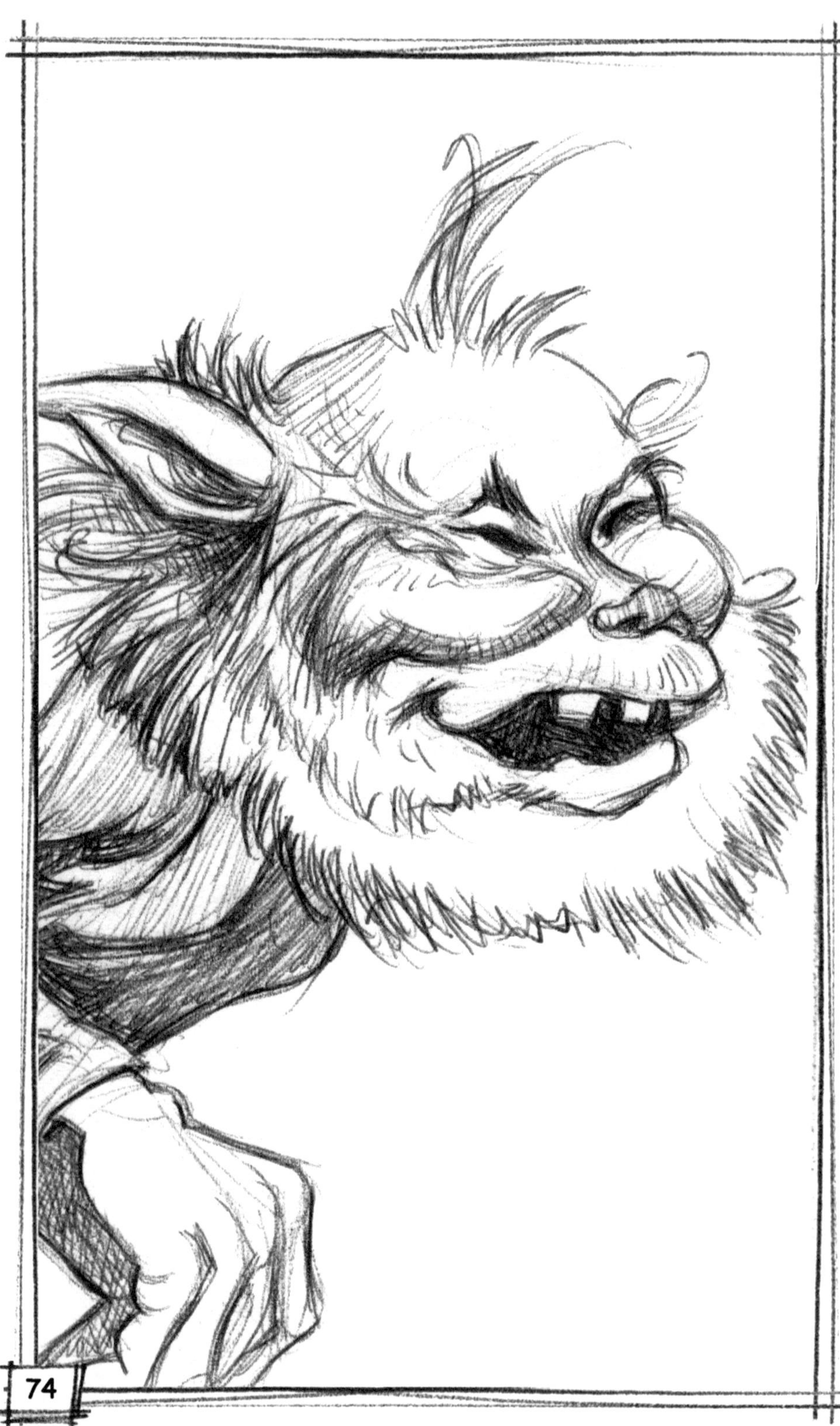

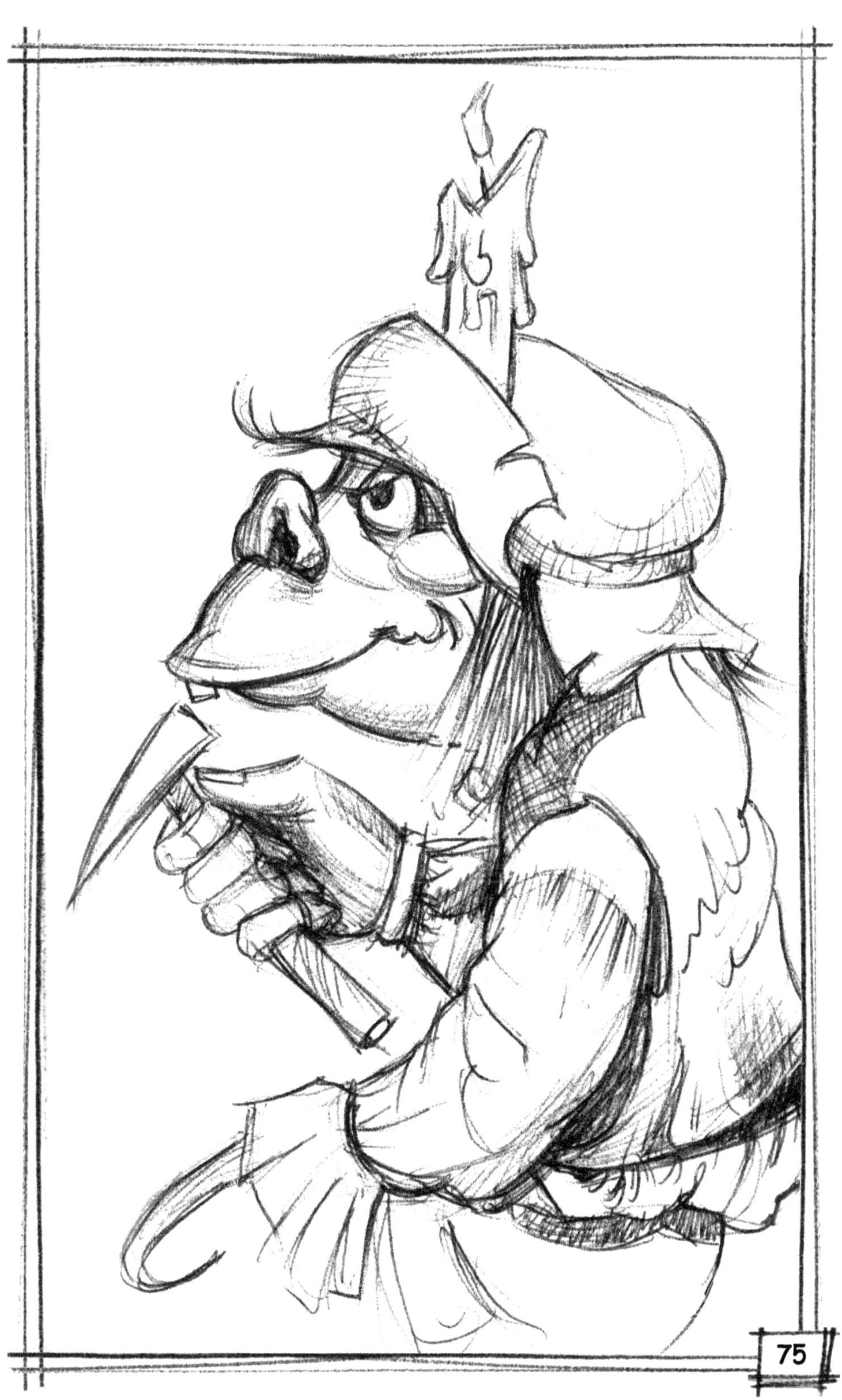

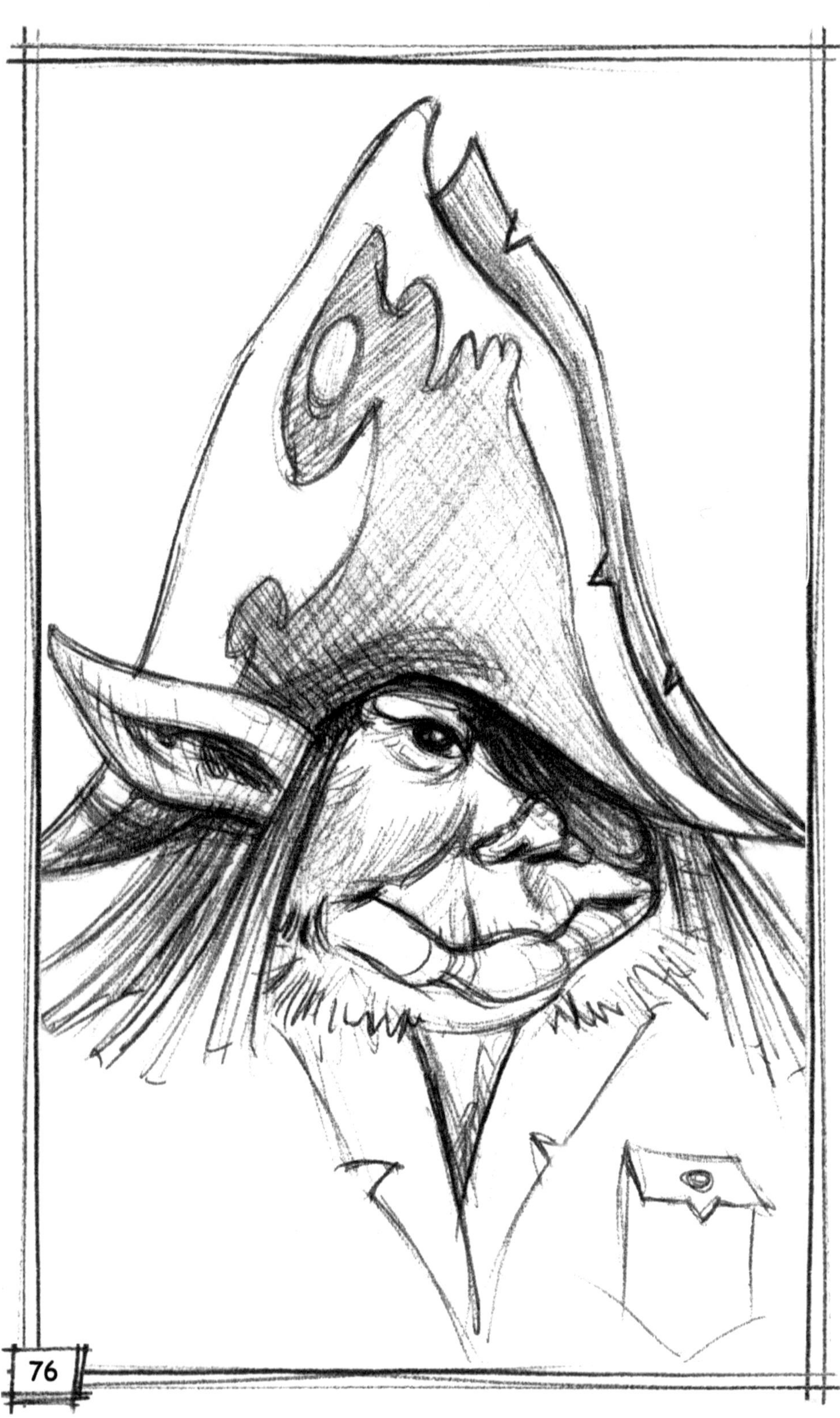

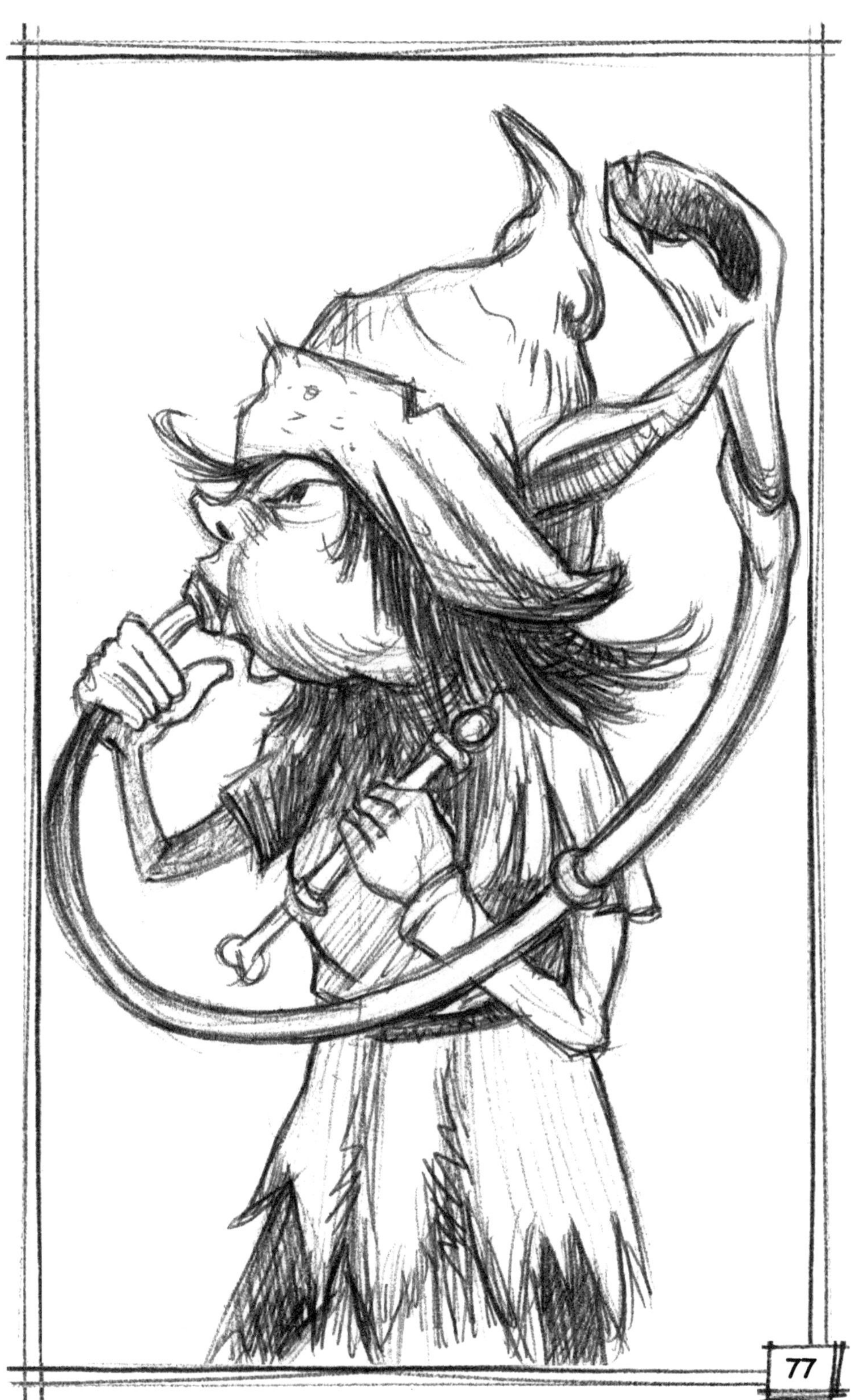

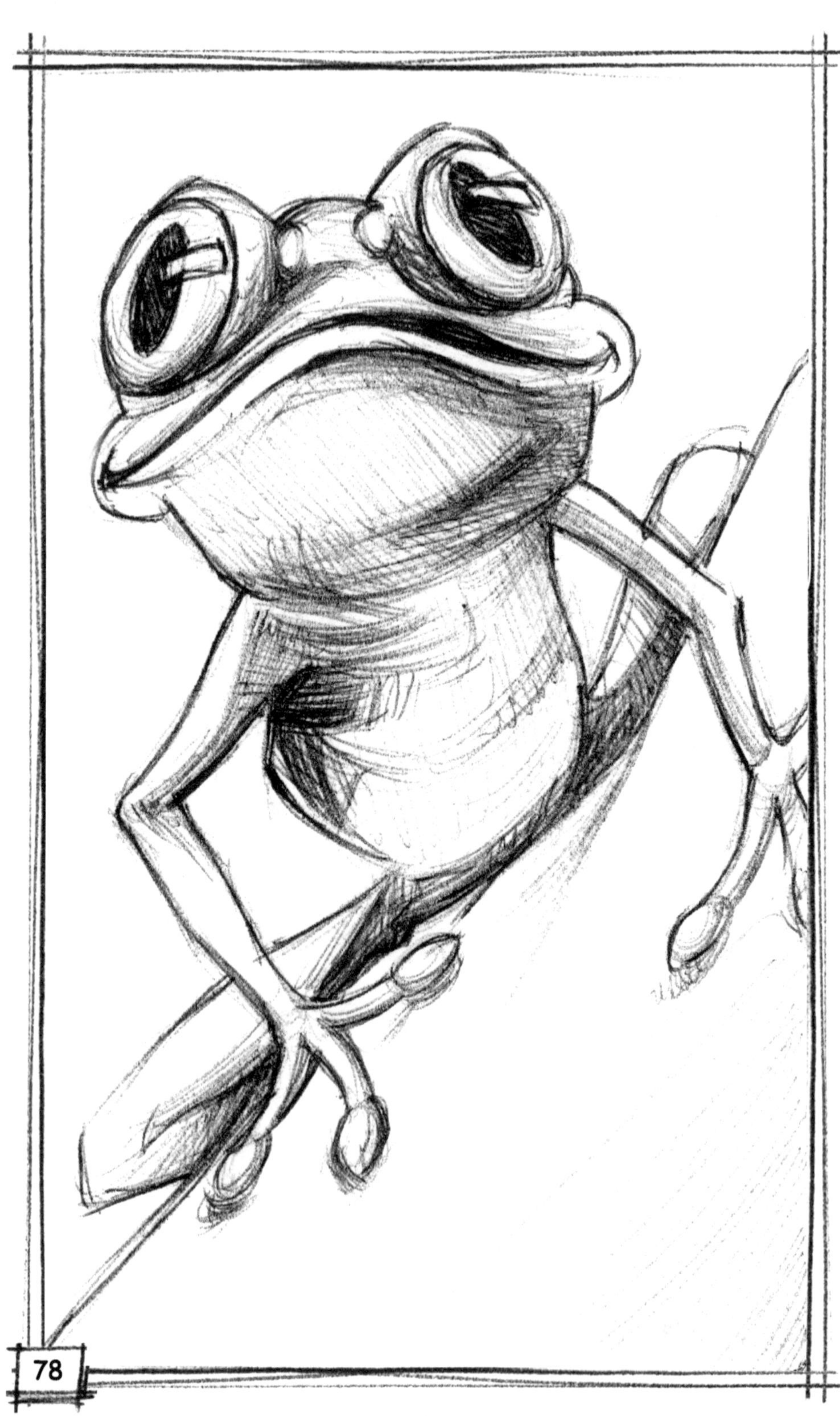

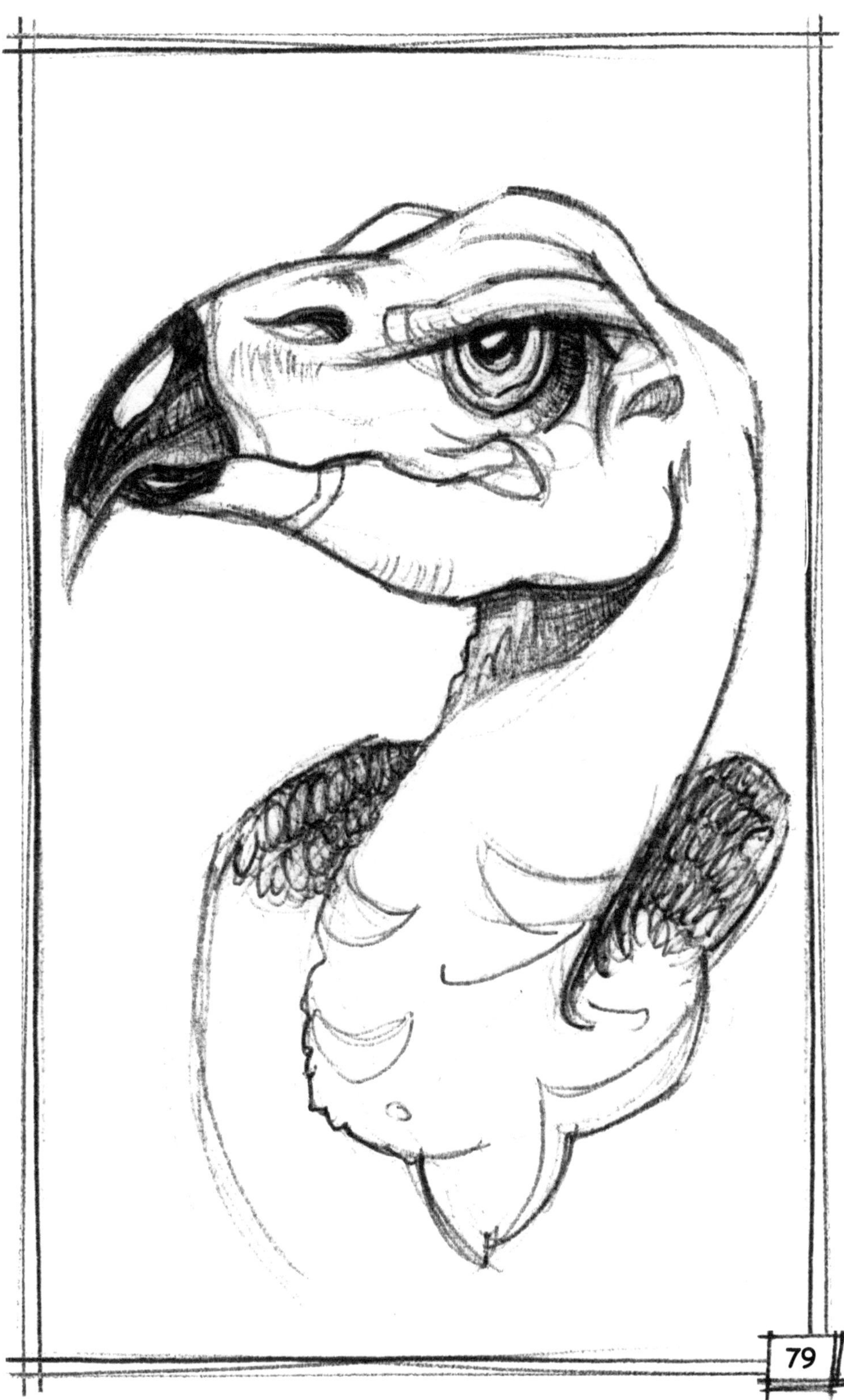

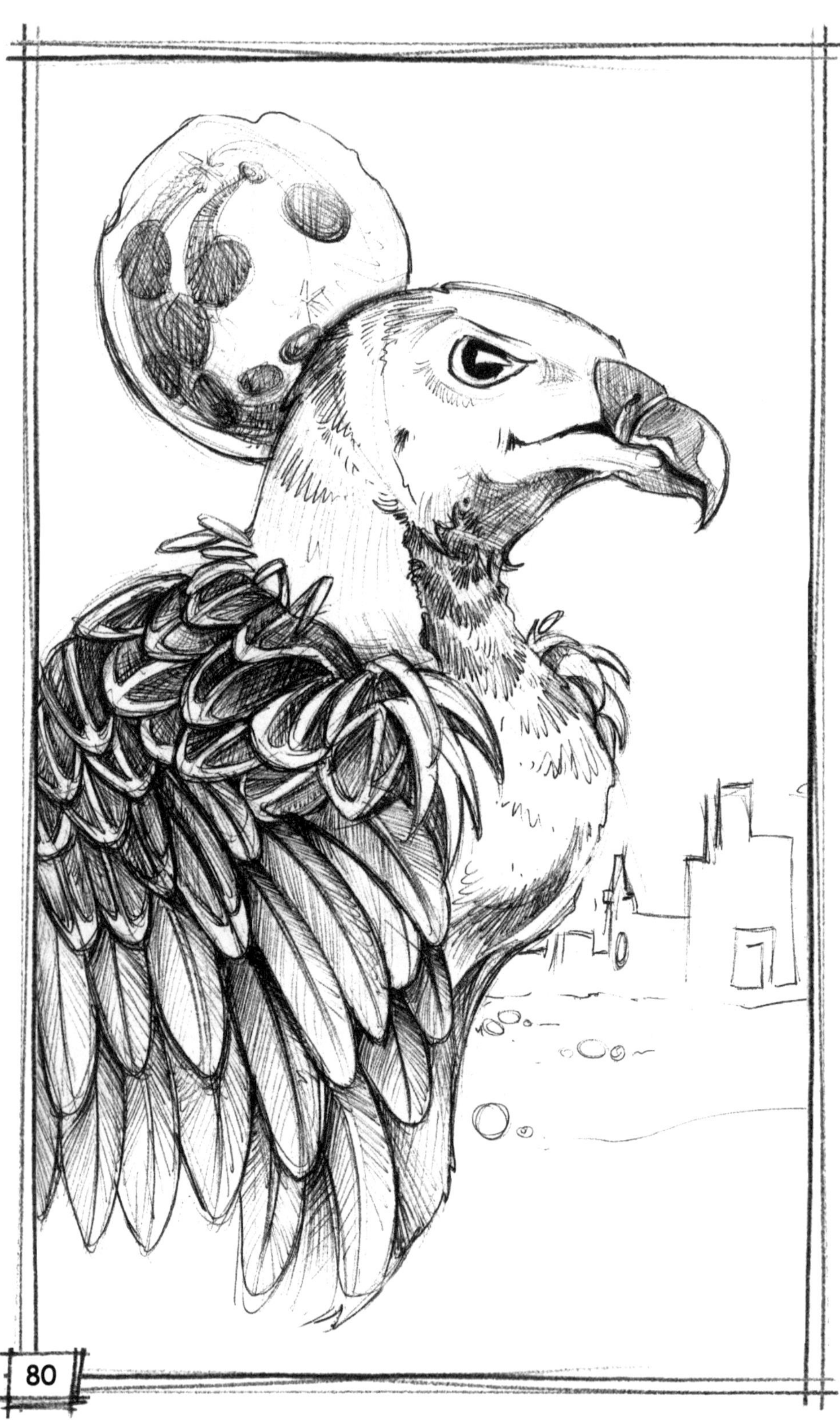

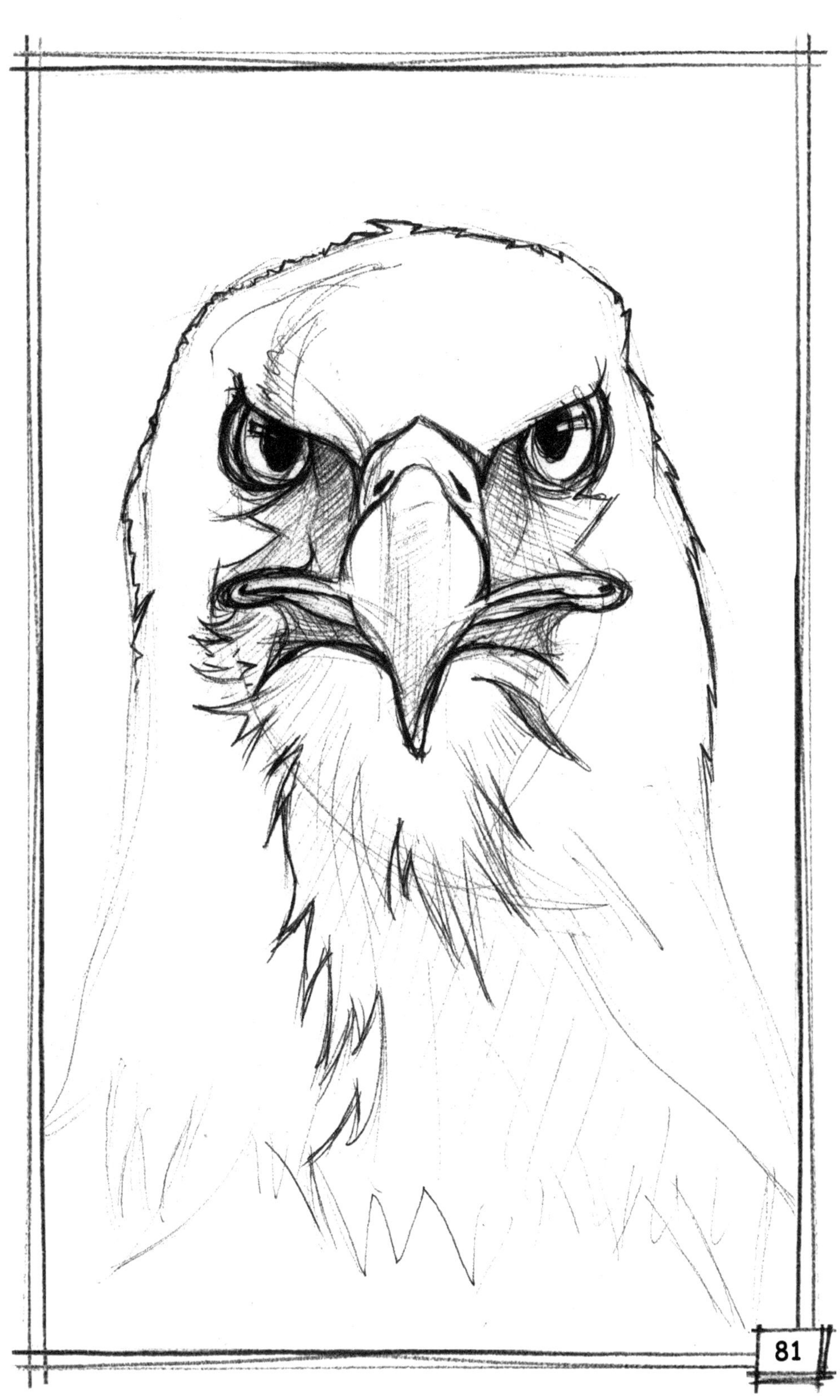

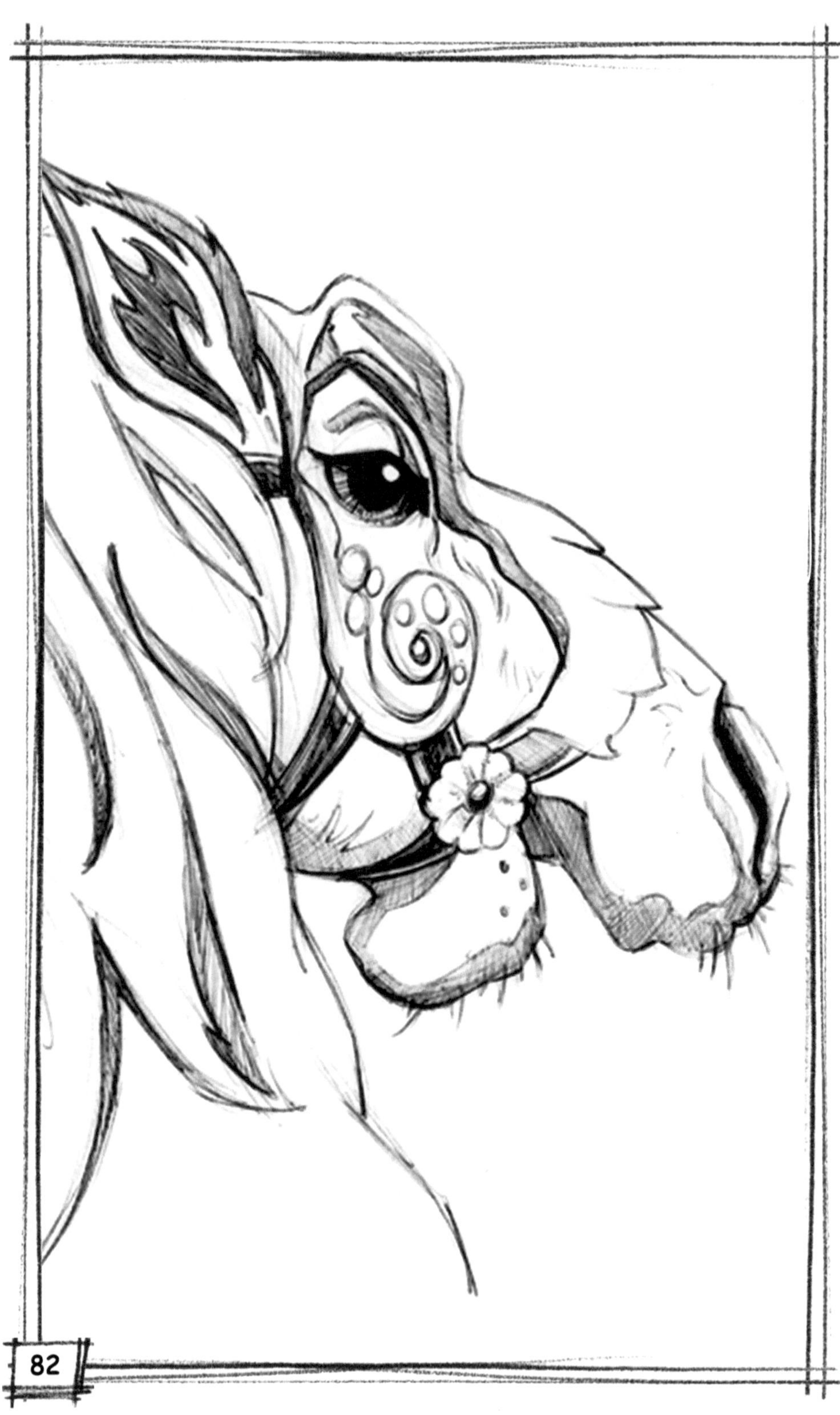

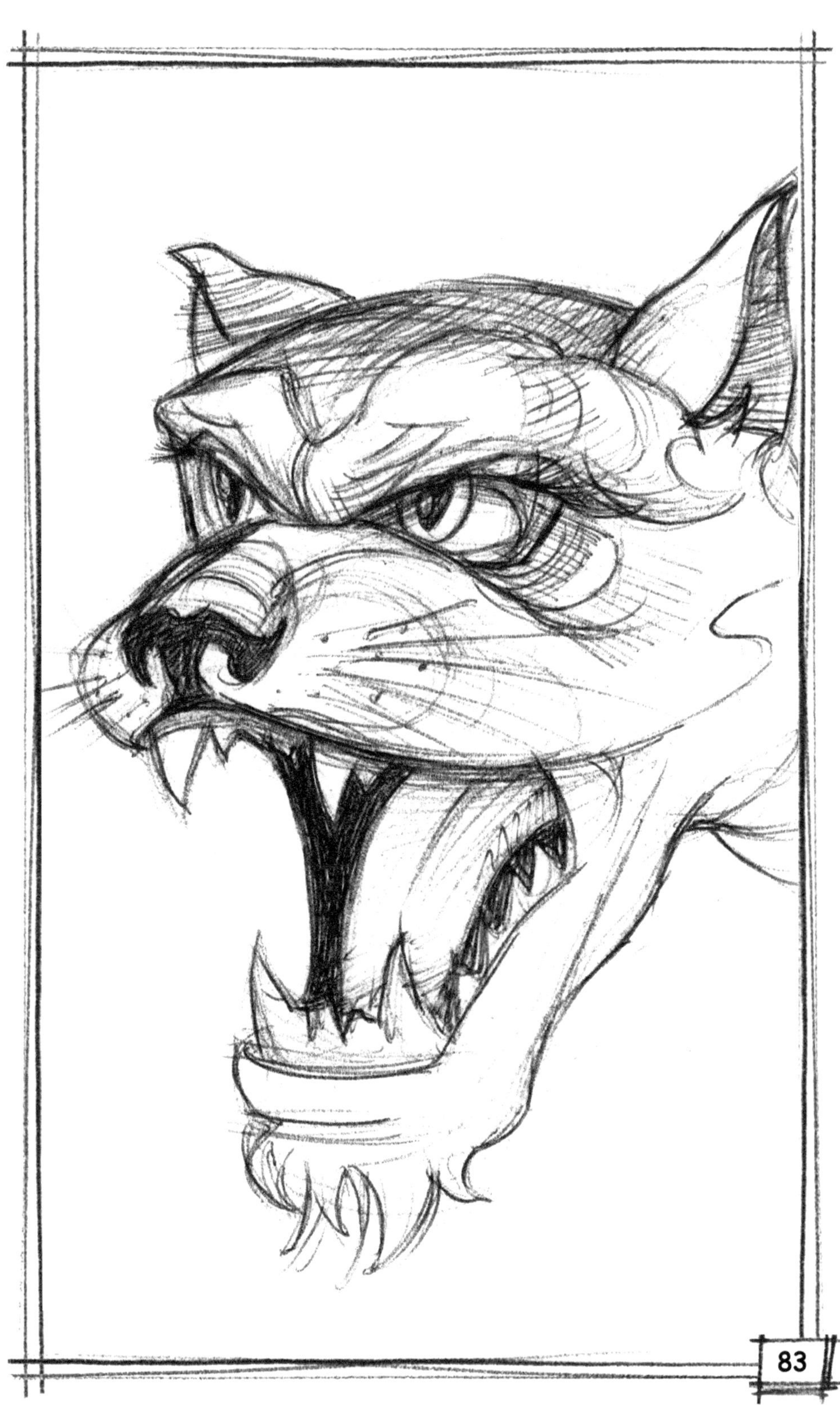

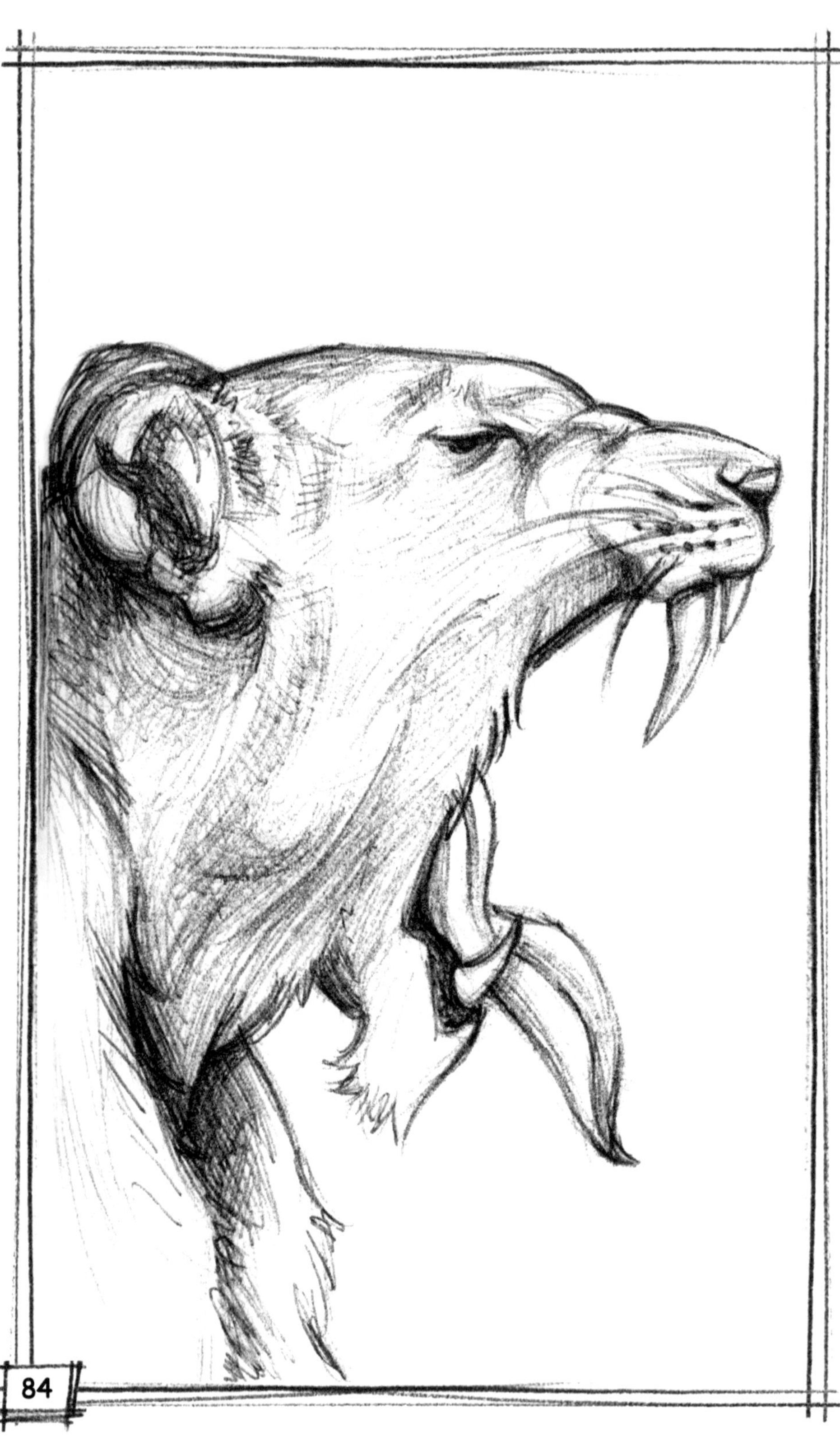

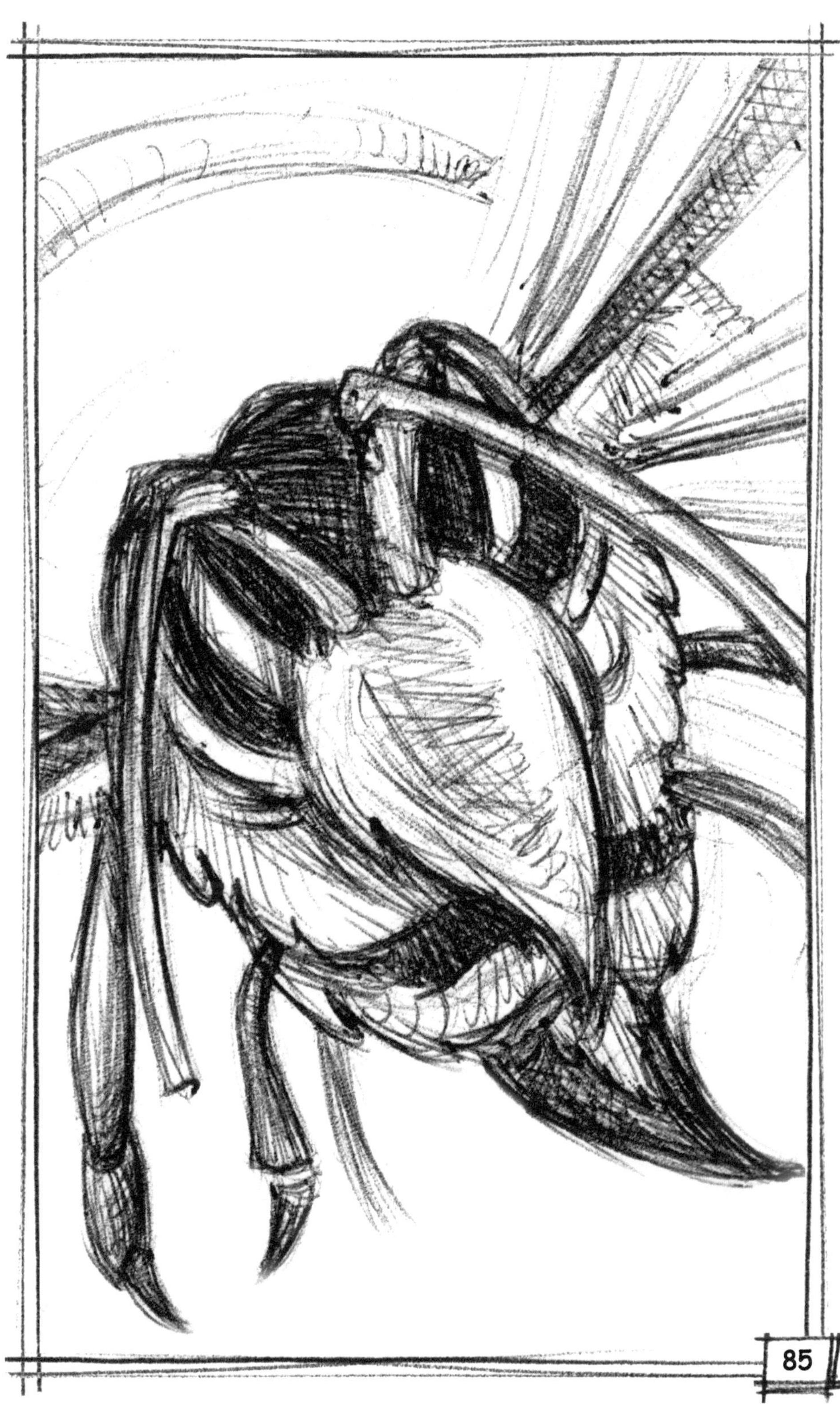

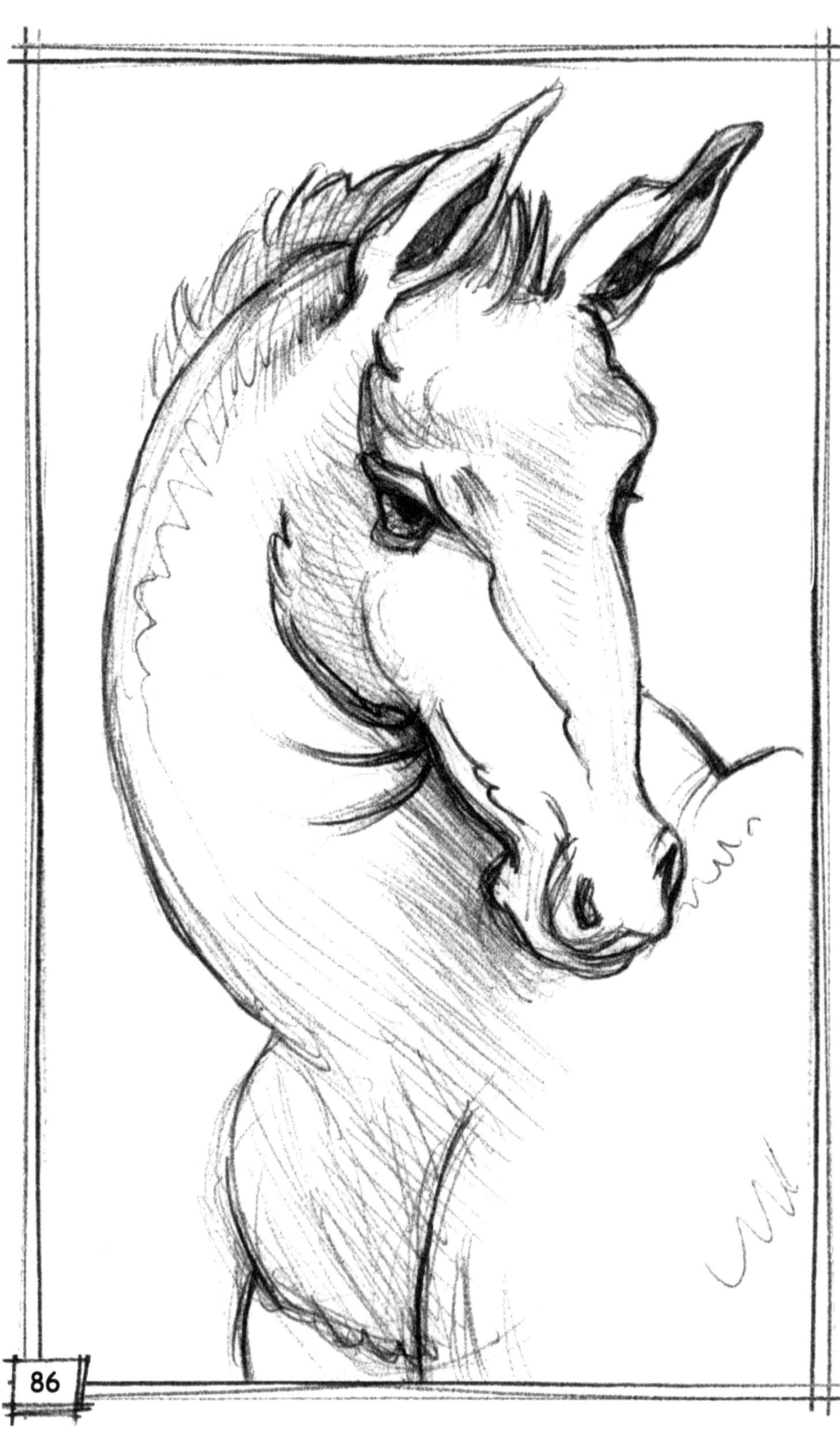

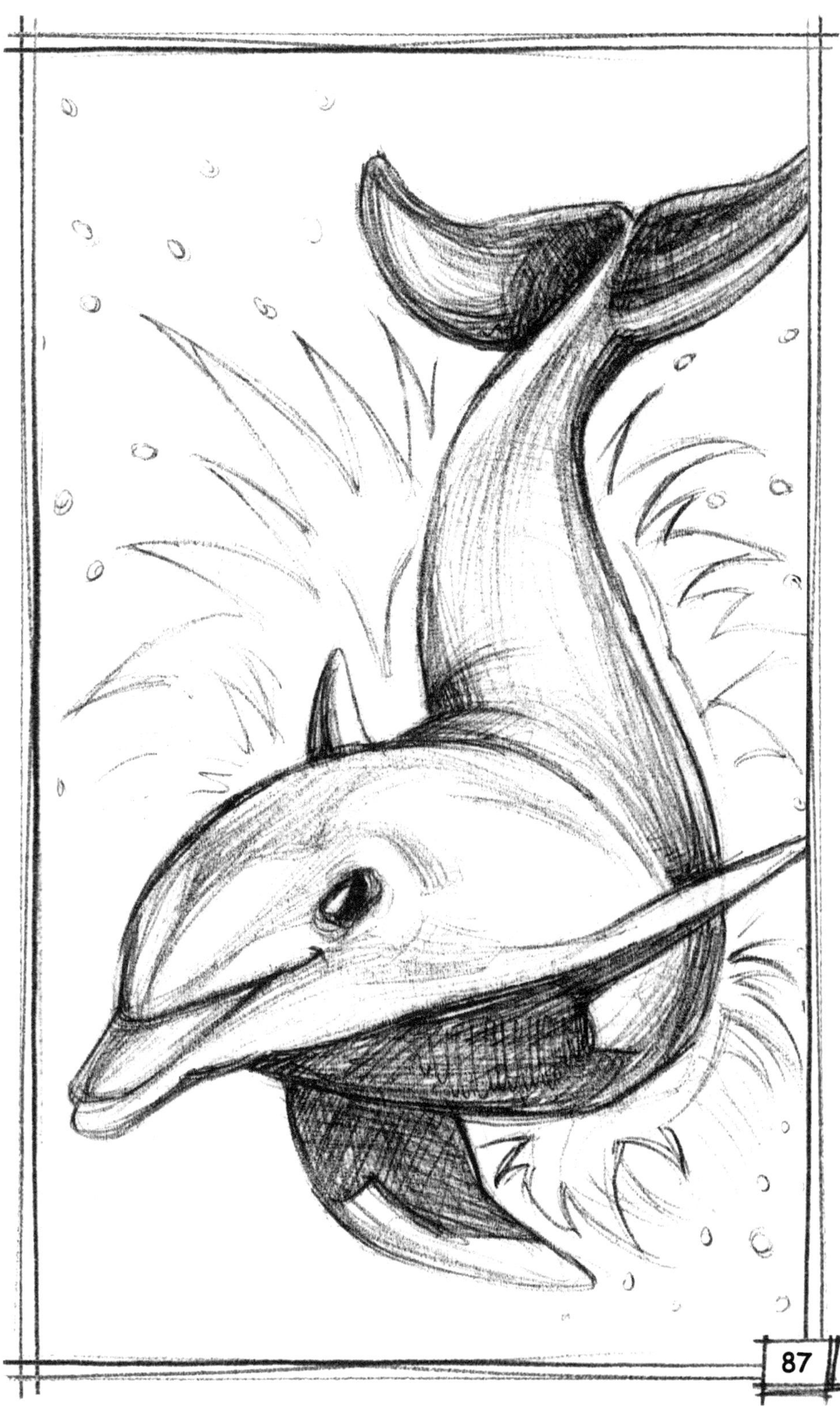

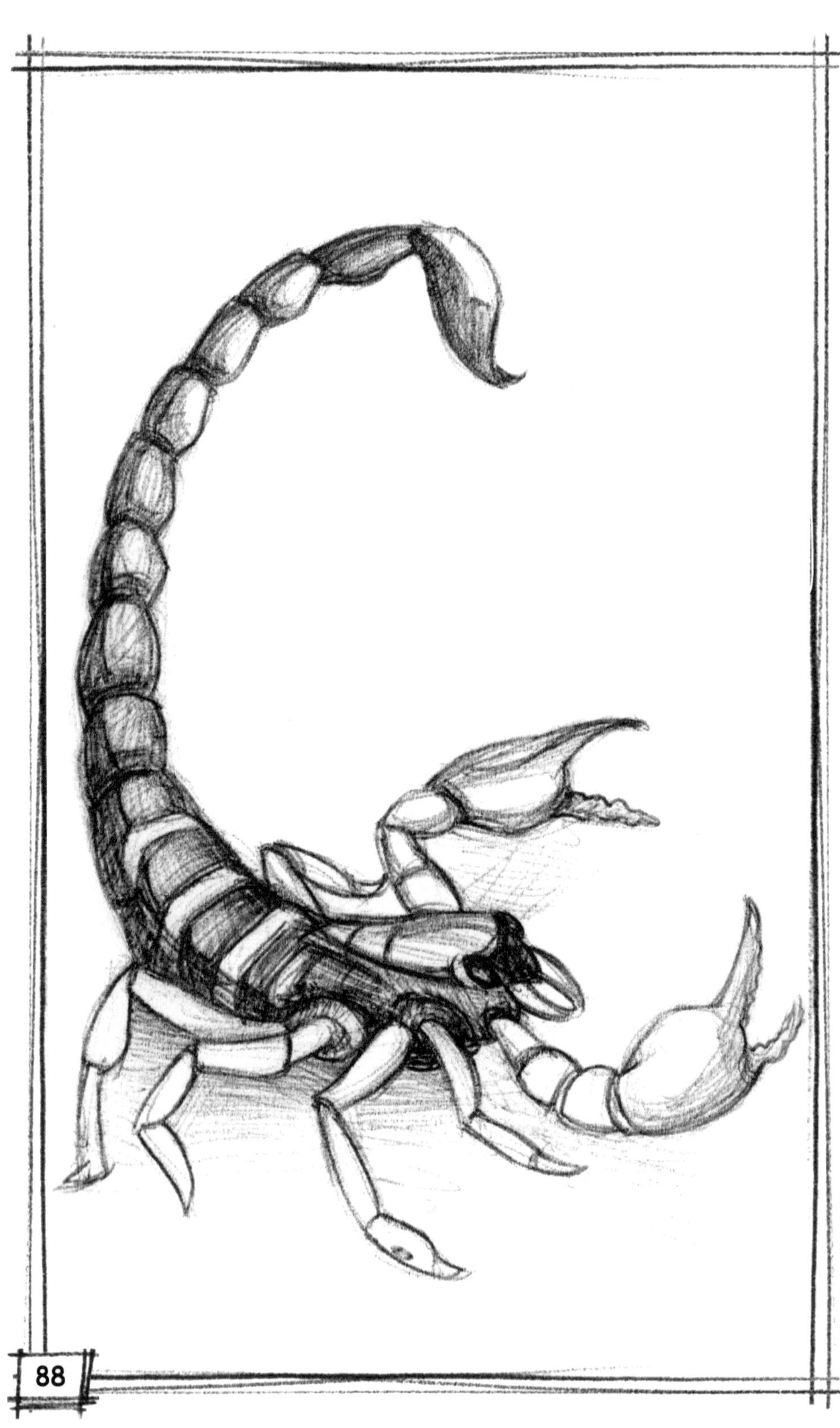

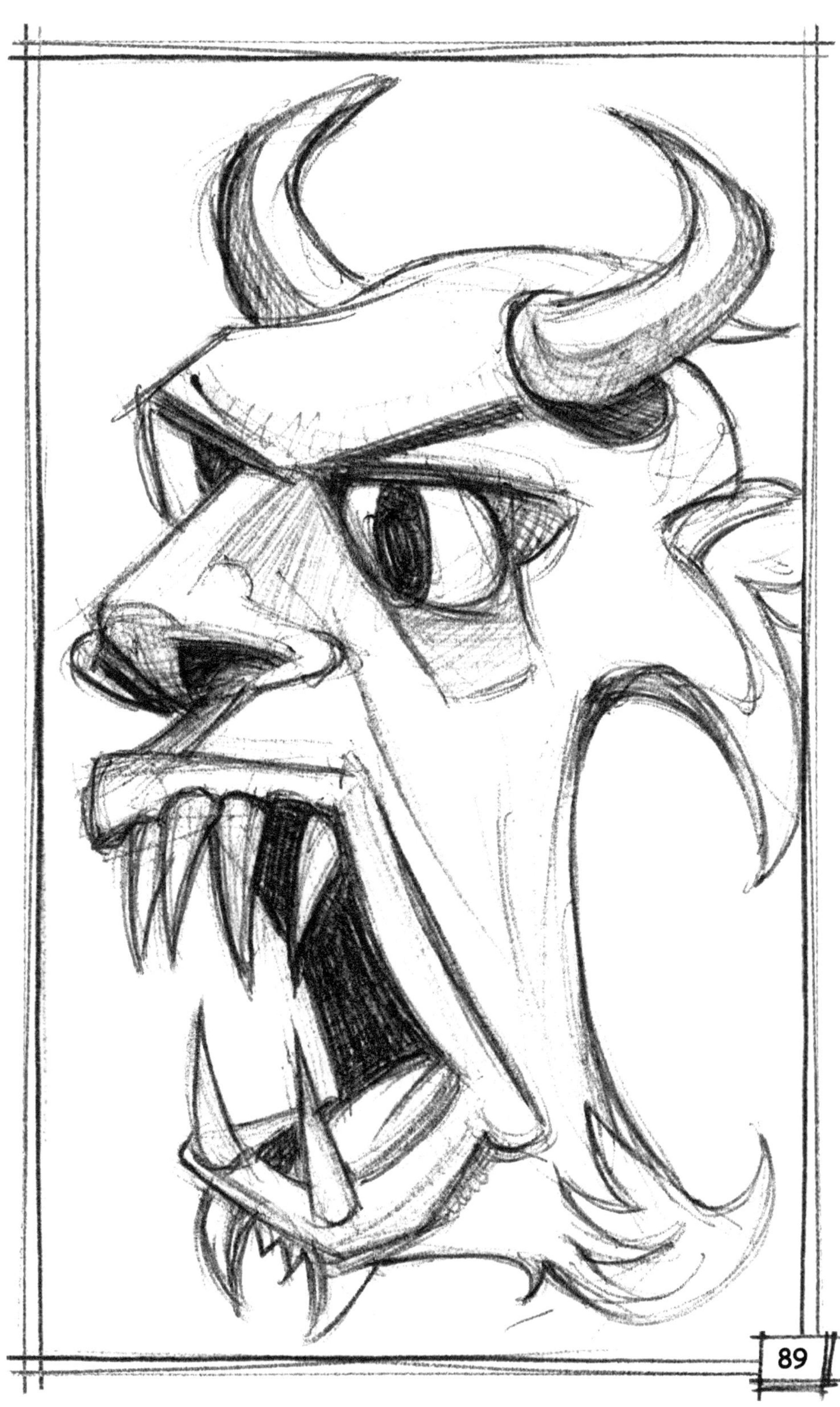

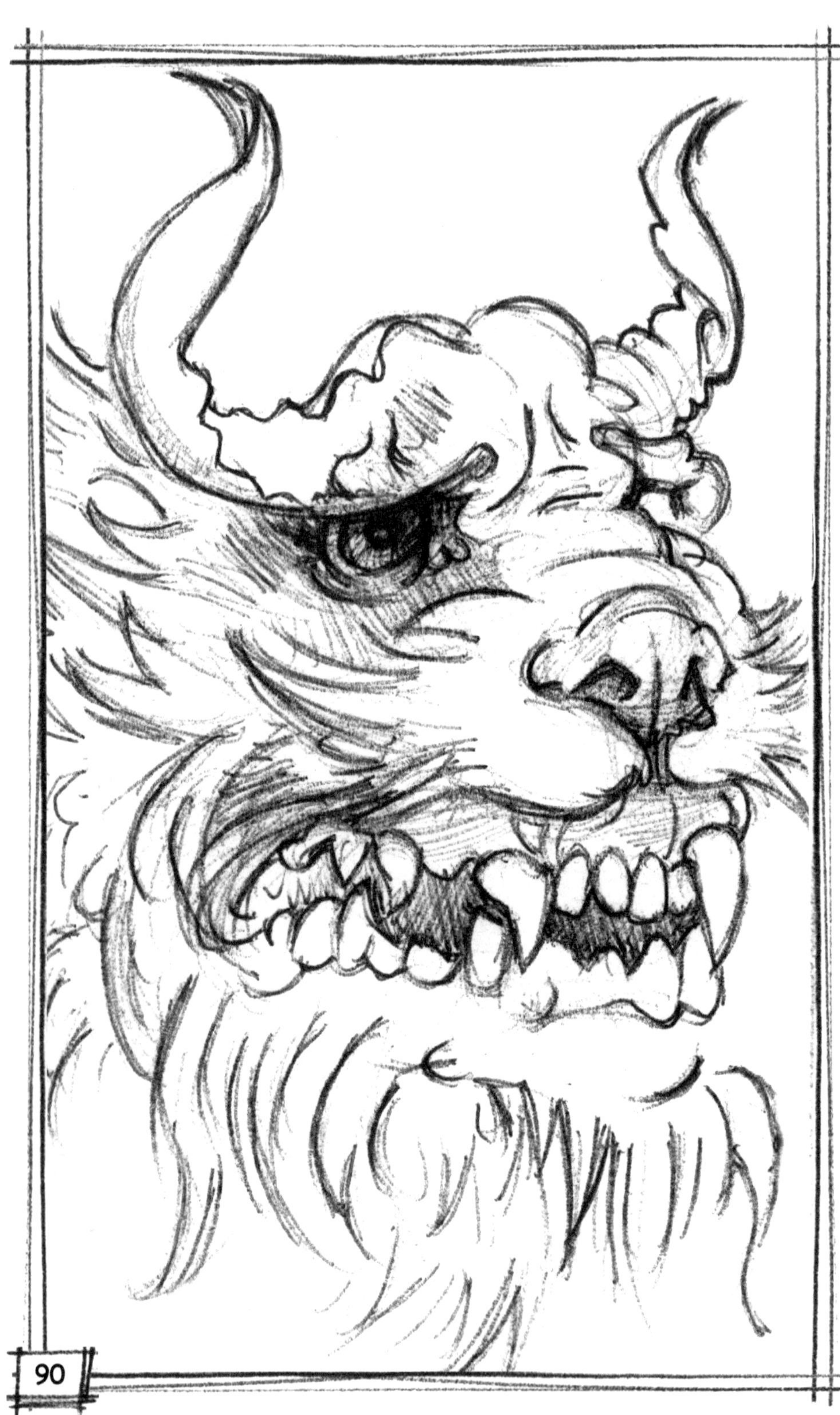

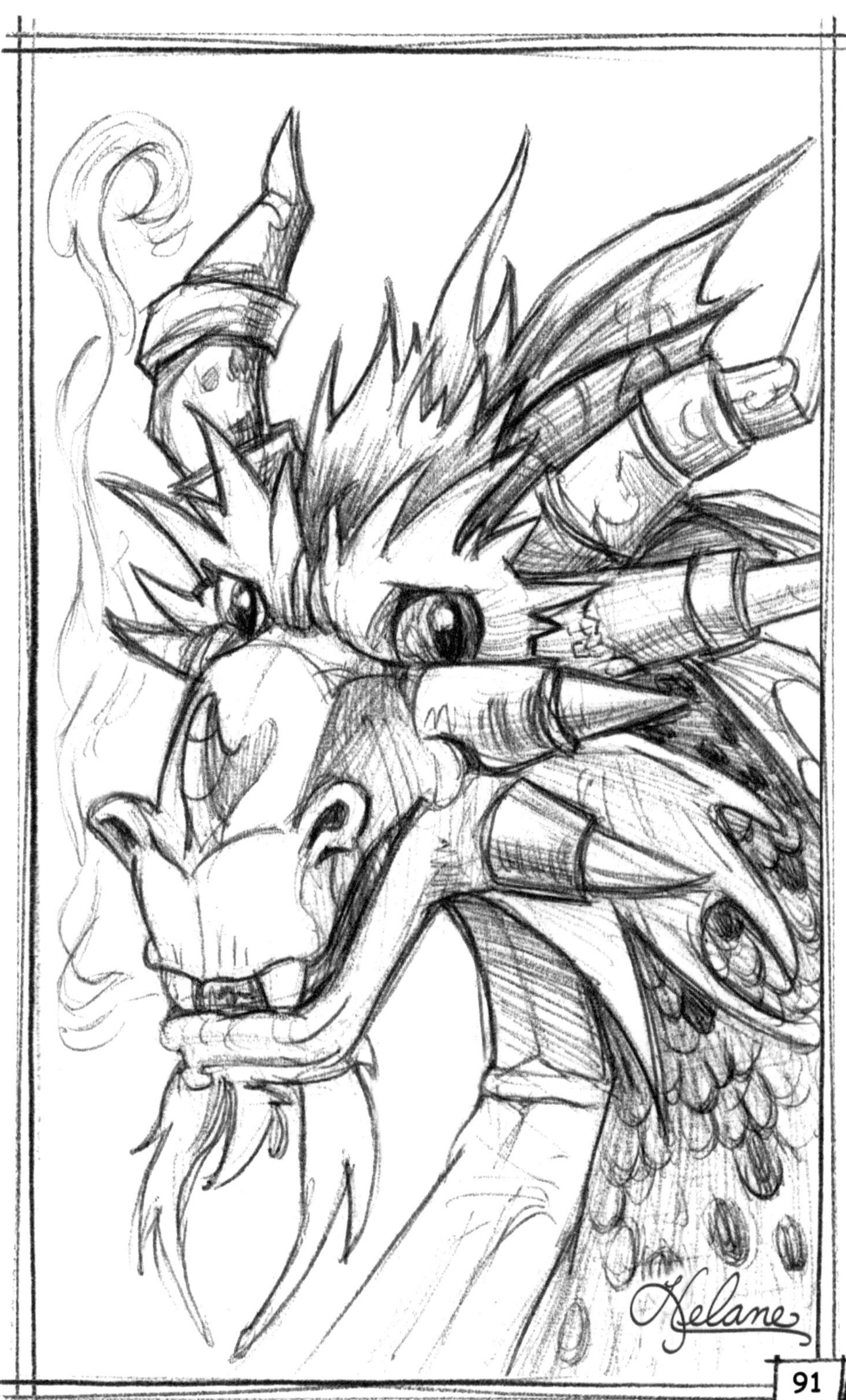
Kelane

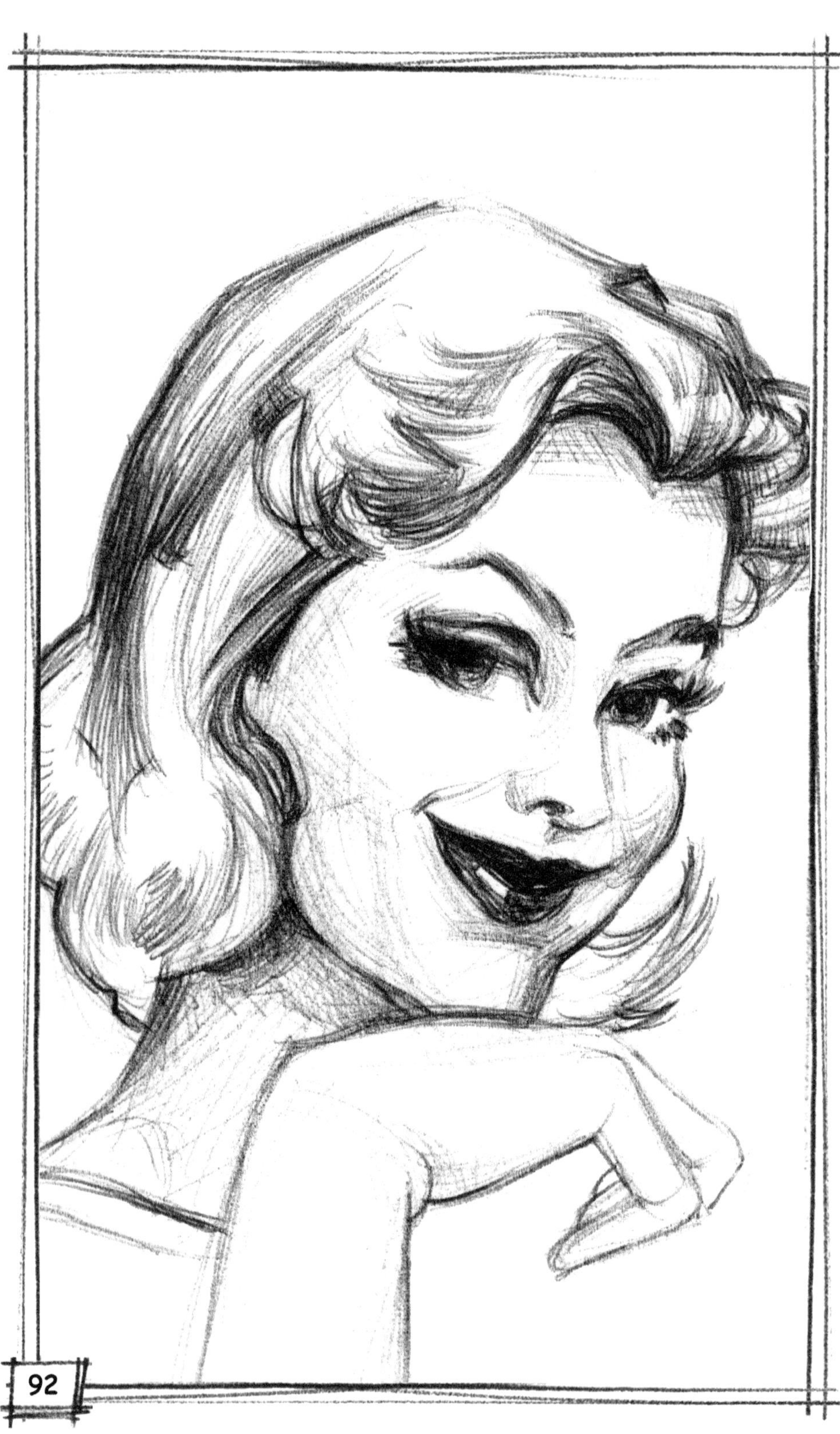

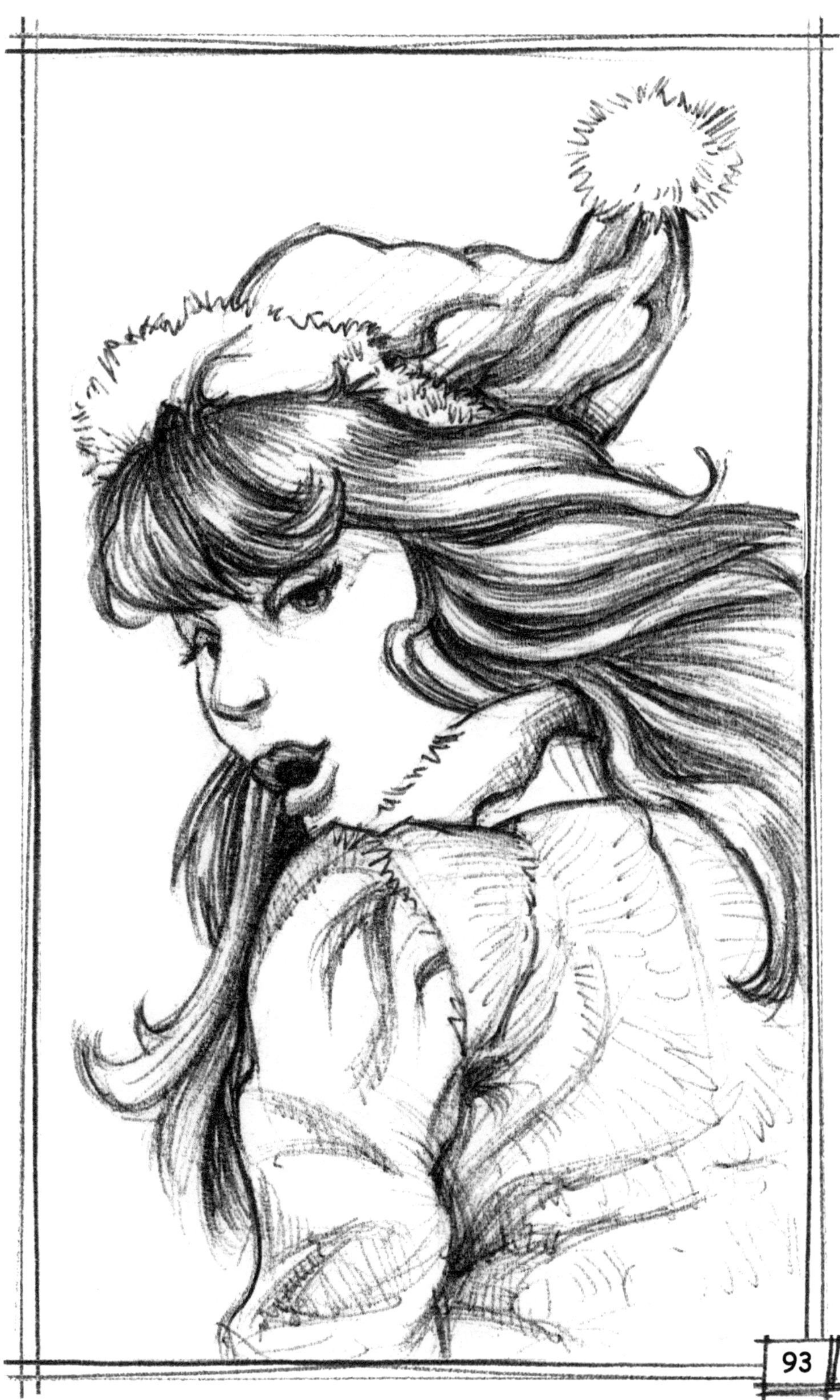

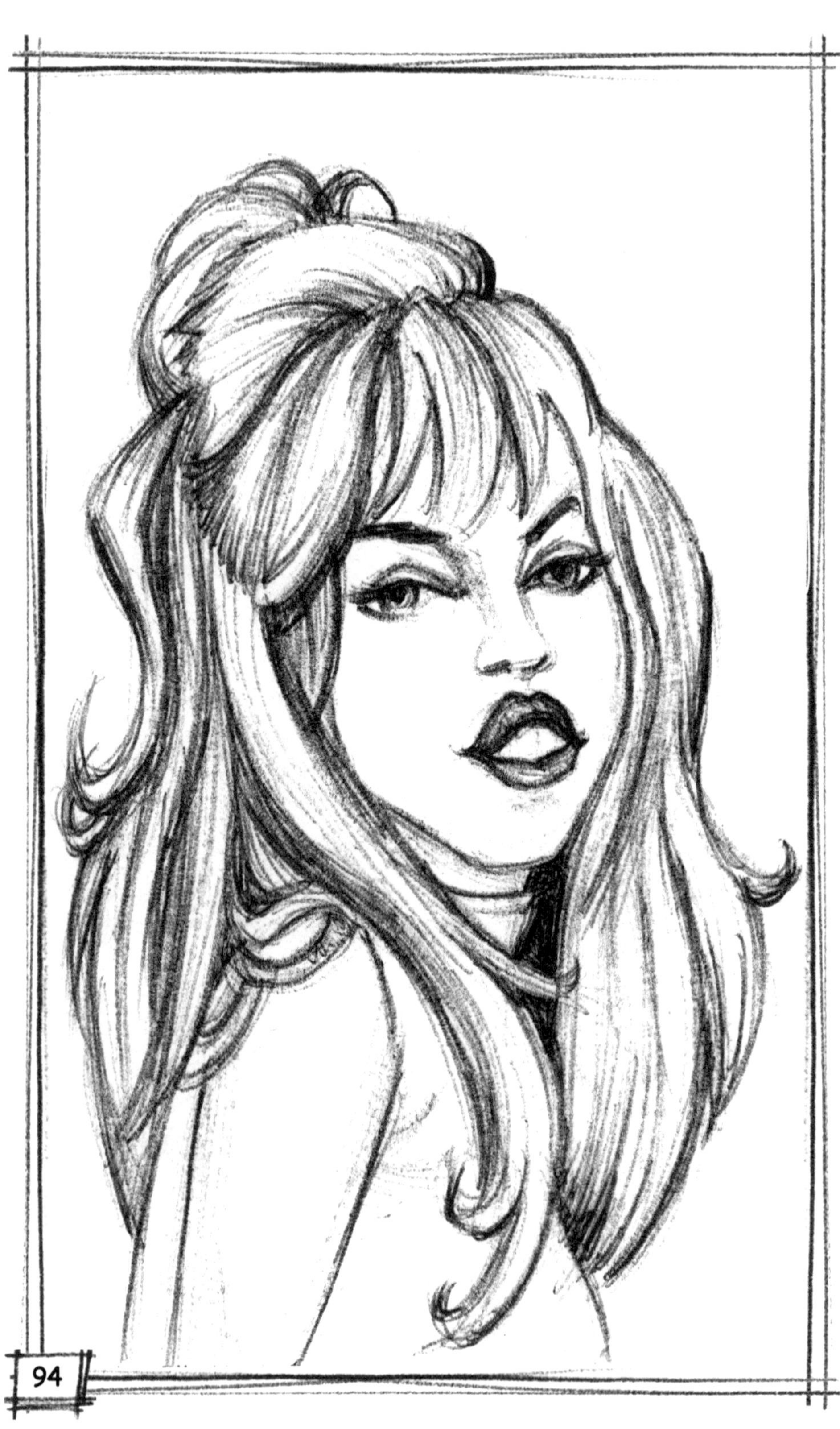

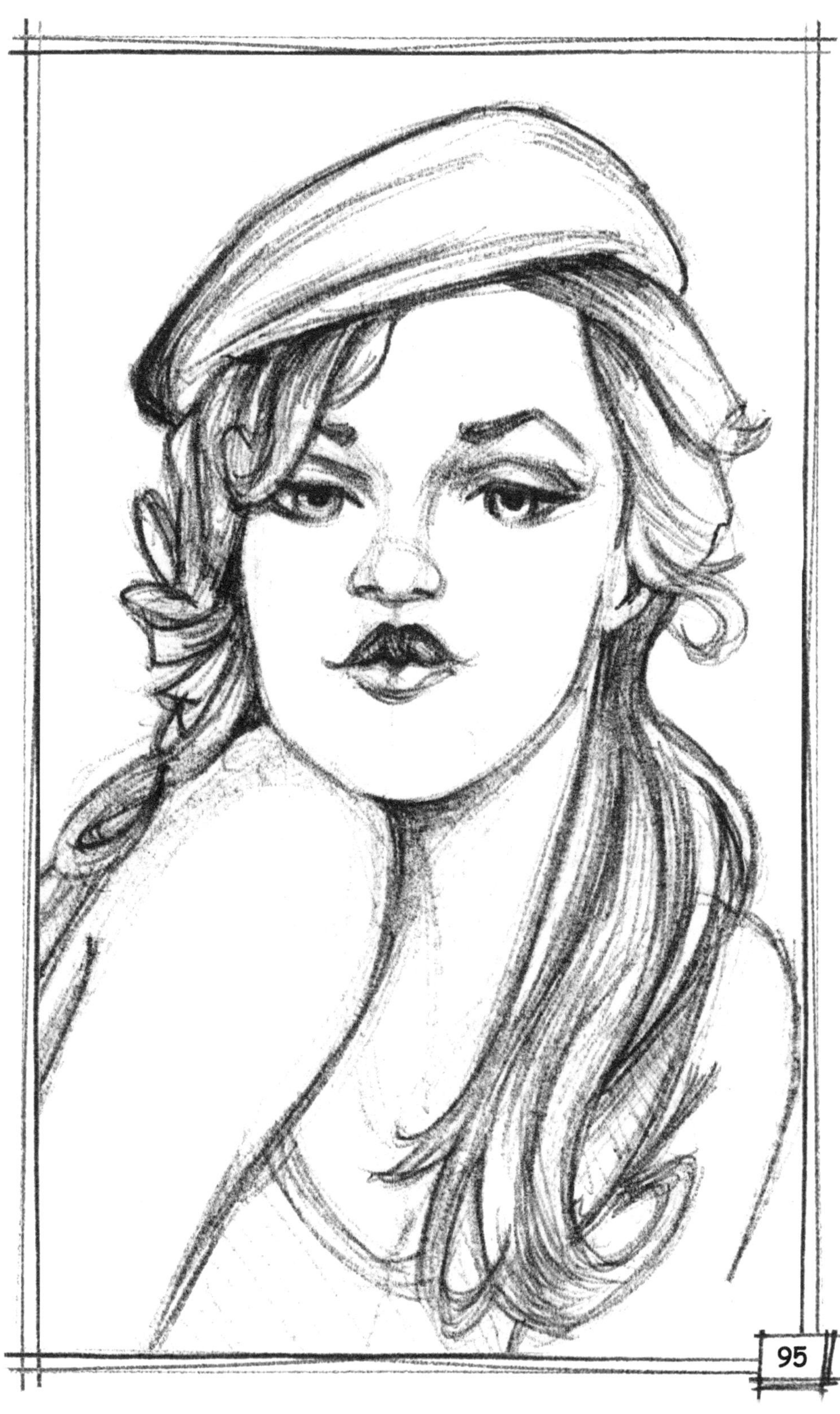

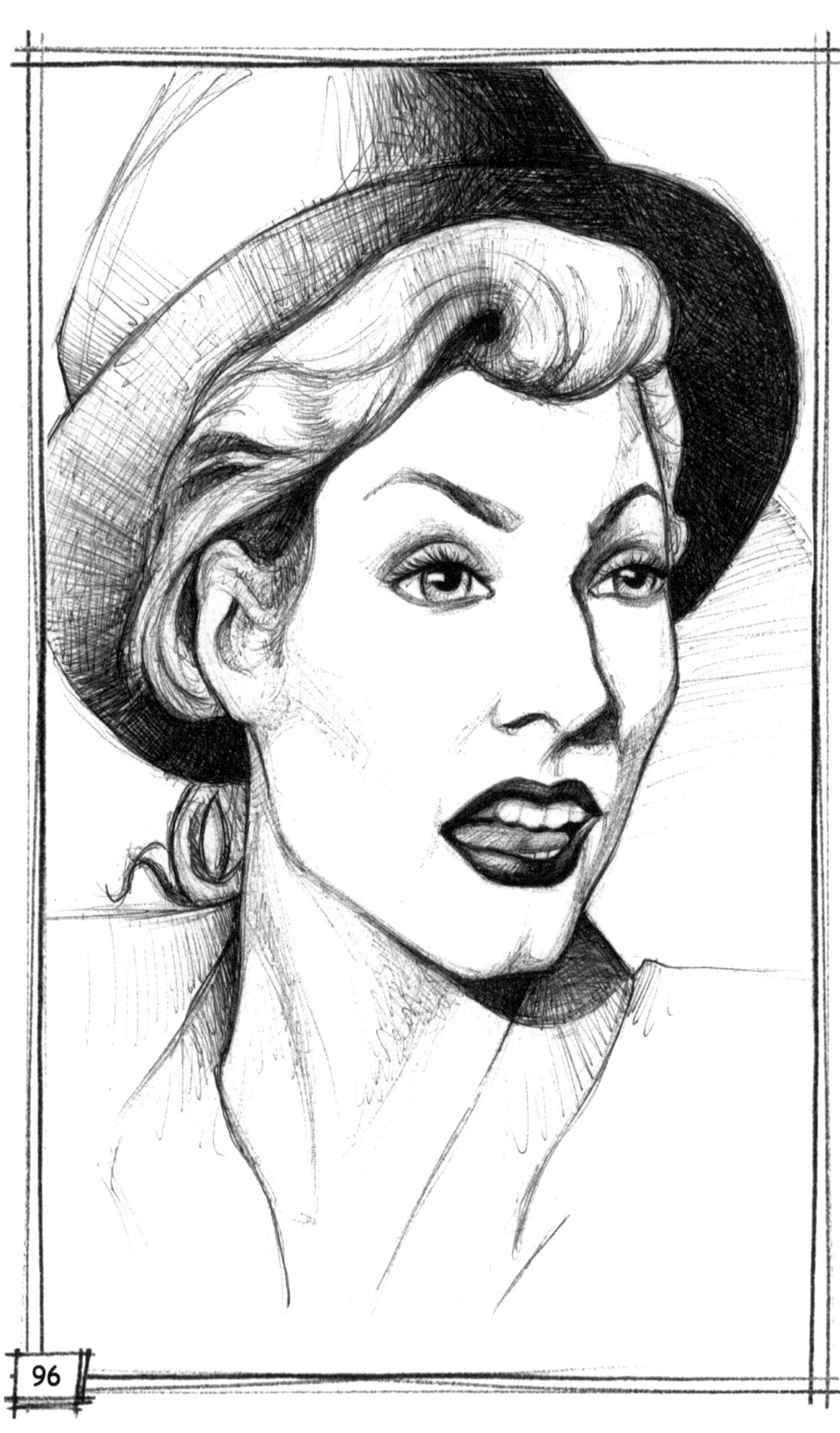

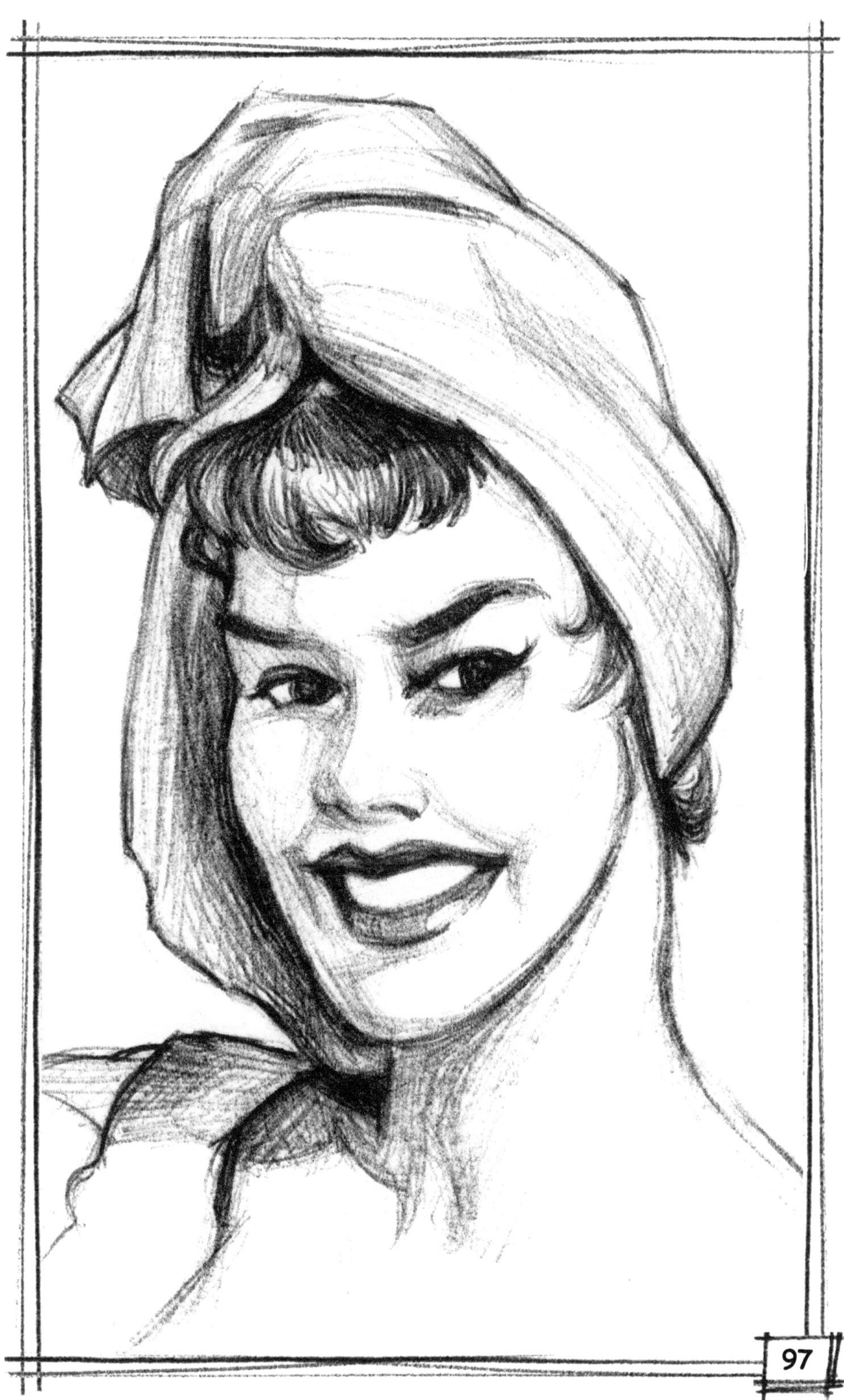

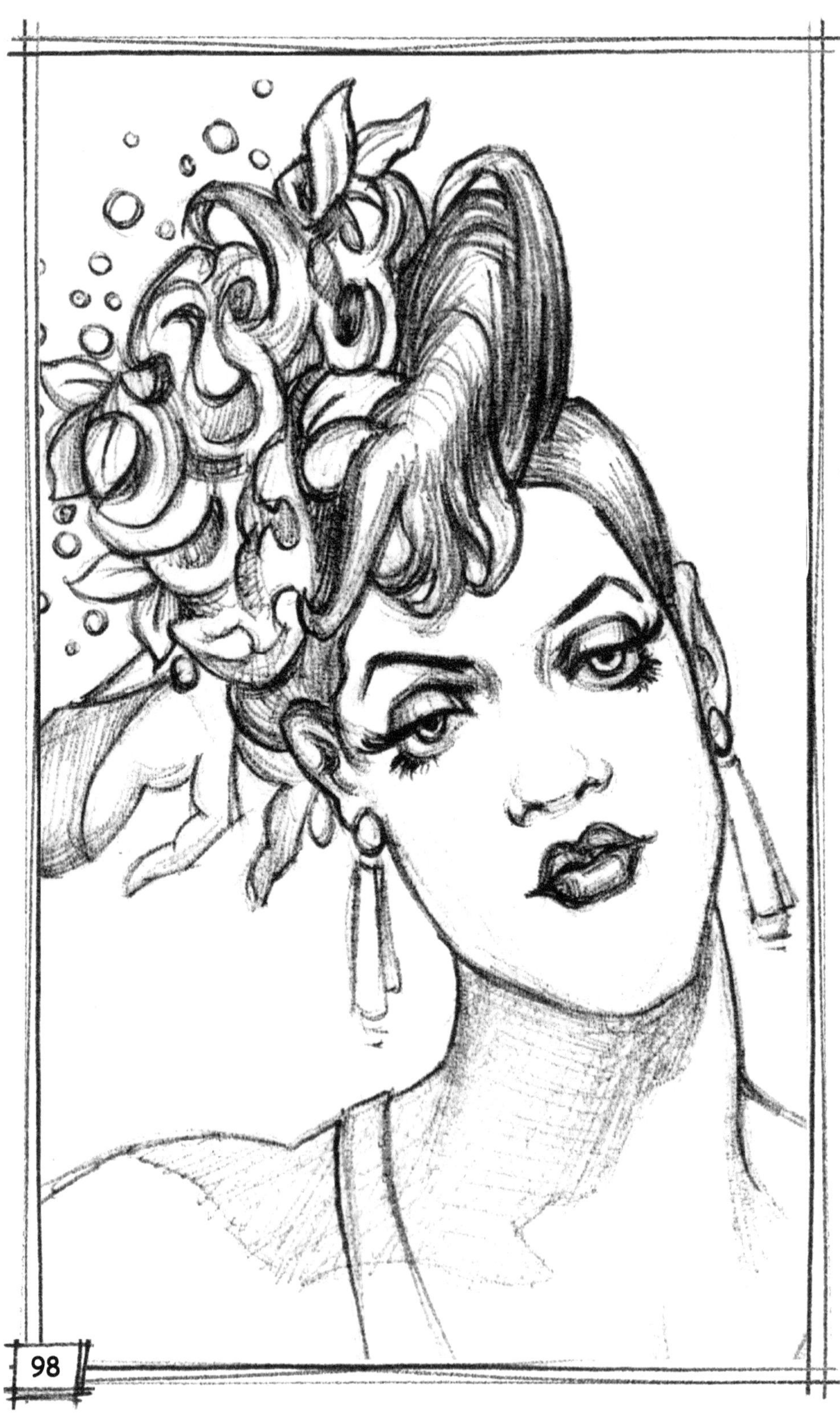

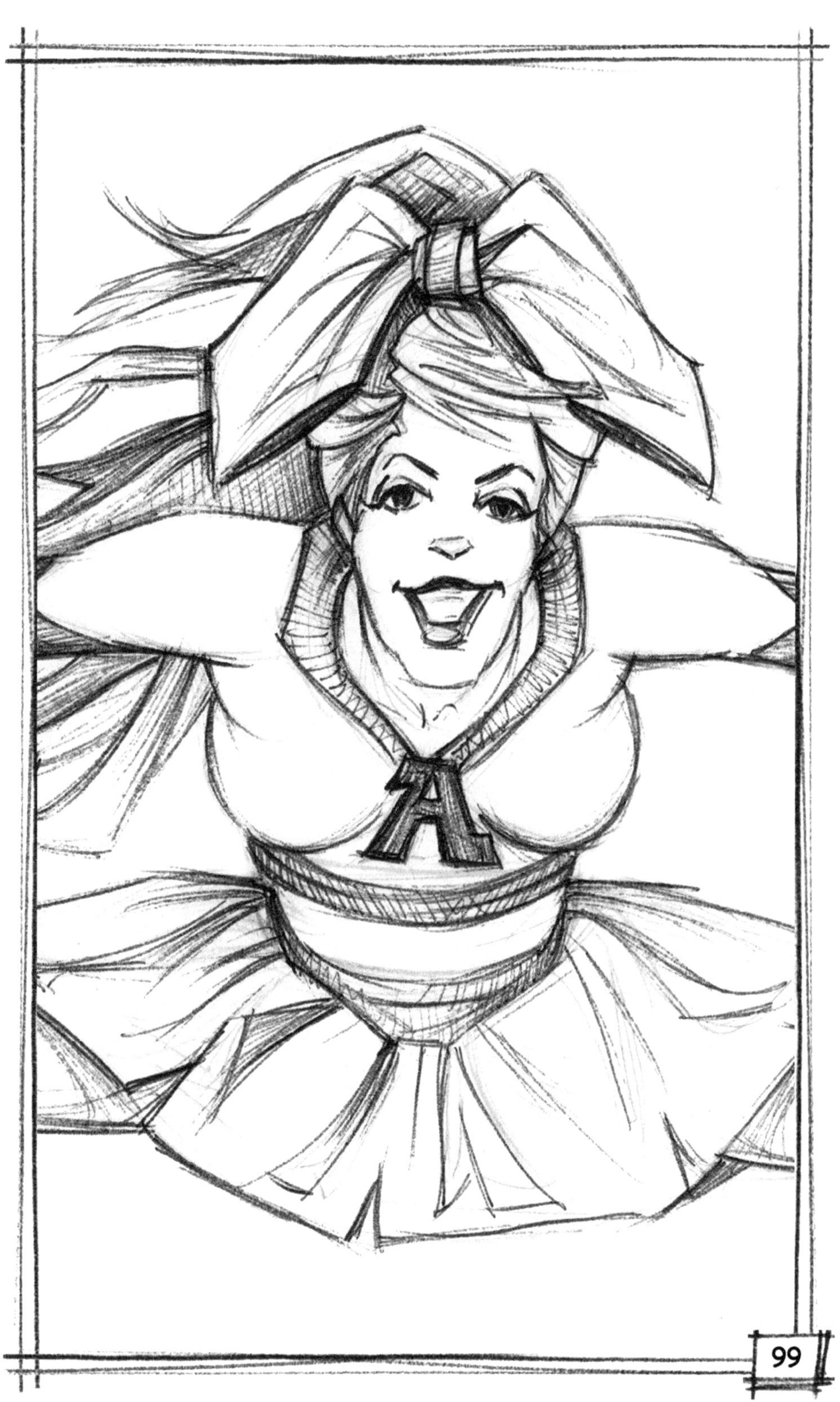

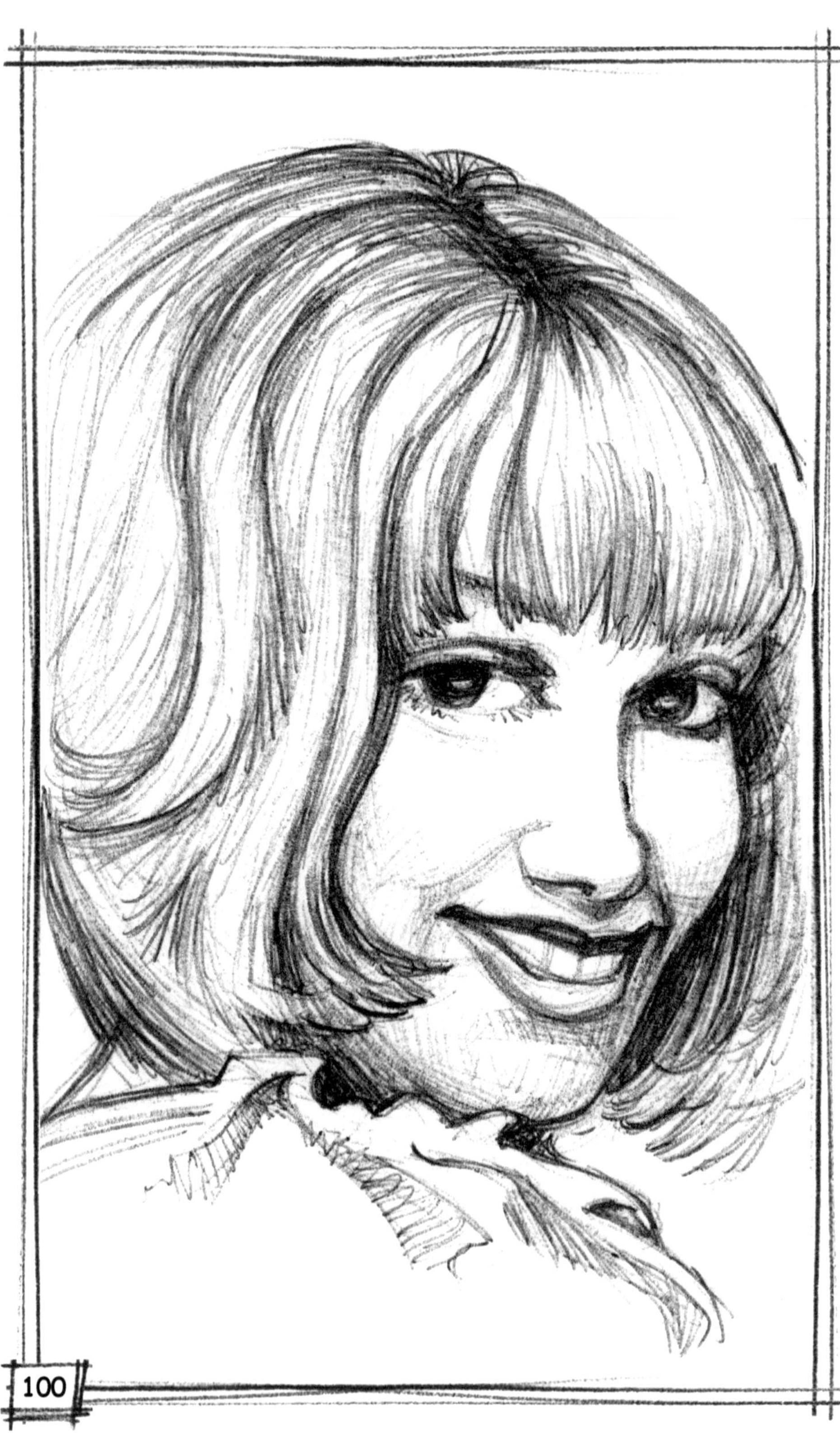

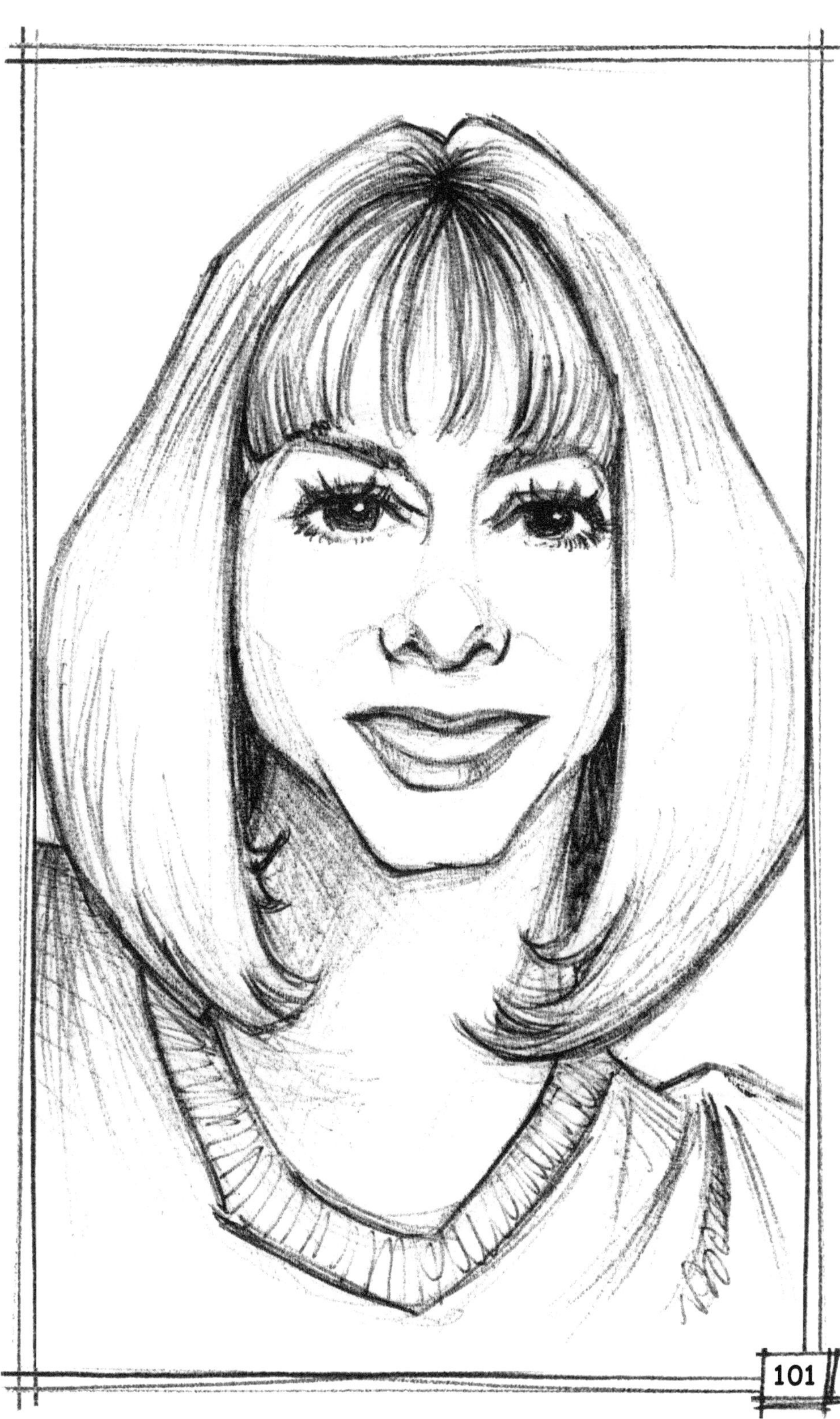

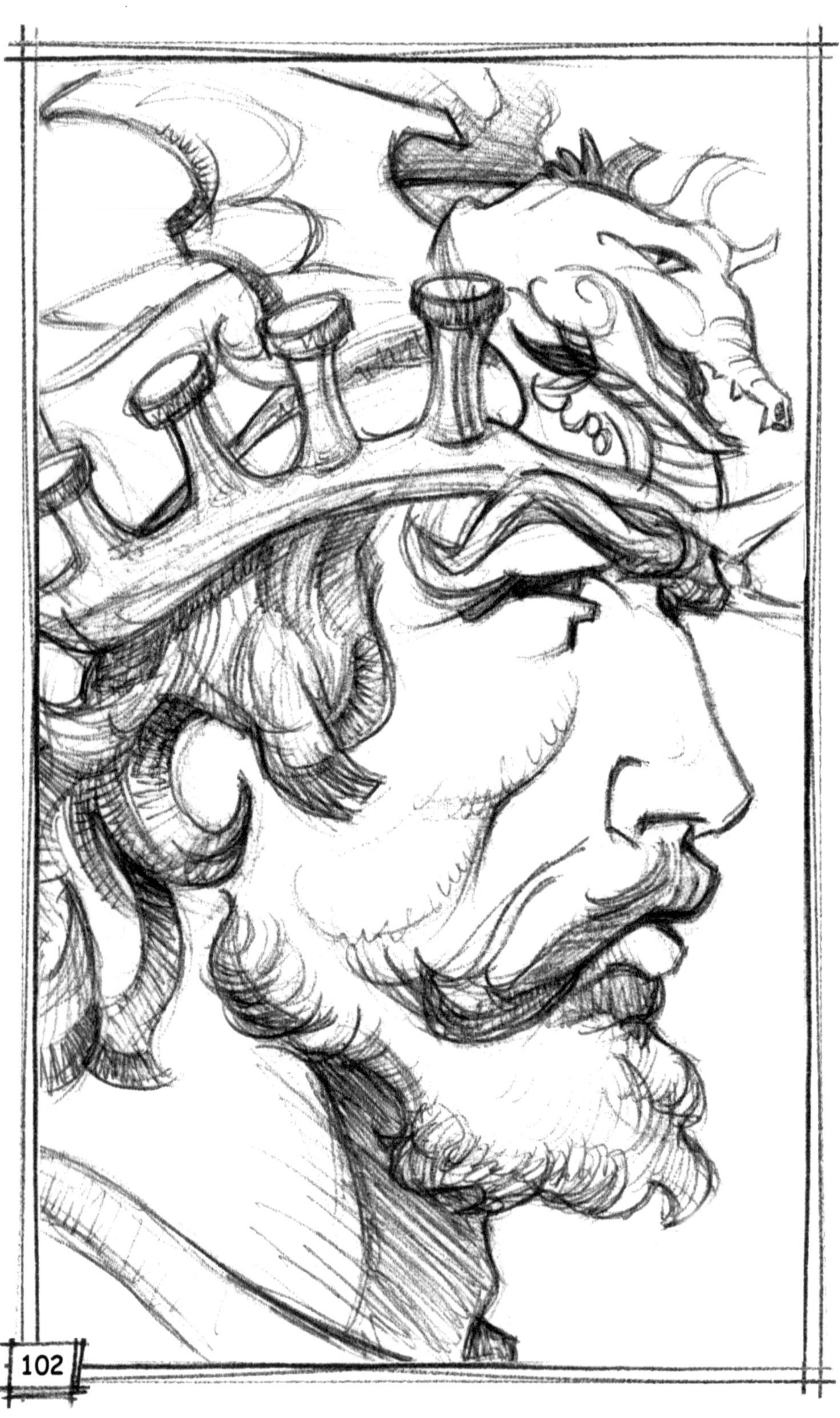

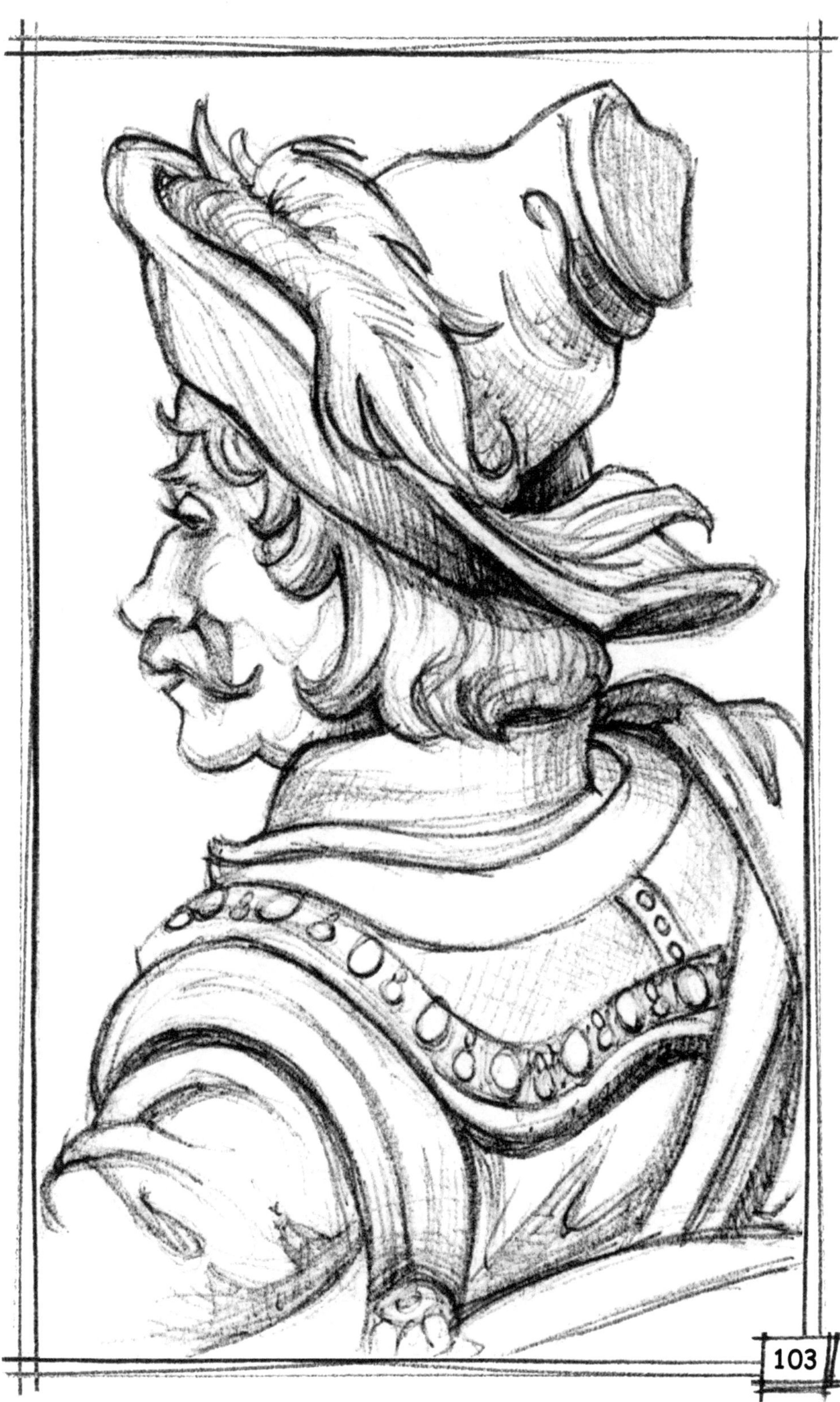

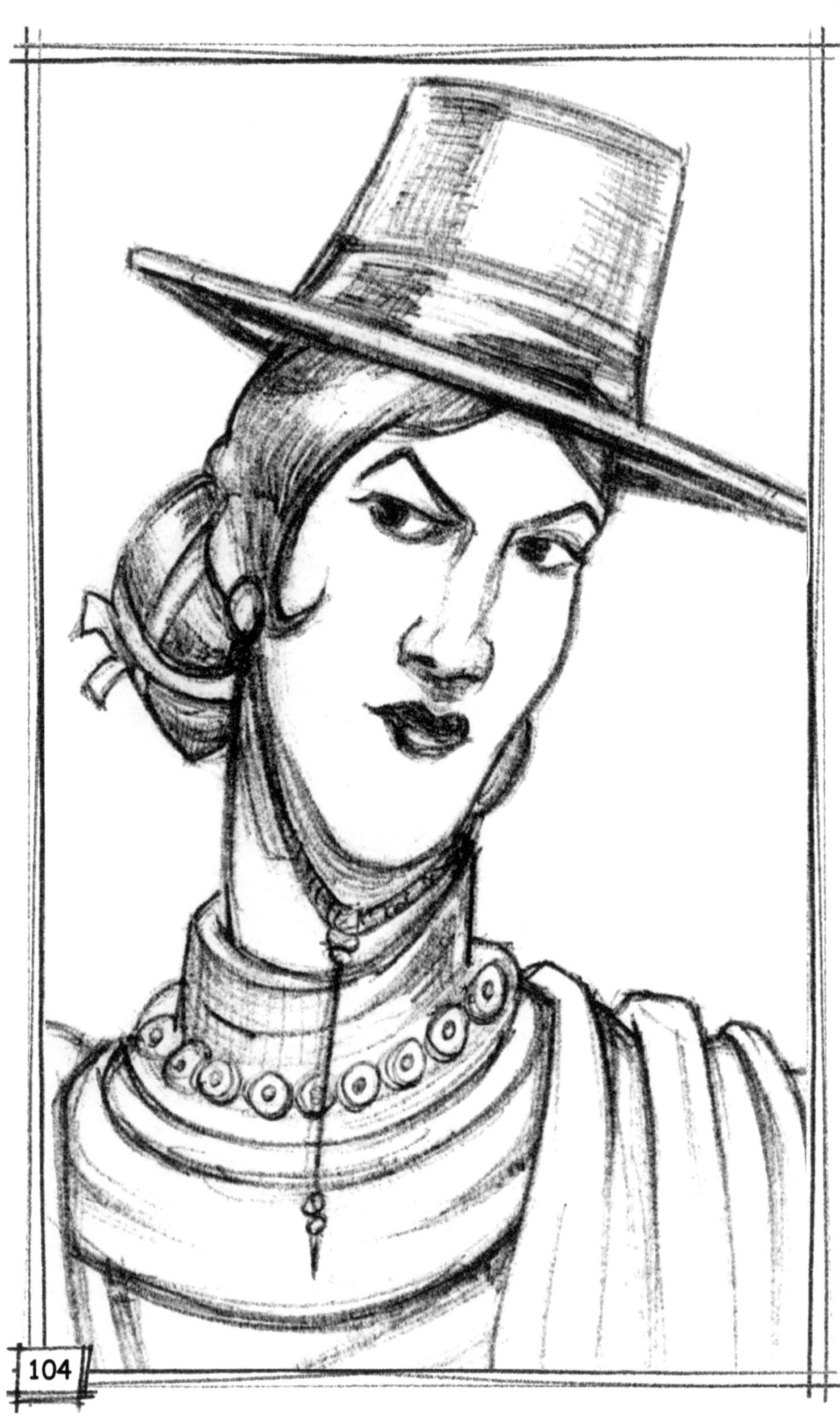

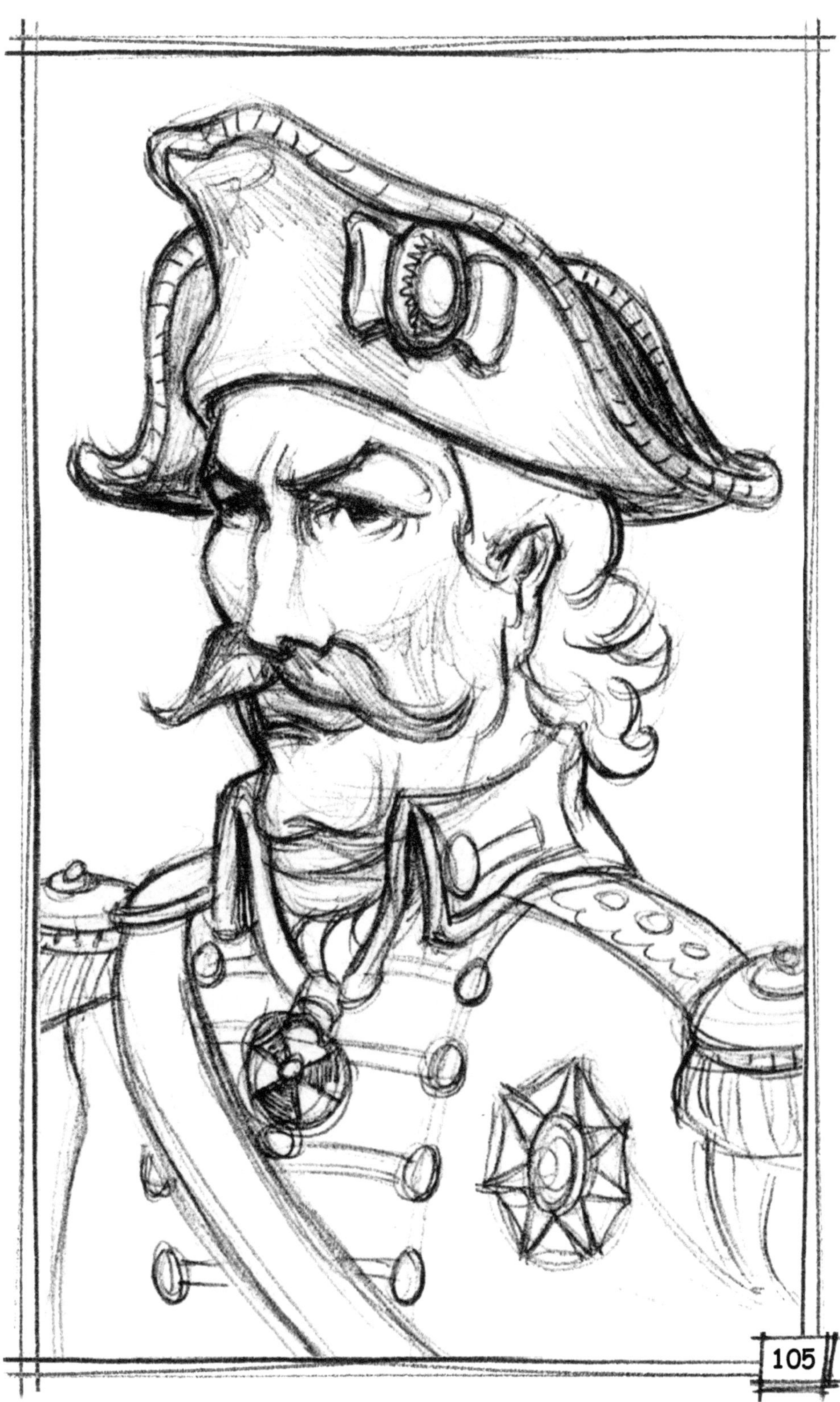

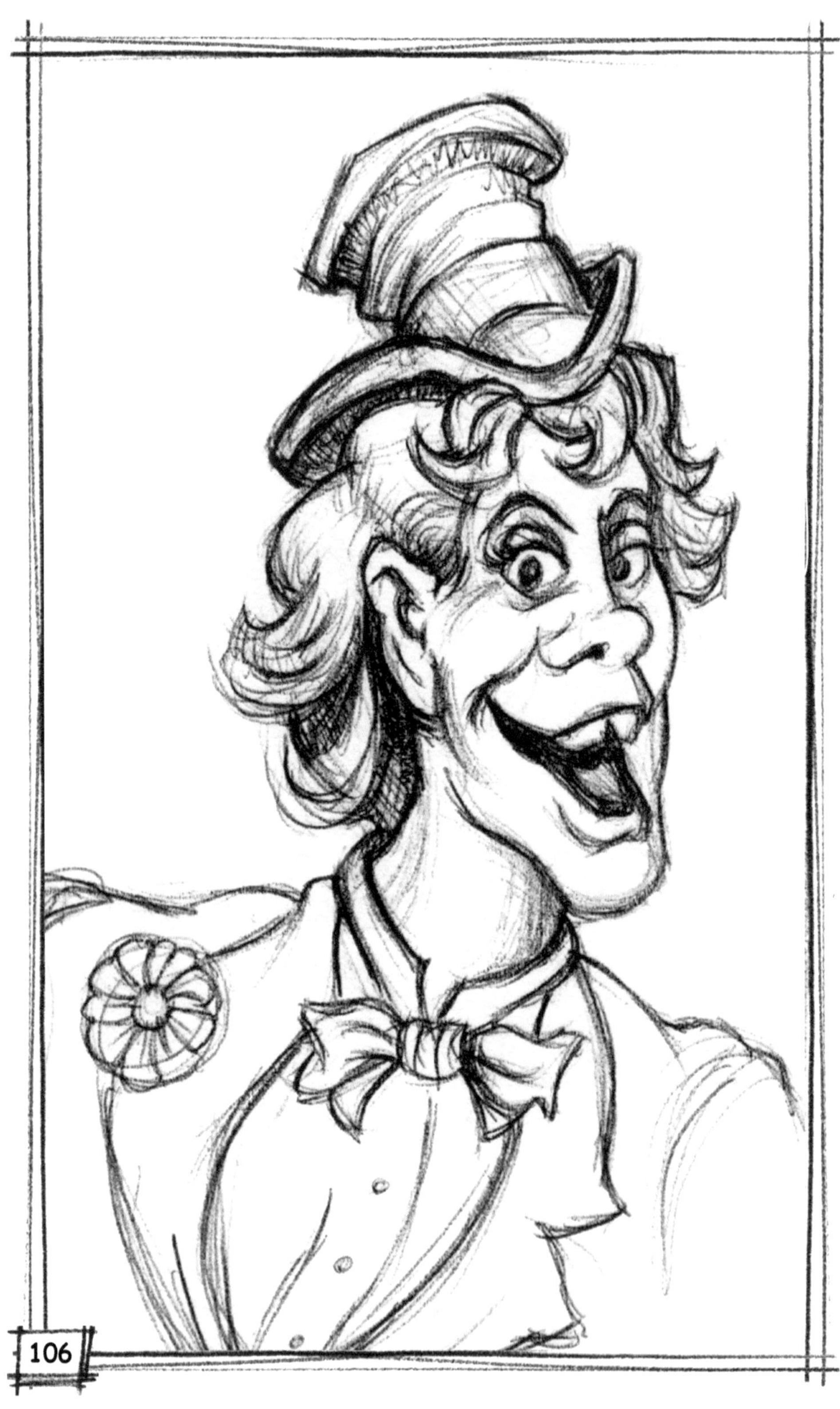

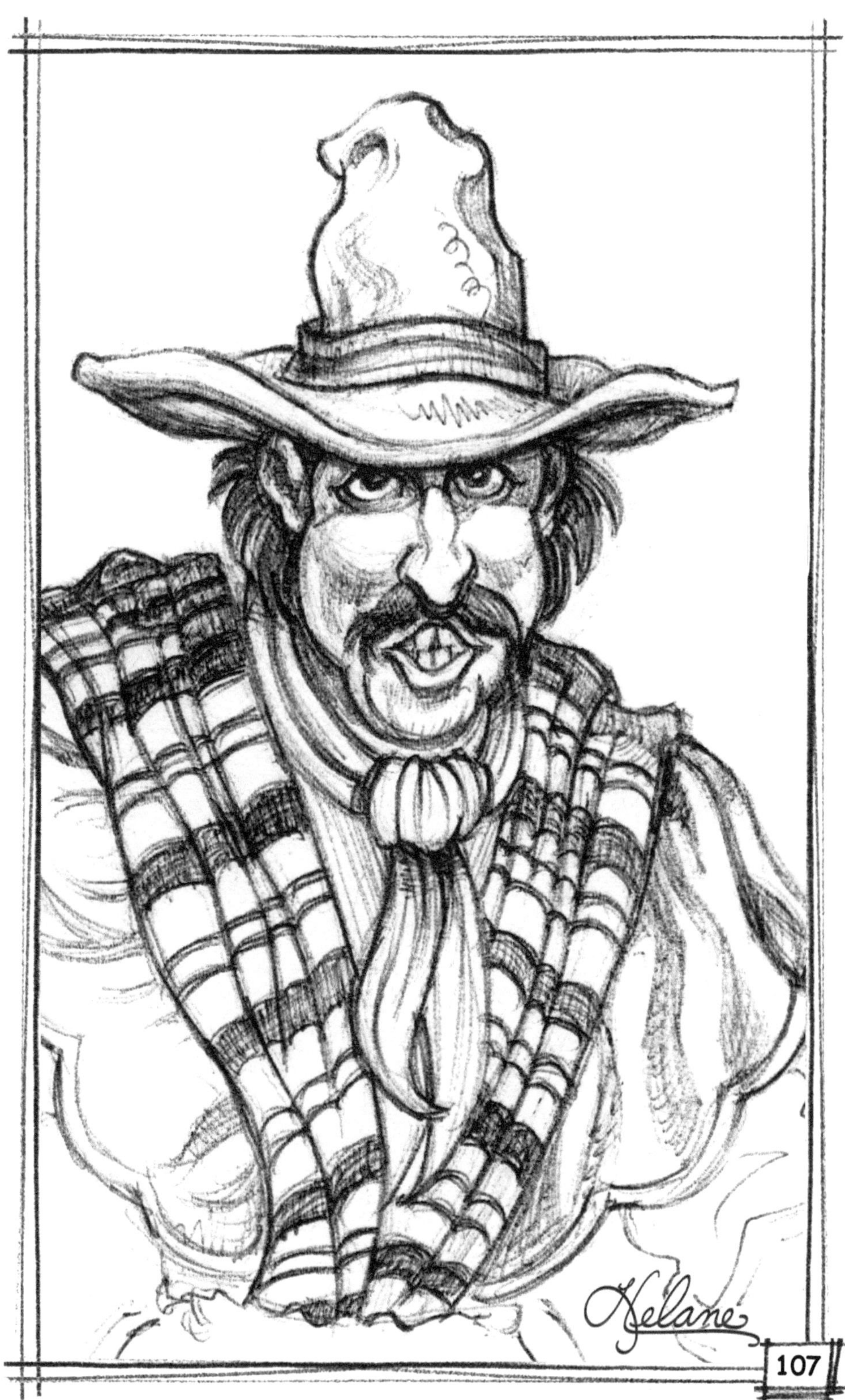

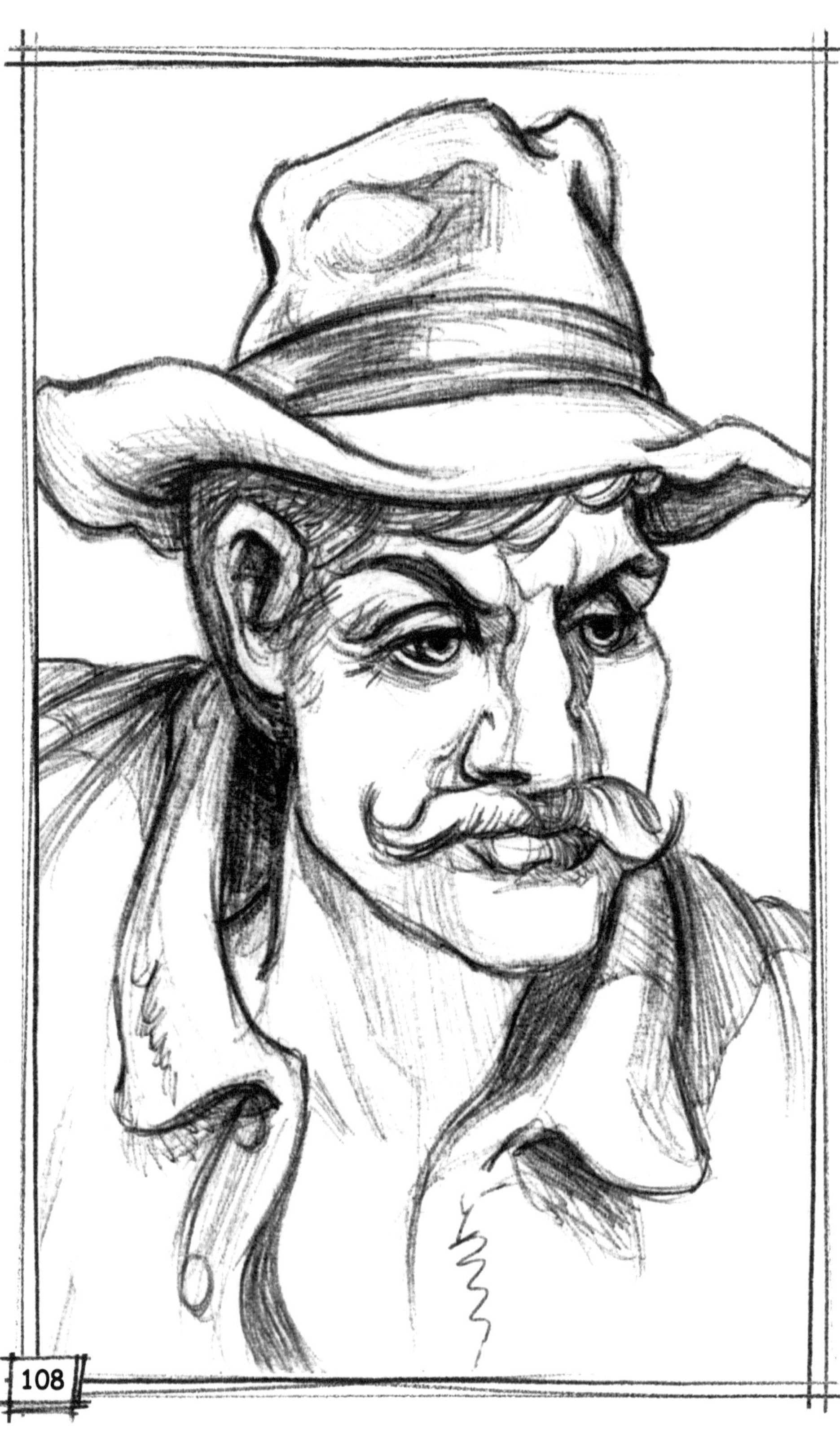

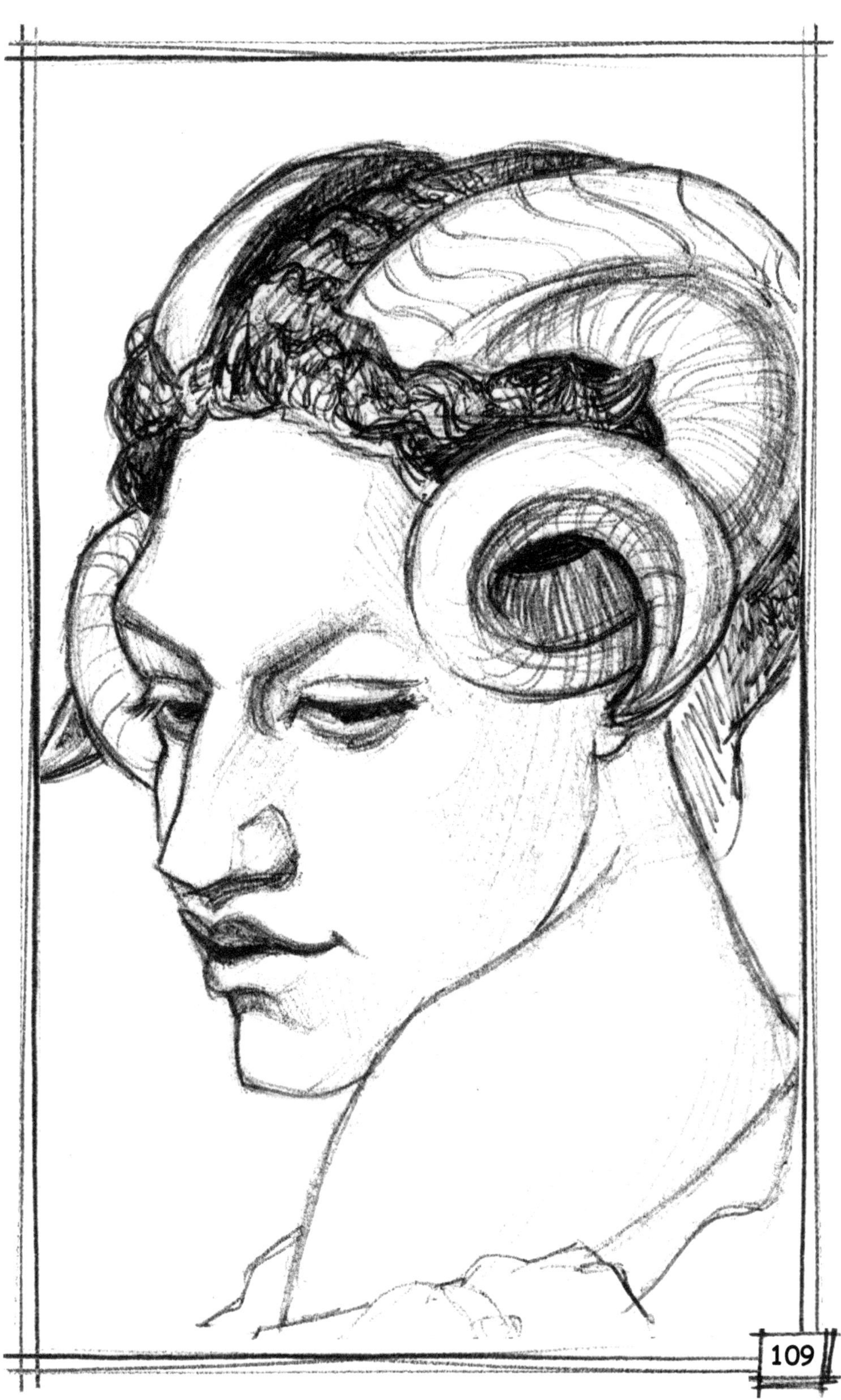

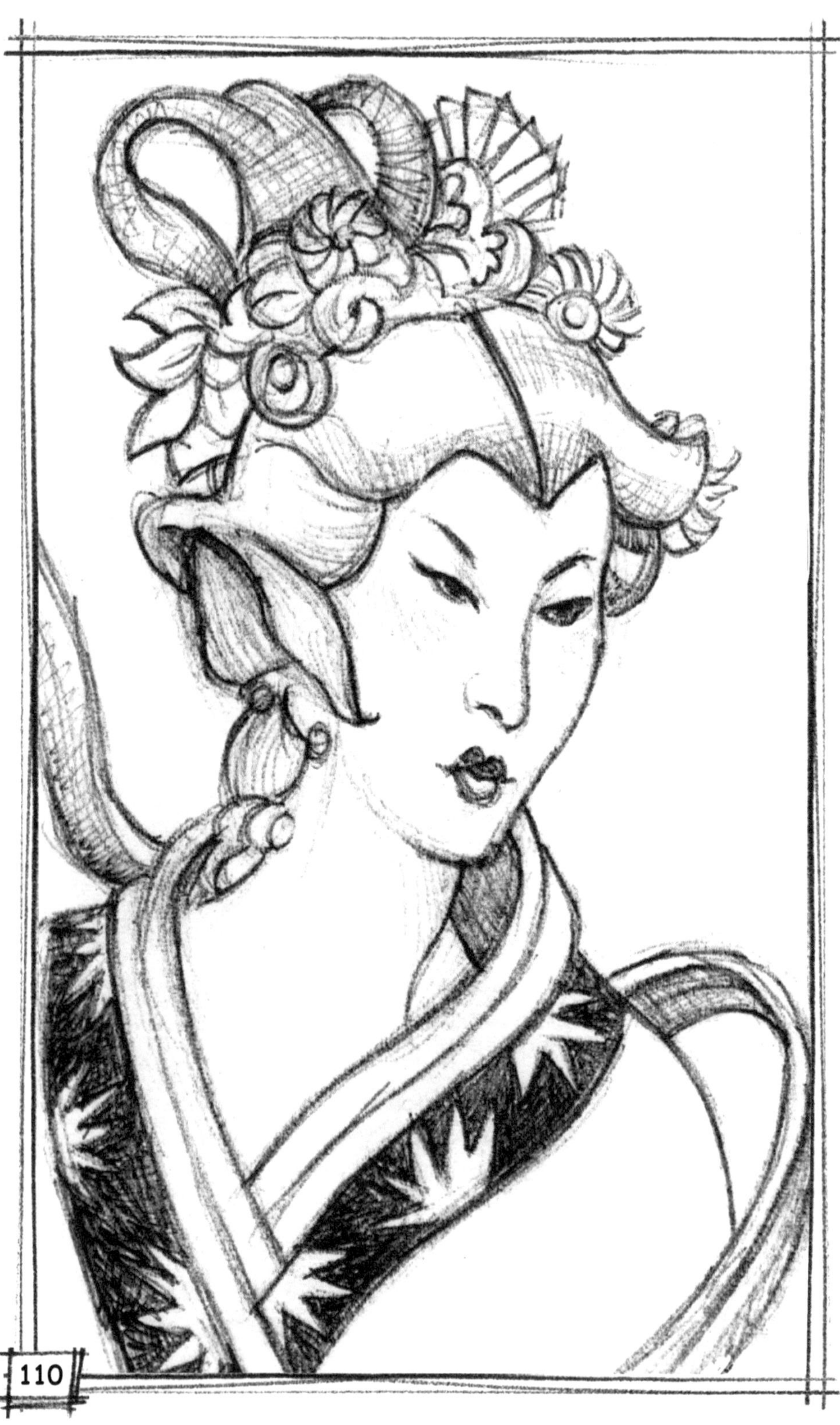

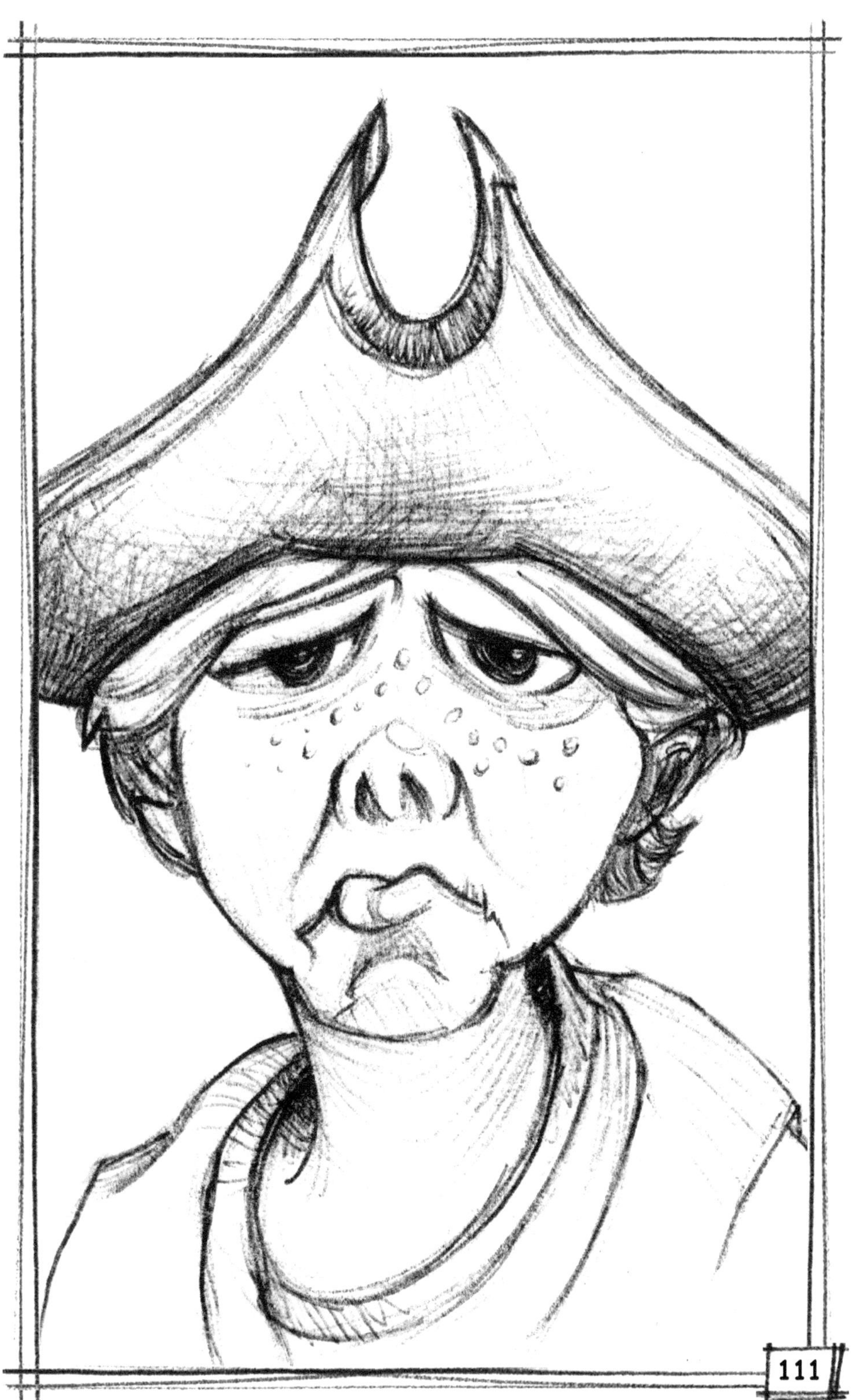

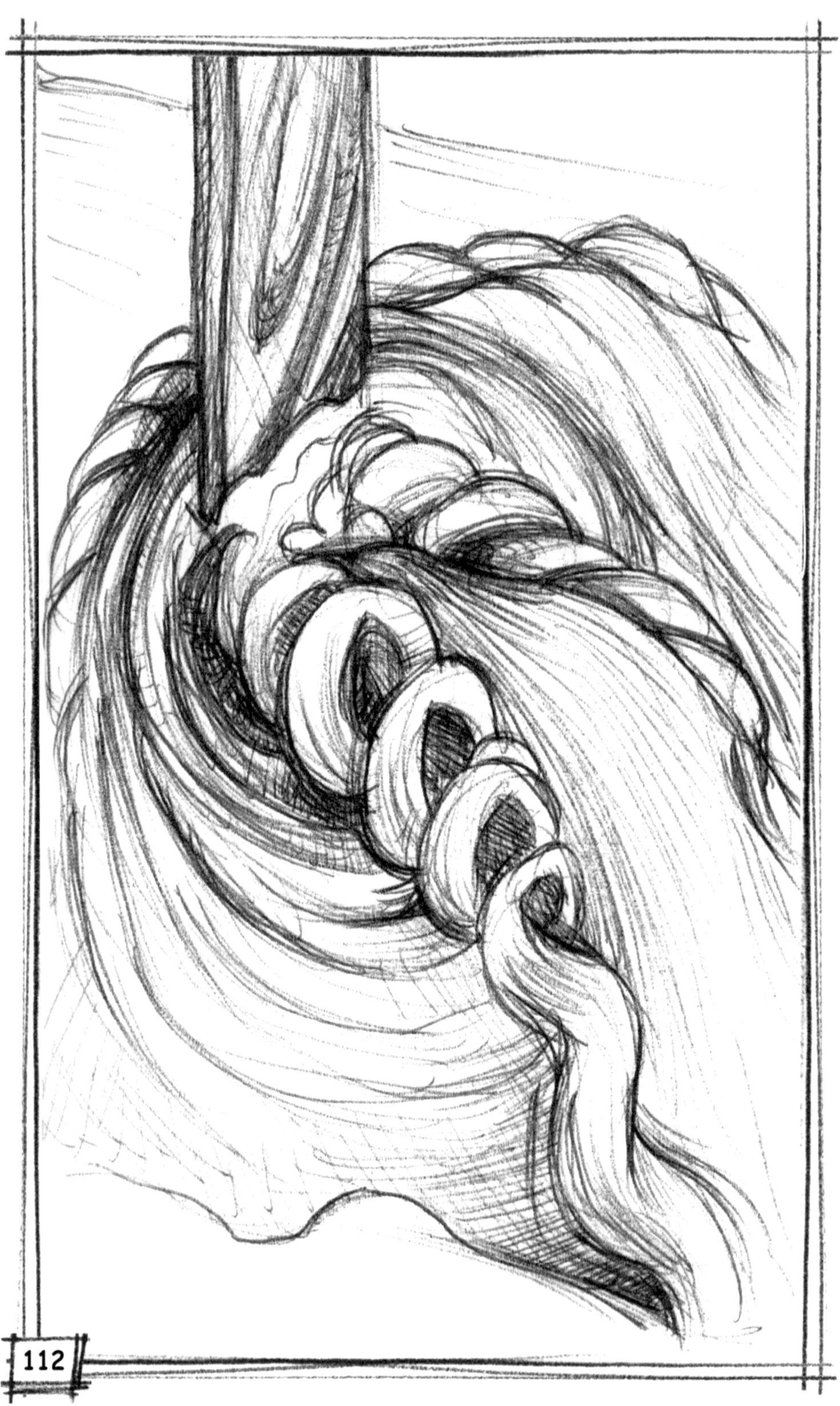

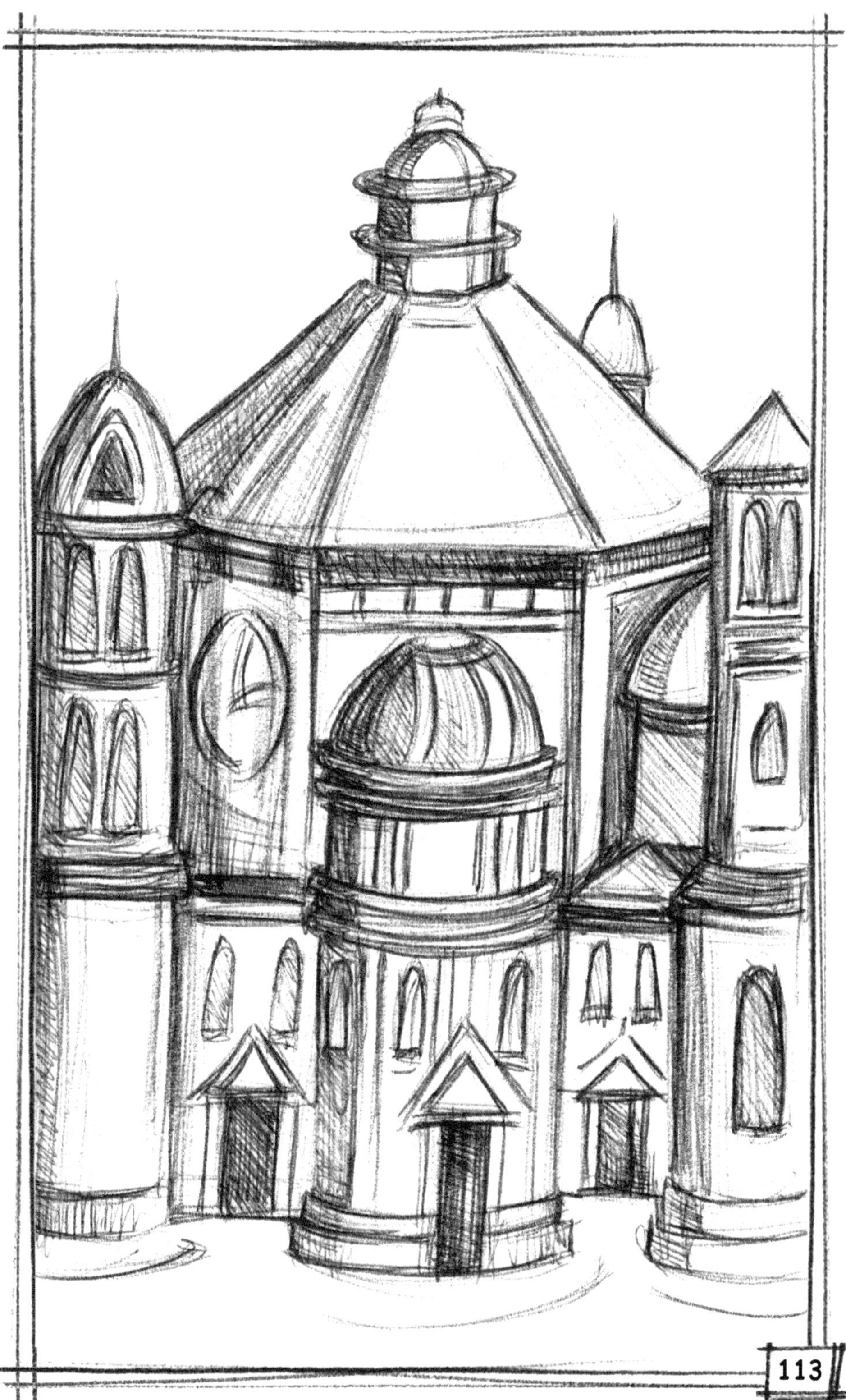

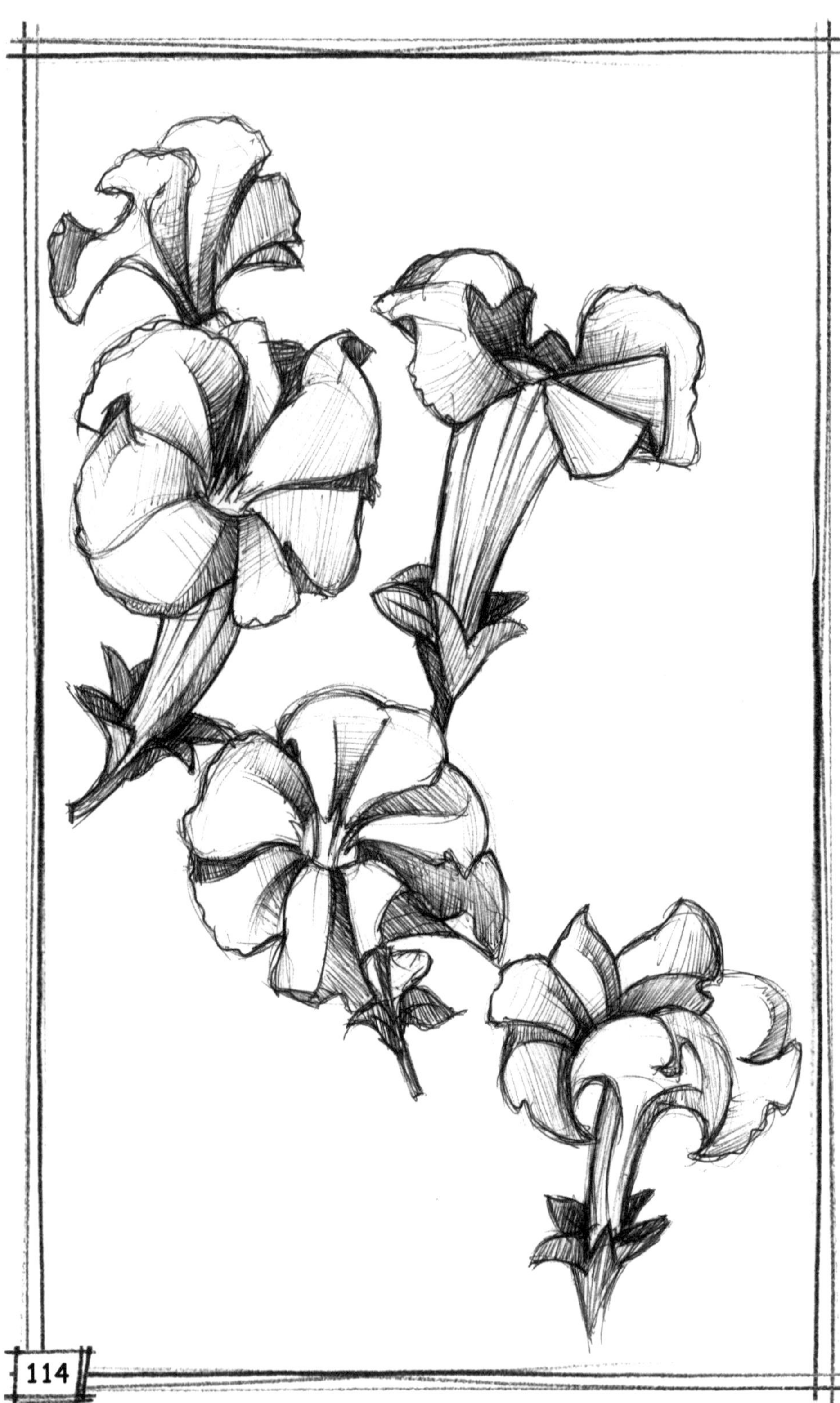

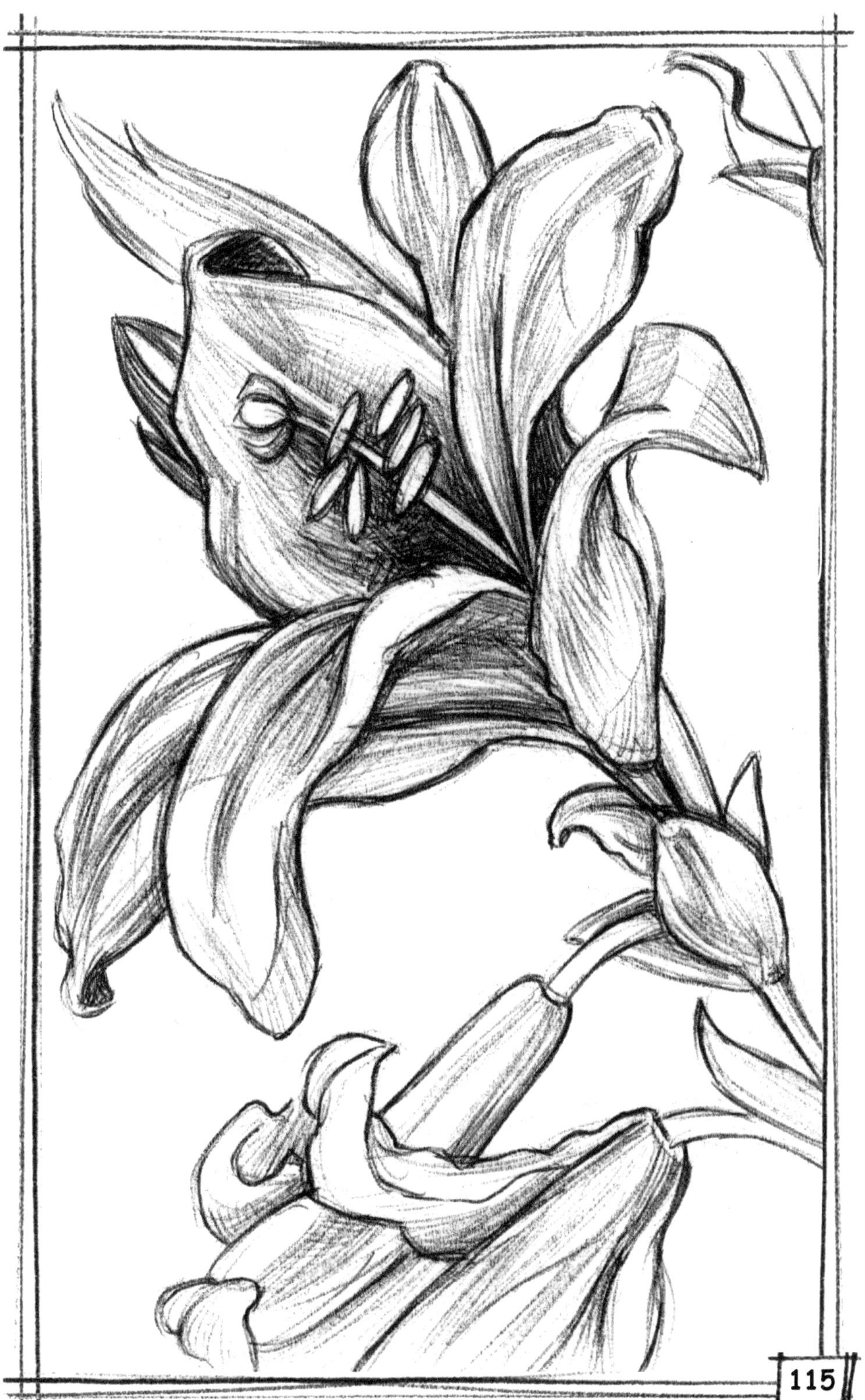

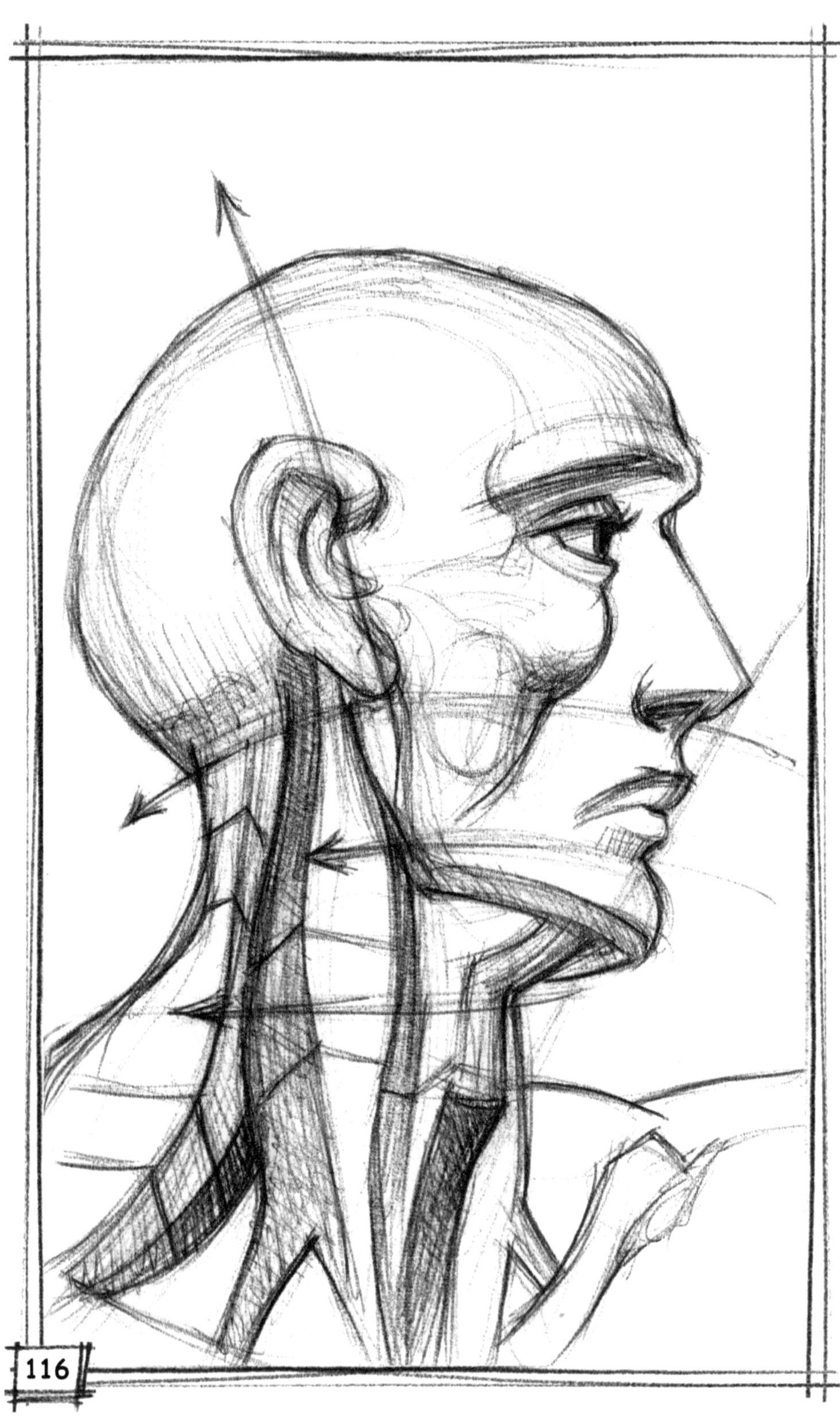

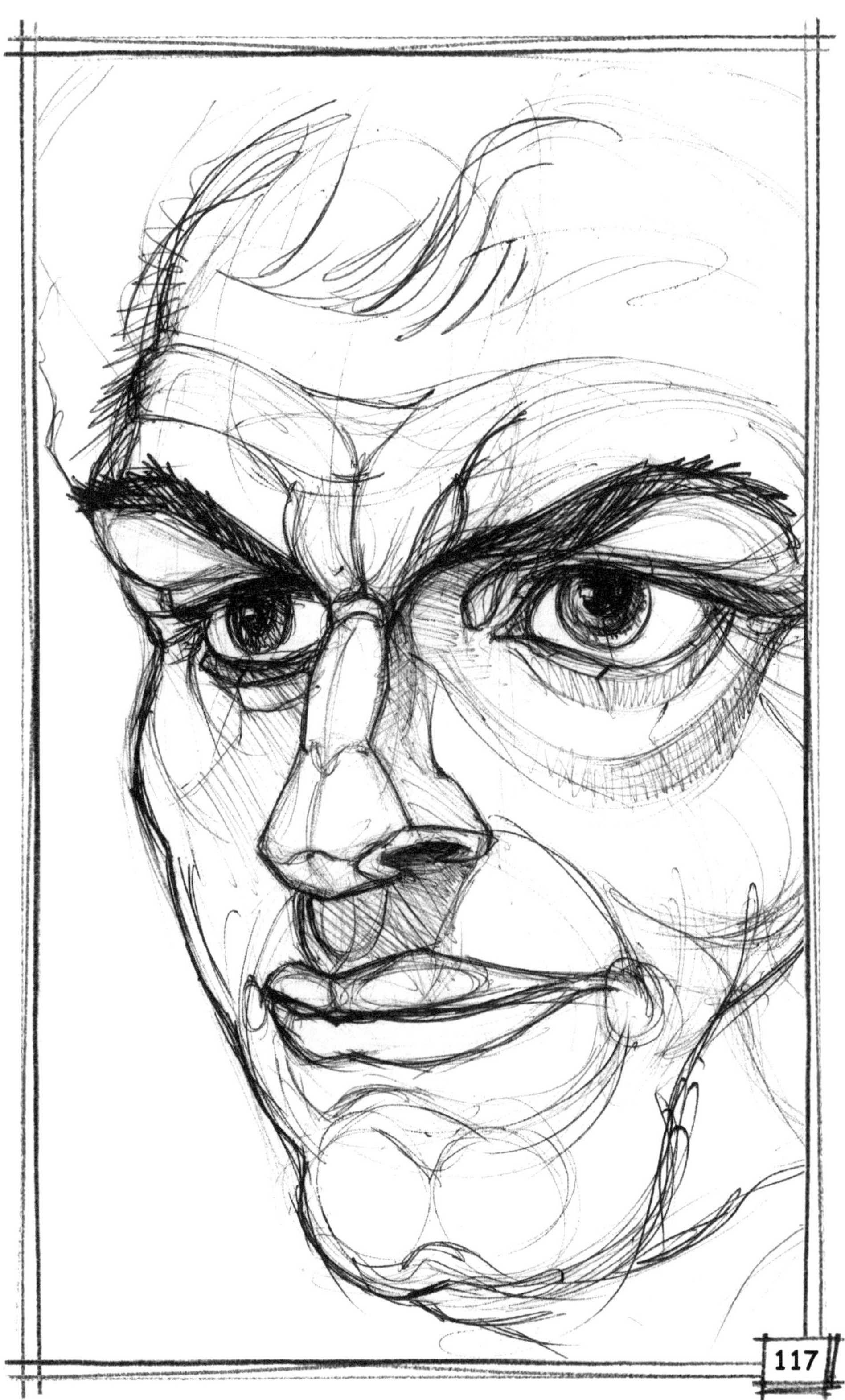

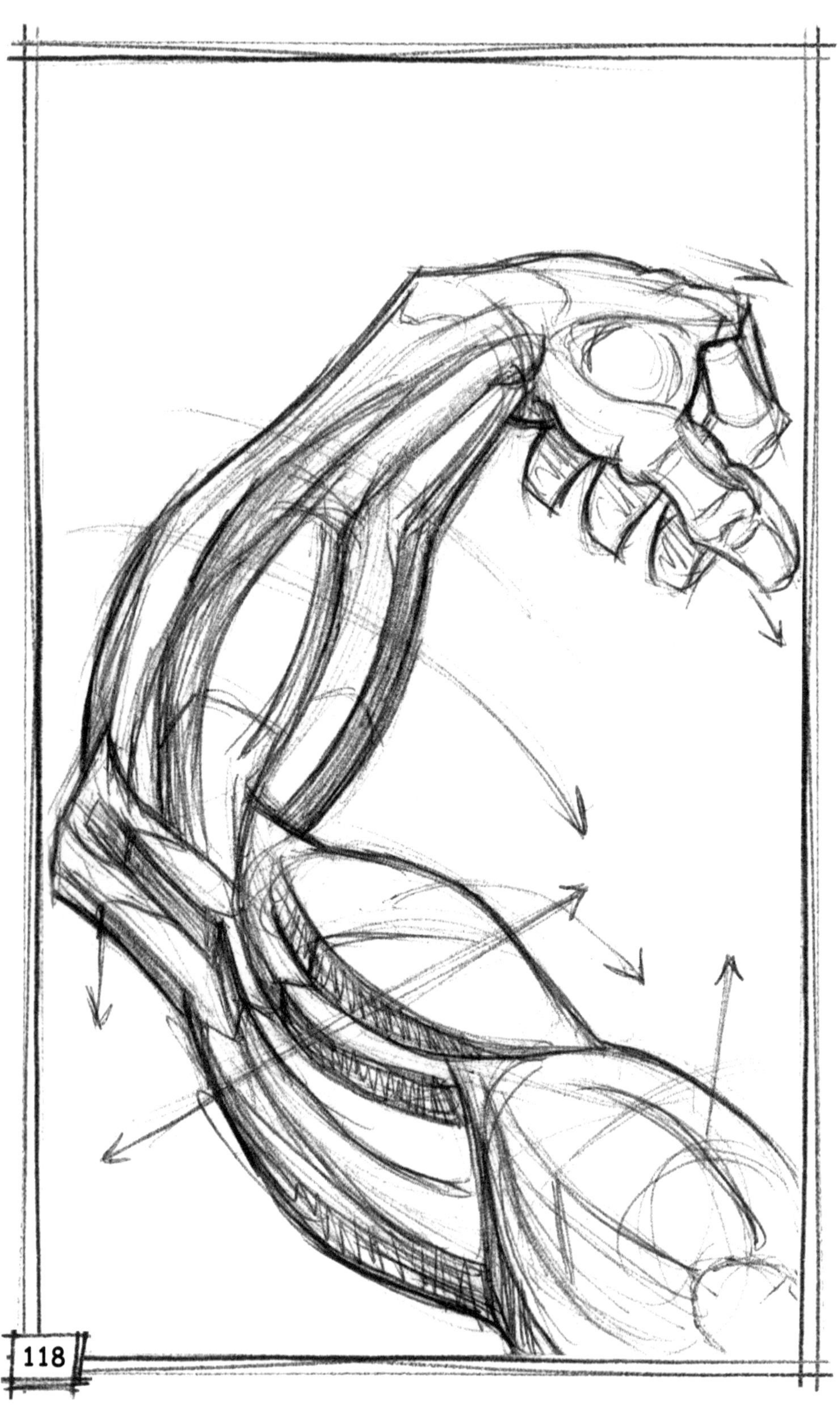

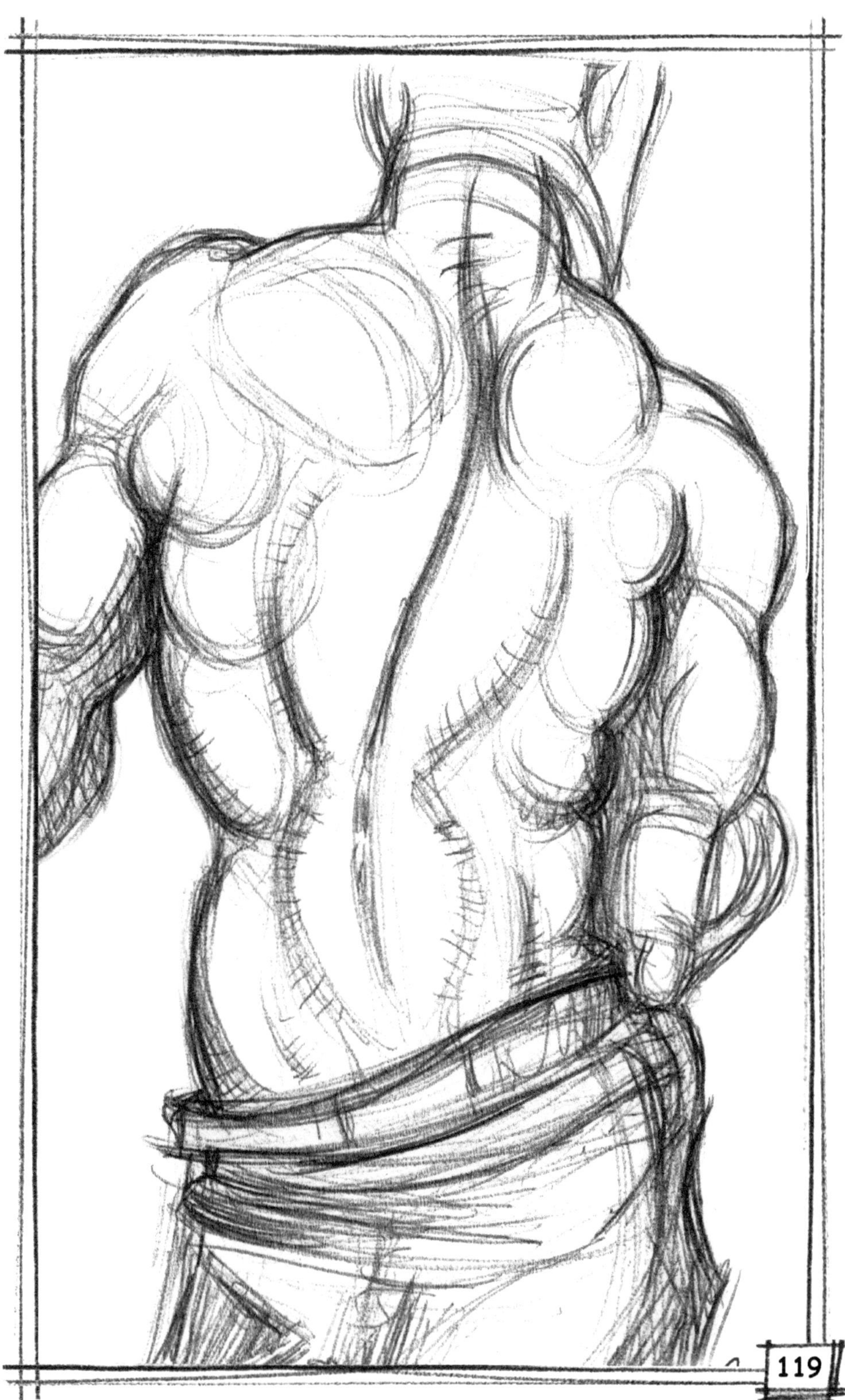

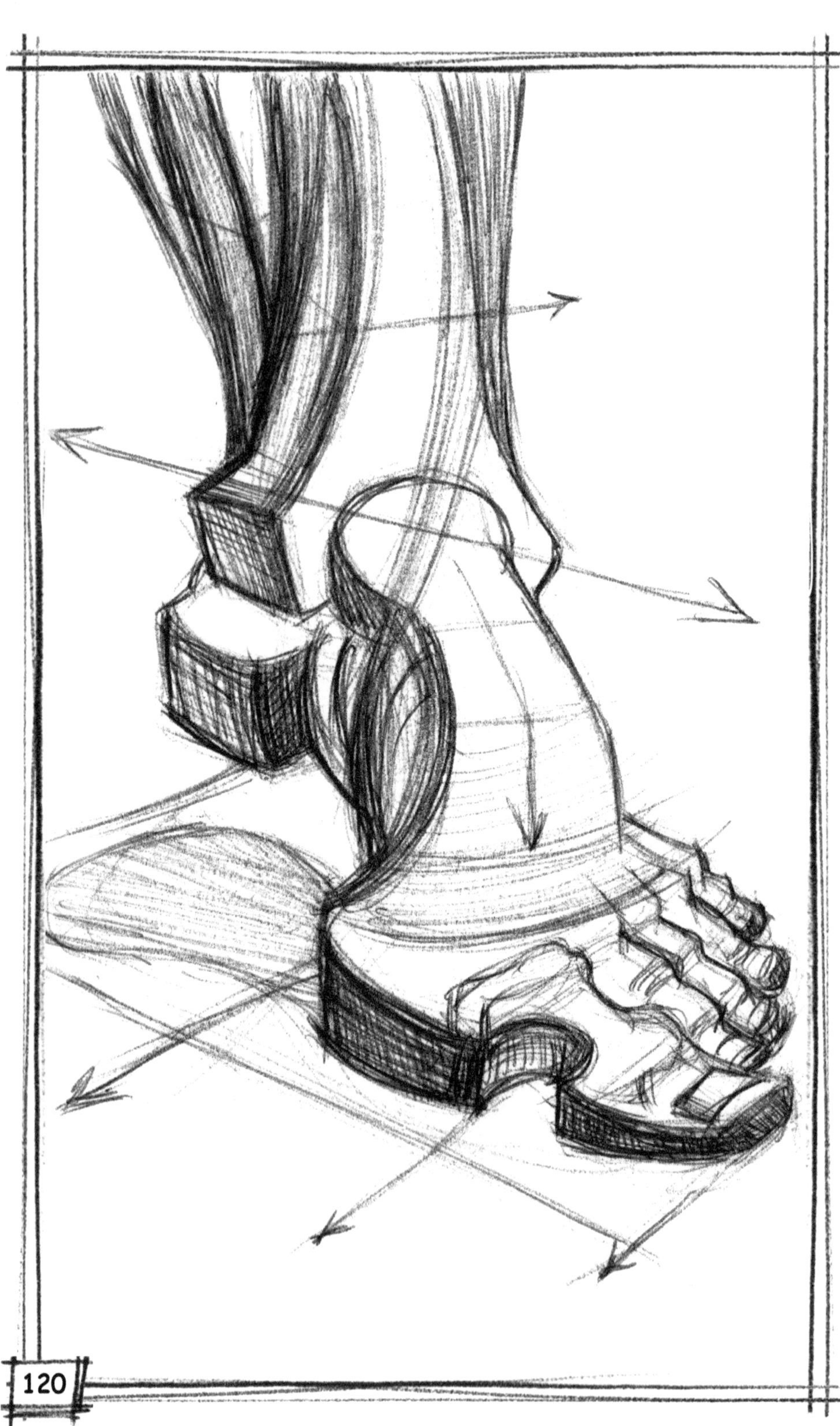

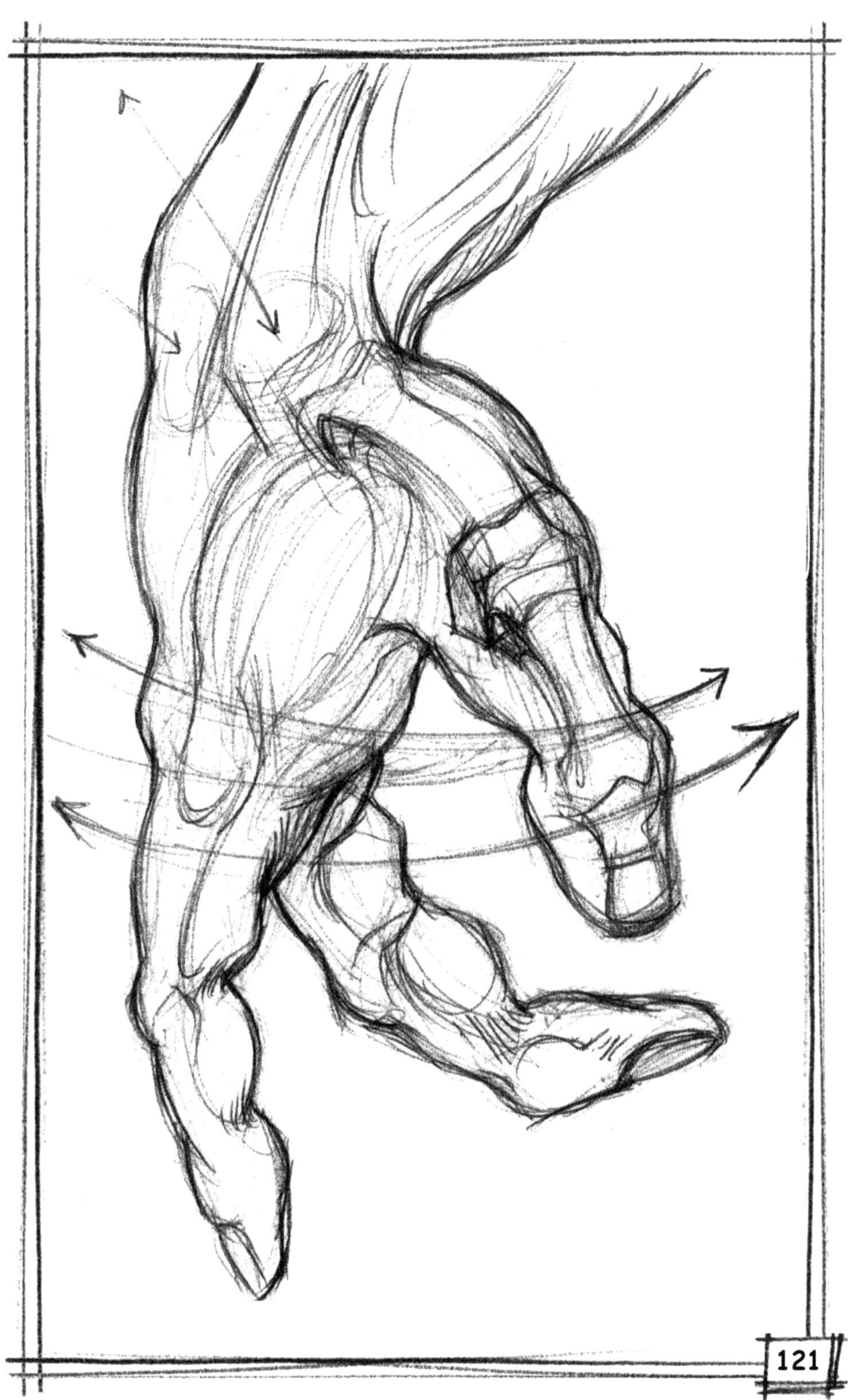